The Supreme Court

Twelfth Edition

CQ Press, an imprint of SAGE, is the leading publisher of books, periodicals, and electronic products on American government and international affairs. CQ Press consistently ranks among the top commercial publishers in terms of quality, as evidenced by the numerous awards its products have won over the years. CQ Press owes its existence to Nelson Poynter, former publisher of the *St. Petersburg Times,* and his wife Henrietta, with whom he founded *Congressional Quarterly* in 1945. Poynter established CQ with the mission of promoting democracy through education and in 1975 founded the Modern Media Institute, renamed The Poynter Institute for Media Studies after his death. The Poynter Institute (*www.poynter.org*) is a nonprofit organization dedicated to training journalists and media leaders.

In 2008, CQ Press was acquired by SAGE, a leading international publisher of journals, books, and electronic media for academic, educational, and professional markets. Since 1965, SAGE has helped inform and educate a global community of scholars, practitioners, researchers, and students spanning a wide range of subject areas, including business, humanities, social sciences, and science, technology, and medicine. A privately owned corporation, SAGE has offices in Los Angeles, London, New Delhi, and Singapore, in addition to the Washington DC office of CQ Press.

The Supreme Court

Twelfth Edition

Lawrence Baum
Ohio State University

Los Angeles | London | New Delhi
Singapore | Washington DC

Los Angeles | London | New Delhi
Singapore | Washington DC

FOR INFORMATION:

CQ Press

An Imprint of SAGE Publications, Inc.

2455 Teller Road

Thousand Oaks, California 91320

E-mail: order@sagepub.com

SAGE Publications Ltd.

1 Oliver's Yard

55 City Road

London EC1Y 1SP

United Kingdom

SAGE Publications India Pvt. Ltd.

B 1/I 1 Mohan Cooperative Industrial Area

Mathura Road, New Delhi 110 044

India

SAGE Publications Asia-Pacific Pte. Ltd.

3 Church Street

#10-04 Samsung Hub

Singapore 049483

Printed in the United States of America

Library of Congress Cataloging-in-Publication Data

Baum, Lawrence, author.
The Supreme Court/Lawrence Baum, Ohio State University.—Twelfth edition.

pages cm
Includes bibliographical references and index.

ISBN 978-1-4833-7611-0 (pbk.: alk. paper)

1. United States. Supreme Court. 2. Constitutional law—United States. 3. Courts of last resort—United States. 4. Judicial review—United States. I. Title.

KF8742.B35 2015
347.73'26—dc23   2015027595

This book is printed on acid-free paper.

Acquisitions Editor: Sarah Calabi

Senior Development Editor: Nancy Matuszak

Production Editor: Tracy Buyan

Copy Editor: Megan Markanich

Typesetter: C&M Digitals (P) Ltd.

Proofreader: Lawrence W. Baker

Cover Designer: Glenn Vogel

Marketing Manager: Amy Whitaker

Certified Sourcing
www.sfiprogram.org
SFI-00453

17 18 19 10 9 8 7 6 5 4 3 2

Contents

Tables, Figures, and Boxes

Tables

Figures

Boxes

Preface

Toward the end of June, the Supreme Court becomes a focus of national interest. As the Court concludes its annual term, it hands down decisions in cases that the justices could not fully resolve until they were faced with a deadline. Those cases usually include some of the most important matters that the Court addressed in its term. June 2015 was no exception. In the last three weekdays of the 2014 term, the Court issued two decisions of extraordinary importance in cases that had received enormous attention. In one set of cases, the Court ruled that states could not prohibit same-sex marriages. Its ruling came after a political and legal conflict that had involved all three branches of government at the federal and state levels. In another case, the Court held that the federal health care law sponsored by President Obama authorized federal subsidies for health insurance in states in which the federal government (rather than state governments) had set up "exchanges" under the law. The Court's decision effectively allowed the law to remain operative in the states that had federal exchanges, two-thirds of all states.

The drama that occurs every June reminds Americans of something they already recognize: the importance of the Supreme Court to the life of the nation. But that recognition is not fully matched by understanding of the Court. It is a complicated institution, one that is more difficult to comprehend than the other branches of government. As a result, people with great interest in American politics—even some who are experts in most aspects of politics—often have only limited knowledge of the Court.

I have written this book to provide a better understanding of the Supreme Court. The book is intended to serve as a short but comprehensive guide both for readers who already know much about the Court as well as those who have a more limited sense of it. I discuss how the Court functions, the work that it does, and the effects of its rulings on the lives of people in the United States. And I probe explanations of the decisions that the Court and its justices make, of actions by other people and groups that affect the Court, and of the Court's impact on government and society.

The book discusses the Court's history in order to provide needed perspective, but it focuses primarily on the current era. With that focus, this edition discusses recent developments in and around the Court. I give particular attention to the Court's major decisions in the past few years and their political context. Some important developments are related to the growth of partisan and ideological polarization in American politics. Senators are increasingly unwilling to vote to confirm nominees to the Court who are appointed by a president from the opposing party. And for the first time in its history, the Court since 2010 has been divided between ideological blocs that also fall along party lines.

The book's first chapter introduces the Supreme Court. In this chapter I discuss the Court's role in general terms, examine its place in the judicial system, analyze the Court as an institution, and present a brief summary of its history.

Each of the other chapters deals with an important aspect of the Court. Chapter 2 focuses on the justices: their selection, their backgrounds and careers, and the circumstances under which they leave the Court. Chapter 3 discusses how cases reach the Court through the actions of parties to cases, the lawyers who represent them, interest groups, and the federal government in its special role. The chapter then considers how and why the Court selects the small number of cases that it will hear and decide.

Chapter 4 examines decision making in the cases that the Court accepts for full consideration. After outlining the Court's decision-making procedures, I turn to the chapter's primary concern: the factors that influence the Court's choices among alternative decisions and policies. Chapter 5 deals with the kinds of issues on which the Court concentrates, the policies it supports, and the extent of its activism in the making of public policy. I give special attention to changes in the Court's role as a policymaker and the sources of those changes. The final chapter examines the ways in which other government policymakers respond to the Court's decisions, as well as the Court's impact on American society as a whole.

The book reflects the very considerable help that many people gave me with earlier editions. This edition was strengthened by suggestions for revision from Gayle Binion, University of California, Santa Barbara; Sara Crook, Peru State College; Sheldon Goldman, University of Massachusetts; Will McLauchlan, Purdue University; Luke Plotica, Virginia Tech; and Lydia Brashear Tiede, University of Houston. In updating information for this edition, I received valuable help from Marcia Coyle, Tony Mauro, and the Public Information Office of the Supreme Court.

As always, the professionals at CQ Press did much to make my life easier and, more important, to make the book better. I appreciate the excellent assistance of Tracy Buyan, Raquel Christie, Megan Markanich, and

Nancy Matuszak in carrying out this revision. I am also grateful for the leadership and encouragement of Sarah Calabi and Charisse Kiino.

I benefit a great deal from the professional community of scholars who study the courts and American politics. The body of high-quality research about the Supreme Court continues to grow, and this edition incorporates a good deal of recent research on the Court. I have learned much from my interactions with other scholars in this community. I have also learned from my colleagues in the political science department at Ohio State, a department and university that provide valuable support for my work. And the students whom I teach have added to my understanding of the Court with their questions and ideas. In this and other ways, they make teaching a great pleasure.

About the Author

Lawrence Baum is professor emeritus of political science at Ohio State University and holds a doctorate from the University of Wisconsin. A widely recognized authority on the court system, Baum is the author of *Specializing the Courts* (2011), *Judges and Their Audiences: A Perspective on Judicial Behavior* (2006), *The Puzzle of Judicial Behavior* (1997), and *American Courts: Process and Policy* (7th ed., 2012) as well as articles on a range of topics related to the courts. He has received the Alumni Award for Distinguished Teaching, the University Distinguished Scholar Award, and the Lifetime Achievement Award from the Law and Courts Section of the American Political Science Association.

To my students

Chapter 1

The Court

In 2010, after a heated battle in Congress, President Obama signed the law that made major changes to the country's health care system. Two years later the Supreme Court addressed arguments that two key provisions of the law went beyond the constitutional powers of Congress. The Court narrowly upheld the law's mandate that most individuals have health insurance, but it struck down a provision that effectively forced states to expand their Medicaid coverage for low-income residents.

In 2015 the Court returned to the law. In thirty-four states, the state government had decided not to set up the "exchanges" under which the health program operated, and the federal government stepped in to set up the exchanges itself under the law. The Treasury Department acted to provide tax credits to people who signed up for insurance in those states, as it did in the other sixteen states. Opponents of the program argued that the law's wording did not allow tax credits in the states with federally created exchanges, but the Court ruled that those tax credits were allowed. In doing so, the Court made it possible for the health care law to function in those thirty-four states.[1]

In ruling on three major issues involving President Obama's most important legislative accomplishment, the Court made itself a major participant in health care politics and policy. By doing so, it maintained a role that it has played through most of its history. In the past half century the Court has issued highly significant rulings on issues such as abortion, capital punishment, gun rights, and funding of political campaigns. One of its decisions ensured that President Richard Nixon would leave office in 1974, and another ensured that George W. Bush would become president in 2001.[2]

Because the Supreme Court plays a key role in American life, it is impossible to understand American government and society without understanding the Court. In this book, I seek to contribute to that understanding. Who serves on the Court, and how do they get there? What determines which cases and issues the Court decides? In resolving the cases before it, how does the Court choose between alternative decisions? In what policy areas does the Court play an active role, and what kinds of policies does it make? Finally, what happens to the Court's decisions after they are handed down, and what impact do those decisions have?

Each of these questions is the subject of a chapter in the book. As I focus on each question, I try to show not only what happens in and around the Court but also why things work the way they do. This first chapter is an introduction to the Court, providing background for the chapters that follow.

A Perspective on the Court

The Supreme Court's place in government is complicated, so it is useful to begin by considering the Court's attributes as an institution and its work as a policymaker.

The Court in Law and Politics

The Supreme Court is, first of all, a court—the highest court in the federal judicial system. Like other courts, it has jurisdiction to hear and decide certain kinds of cases. And like other courts, it can decide legal issues only in cases that are brought to it.

As a court, the Supreme Court makes decisions within a legal framework. Congress writes new law, but the Court interprets existing law. In this respect the Court operates within a constraint from which legislators are free.

In another respect, however, the justices have more autonomy than most other policymakers: the widespread belief that courts should be insulated from the political process gives the Court a degree of actual insulation. In particular, the justices' appointments for life allow them some freedom from concerns about whether political leaders and voters approve of their decisions.

The Court's insulation from politics is far from total, however. People sometimes speak of courts as if they are, or at least ought to be, "nonpolitical." In a literal sense, this is impossible: As a part of government, courts are political institutions by definition. What people really mean when they refer to courts as nonpolitical is that courts are separate from the political process and that their decisions are affected only by legal considerations. This too is impossible for courts in general and certainly for the Supreme Court.

The Court is political in this sense primarily because it makes important decisions on major issues. People care about those decisions and want to influence them. As a result, political battles regularly arise over appointments to the Court. Interest groups bring cases and present arguments to the Court in an effort to help shape its policies. Members of Congress pay attention to the Court's decisions and hold powers over the

Court, and for that reason the justices may take Congress into account when they decide cases. Finally, the justices' political values affect the votes they cast and the opinions they write in the Court's decisions.

Thus, the Supreme Court is both a legal institution and a political institution. The political process and the legal system each influence what the Court does. This ambiguous position adds to the Court's complexity. It also makes the Court an interesting case study in political behavior.

The Court as a Policymaker

This book examines the Supreme Court broadly, but it emphasizes the Court's role in making public policy—the authoritative rules by which people in government institutions seek to influence government itself and to shape society as a whole. Legislation to fund schools, a trial court's ruling in an auto accident case, and a Supreme Court decision on labor law are all examples of public policy. The Court is part of a policymaking system that includes lower courts and the other branches of government.

As I have noted, the Supreme Court makes public policy by interpreting provisions of law. Issues of public policy come to the Court in the form of legal questions.

The Court does not rule on legal questions in the abstract. Rather, it addresses these questions in the process of settling specific controversies between parties (sometimes called litigants) that bring cases to it. In a sense, then, every decision by the Court has three aspects: it is a judgment about the specific dispute brought to it, an interpretation of the legal issues in that dispute, and a position on the policy questions that are raised by the legal issues.

These three aspects of the Court's rulings are illustrated by a 2014 decision, *Sandifer v. United States Steel Corp.* Some current and former employees of U.S. Steel brought a lawsuit against the company under the federal Fair Labor Standards Act (FLSA), arguing that they should be paid for the time they spent putting on, and taking off, protective gear required for their jobs. However, U.S. Steel and the United Steelworkers, the employees' union, had agreed that workers should not be paid for that time, and a provision of the FLSA held that such agreements overrode workers' pay rights if they involved "changing clothes" at the beginning and end of the workday. The Supreme Court ruled that most of the protective gear qualified as "clothes" under that provision and that the time workers spent on the other gear was minimal, so it ruled against the employees.

In the first aspect of its decision, the Supreme Court affirmed the court of appeals decision against the employees who had brought the lawsuit. As a result, the employees lost the case. If the Supreme Court had reversed the court of appeals decision, the case would have gone back to the lower courts to consider the employees' claim for back pay.

A steelworker at an Ohio plant. The Supreme Court's 2014 decision on pay for the time that steelworkers spend putting on protective gear and taking it off had a direct effect on the parties to that case and broader effects on labor law and policy.

The Court's decision was also a judgment about the meaning of the provision of the FLSA that was in question, section 203(o) of Title 29 of the United States Code. Its interpretation of "changing clothes" as applied to protective gear became the authoritative standard, one that lower courts were obliged to follow in any future case involving that language.

Finally, the Supreme Court's decision shaped federal policy on requirements for payment of employees. The decision meant that the employees covered by the FLSA—most of the nation's workforce—generally had no legal right to be paid for the time spent putting on protective gear and taking it off if their union had agreed to give up that right in negotiations with a company. Thus, by making its decision the Court acted as a policy-maker on labor law.

Like most of the Court's decisions, the ruling in *Sandifer* was undramatic and received little coverage from the news media. In contrast, some decisions receive widespread attention and become the subjects of heated debate. But through both types of decisions, singly and in combination with each other, the Court contributes to the content of government policy.

This role for the Court reflects several circumstances. For one thing, as the French observer Alexis de Tocqueville noted early in the nation's history, "Scarcely any political question arises in the United States that is not resolved, sooner or later, into a judicial question."[3] In part, this is because the United States has a written constitution that can be used to challenge the legality of government actions. Because so many policy questions come to the courts and ultimately to the Supreme Court, the Court shapes a wide range of policies.

Yet the Court's role in policymaking is limited by several conditions, two of which are especially important. First, the Court can do only so much with the relatively few decisions it makes in a year. The Court currently issues decisions with full opinions in an average of fewer than eighty cases each year. In deciding such a small number of cases, the Court addresses only a select group of policy issues. Inevitably, there are whole fields of policy that it barely touches. Even in the areas in which the Court does act, it deals with only a limited number of the issues that exist at a given time.

Second, the actions of other policymakers narrow the impact of the Court's decisions. The Court is seldom the final government institution to deal with the policy issues it addresses. Its decisions are implemented by lower-court judges and administrators, who often have considerable discretion over how they put a ruling into effect. Congress and the president influence how the Court's decisions are carried out. They can also overcome its interpretations of federal statutes, laws enacted by Congress, simply by amending those statutes. As a result, there may be a great deal of difference between what the Court rules on an issue and the public policy that ultimately results from government actions on that issue.

For these reasons, those who see the Supreme Court as the dominant force in the U.S. government surely are wrong. But the Court does contribute a good deal to the making of public policy through its decisions.

The Court in the Judicial System

The Supreme Court is part of a court system, and its place in that system structures its role by determining what cases it can hear and the routes those cases take.

State and Federal Court Systems

The United States has a federal court system and a separate court system for each state. Federal courts can hear only those cases that Congress has put under their jurisdiction. Nearly all of the federal courts' jurisdiction falls into three categories.

First are the criminal and civil cases that arise under federal laws, including the Constitution. All prosecutions for federal crimes are brought to federal court. Some types of civil cases based on federal law, such as those involving antitrust and bankruptcy, must go to federal court. Other types can go to either federal or state court, but most are brought to federal court.

Second are cases to which the U.S. government is a party. When the federal government brings a lawsuit, it nearly always does so in federal court. When someone sues the federal government, the case must go to federal court.

Third are civil cases involving citizens of different states in which the amount in question is more than $75,000. If this condition is met, either party may bring the case to federal court. If a citizen of New Jersey sues a citizen of Texas for $100,000 for injuries from an auto accident, the plaintiff (the New Jersey resident) might bring the case to federal court, or the defendant (the Texan) might have the case "removed" from state court to federal court. If neither does so, the case will be heard in state court—generally in the state where the accident occurred or the defendant lives.

Only a small proportion of all court cases fit in any of those categories. The most common kinds of cases—criminal prosecutions, personal injury suits, divorces, actions to collect debts—typically are heard in state court. The trial courts of a single populous state such as Illinois or Florida hear far more cases than the federal trial courts. However, federal cases are more likely than state cases to raise major issues of public policy.

State court systems vary considerably in their structure, but some general patterns exist (see Figure 1-1). Each state system has courts that are

FIGURE 1-1
The Most Common State Court Structures

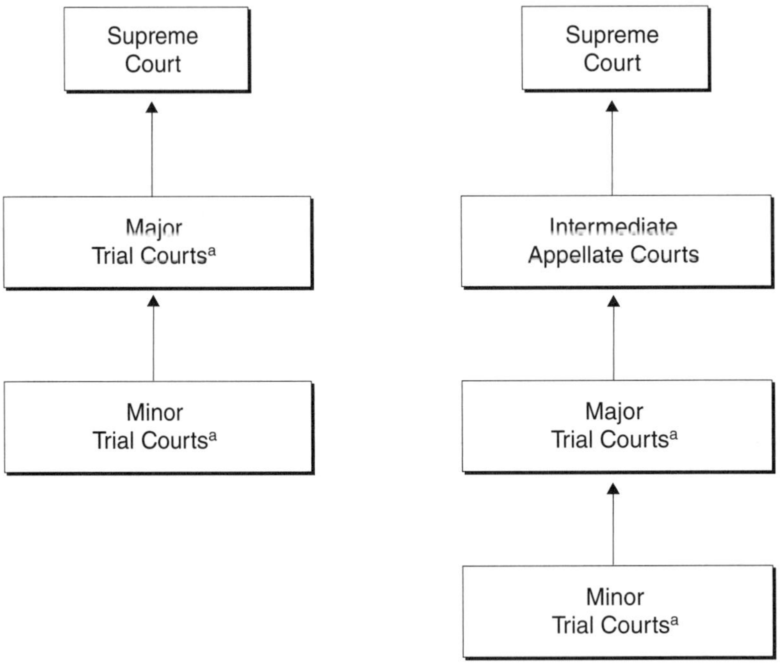

Note: Arrows indicate the most common routes of appeals.

a. In many states, major trial courts or minor trial courts (or both) are composed of two or more different sets of courts. For instance, New York has several types of minor trial courts.

primarily trial courts, which hear cases initially as they enter the court system, and courts that are primarily appellate courts, which review lower-court decisions that are appealed to them. Most states have two sets of trial courts—one to handle major cases and the other to deal with minor cases. Major criminal cases usually concern what the law defines as felonies. Major civil cases are generally those involving large sums of money. Most often, appeals from decisions of minor trial courts are heard by major trial courts.

Appellate courts are structured in two ways. Ten states, generally those with small populations, have a single appellate court—usually called the state supreme court. All appeals from major trial courts go to this supreme court. The other forty states have intermediate appellate courts below the supreme court. These intermediate courts initially hear most appeals from major trial courts. In those states supreme courts have discretionary jurisdiction over most challenges to the decisions of intermediate courts. Discretionary jurisdiction means that a court can choose which cases to hear; cases that a court is required to hear fall under its mandatory jurisdiction.

The structure of federal courts is shown in Figure 1-2. At the base of the federal court system are the federal district courts. The United States has ninety-four district courts. Each state has between one and four district courts, and there is a district court in the District of Columbia and in some of the territories, such as Puerto Rico. District courts hear all federal cases at the trial level, with the exception of a few types of cases that are heard in specialized courts.

Above the district courts are the twelve courts of appeals, each of which hears appeals in one of the federal judicial circuits. The District of Columbia constitutes one circuit; each of the other eleven circuits covers three or more states. The Second Circuit, for example, includes Connecticut, New York, and Vermont. Appeals from the district courts in one circuit generally go to the court of appeals for that circuit, along with appeals from the Tax Court and from some administrative agencies. Patent cases and some claims against the federal government go from the district courts to the specialized Court of Appeals for the Federal Circuit, as do appeals from three specialized trial courts. The Court of Appeals for the Armed Forces hears cases from lower courts in the military system.

The Supreme Court's Jurisdiction

The Supreme Court stands at the top of the federal judicial system. Its jurisdiction, summarized in Table 1-1, is of two types. First is the Court's original jurisdiction: the Constitution gives the Court jurisdiction over a few categories of cases as a trial court, so these cases may be brought directly to the Court without going through lower courts. The Court's original jurisdiction includes some cases to which a state is a party and cases involving foreign diplomatic personnel.

FIGURE 1-2
Basic Structure of the Federal Court System

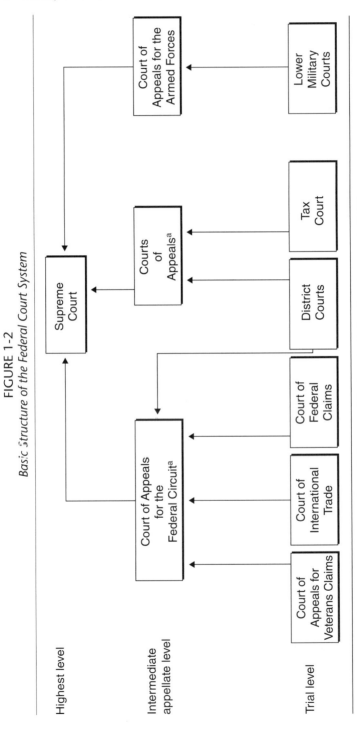

Note: Arrows indicate the most common routes of appeals. Some specialized courts of minor importance are excluded.

a. These courts also hear appeals from administrative agencies.

TABLE 1-1
Summary of Supreme Court Jurisdiction

Types of jurisdiction	Categories of cases
Original	Disputes between states[a]
	Some types of cases brought by a state
	Disputes between a state and the federal government
	Cases involving foreign diplomatic personnel
Appellate[b]	All decisions of federal courts of appeals and specialized federal appellate courts
	All decisions of the highest state court with jurisdiction over a case, concerning issues of federal law
	Decisions of special three-judge federal district courts (mandatory)

a. It is unclear whether these cases are mandatory, and the Court treats them as discretionary.
b. Some minor categories are not listed.

Most cases within the Court's original jurisdiction can be heard alternatively by a district court. Lawsuits between two states can be heard only by the Supreme Court, and these lawsuits account for most of the decisions based on the Court's original jurisdiction. These cases often involve disputes over state borders, though water rights have been the most common issue in recent years. The Court frequently refuses to hear cases under its original jurisdiction, even some lawsuits by one state against another. In part for this reason, full decisions in these cases are not plentiful—fewer than 200 in the Court's history. When the Court does accept a case under its original jurisdiction, it ordinarily appoints a "special master" to gather facts and propose a decision to the Court. These cases can take a long time to resolve. A dispute over water rights involving Kansas, Nebraska, and Colorado that came to the Court in 1999 was back in the Court fifteen years later because of a continuing dispute over compliance with a 2002 settlement agreement in the case.[4]

All the other cases that come to the Court are under the second type of jurisdiction: appellate jurisdiction. Under its appellate jurisdiction the Court hears cases brought by parties that are dissatisfied with the lower-court decisions in their cases. Within the federal court system such cases can come from the federal courts of appeals and from the two specialized appellate courts. Cases may also come directly from special three-judge district courts; most of these cases involve voting and election issues.

State cases can come to the Supreme Court after decisions by state supreme courts if they involve claims based on federal law, including the Constitution. If a state supreme court chooses not to hear a case, the losing party can then go to the Supreme Court. Table 1-2 shows that a substantial majority of the cases that come to the Court—and an even larger majority of the cases that it hears—originated in federal court rather than in state court.

The rule under which state cases come to the Supreme Court may be confusing, because cases based on federal law ordinarily start in federal court. But cases brought to state courts on the basis of state law sometimes contain issues of federal law as well. This situation is common in criminal cases. A person accused of burglary under state law will be tried in a state court. During the state court proceedings, the defendant may argue that the police violated rights protected by the U.S. Constitution during a search. The case eventually can be brought to the Supreme Court on that issue. If it is, the Court will have the power to rule only on the federal issue, not on the issues of state law involved in the case. Thus, the Court cannot rule on whether the defendant actually committed the burglary.

Nearly all cases brought to the Court under its appellate jurisdiction also are under its discretionary jurisdiction, so it can choose whether or not to hear them. With occasional exceptions discretionary cases come to the Court in the form of petitions for a writ of certiorari, a writ through which the Court calls up a case for decision from a lower court. The cases that the Court is required to hear are called appeals. In a series of steps culminating in 1988, Congress converted the Court's jurisdiction from mostly mandatory to almost entirely discretionary. Today, appeals can be brought in only the few cases that come directly from three-judge district courts.

The Supreme Court hears only a fraction of 1 percent of the cases brought to federal and state courts. As this figure suggests, courts other

TABLE 1-2
Sources of Supreme Court Cases in Recent Periods (in Percentages)

	Federal courts			
	Courts of appeals	District courts	Specialized courts	State courts
Cases brought to the Court[a]	74	0	2	24
Cases decided on the merits[b]	79	1	7	13

Source: Data on cases decided on the merits are from SCOTUSblog, http://www.scotusblog.com/reference/stat-pack.

Note: Original jurisdiction cases are not included. Nonfederal courts of the District of Columbia and of U.S. territories are treated as state courts. For cases heard by the Court, each oral argument is counted once unless it involves consolidated cases from two different categories of courts.

a. Cases in which the Court ruled on petitions for hearings, October 6, 2014 (1,657 cases).
b. Cases that the Court decided on the merits, including summary reversals, 2012 and 2013 terms (151 cases).

than the Supreme Court have ample opportunities to make policy on their own. Moreover, their decisions help determine the ultimate impact of the Court's policies. Important though it is, the Supreme Court certainly is not the only court that matters.

An Overview of the Court

Several attributes of the Court should be examined to provide an understanding of the Court as an institution. Especially important are the activities of justices and the people who help them do their work.

The Court's Building

The Supreme Court did not move into its own building until 1935. In its first decade the Court met first in New York and then in Philadelphia. The Court moved to Washington, D.C., with the rest of the federal government at the beginning of the nineteenth century. For the next 130 years, it sat in the Capitol, a tenant of Congress.

The Court's accommodations in the Capitol were not entirely adequate. Among other things, the lack of office space meant that justices did most of their work at home. After an intensive lobbying effort by Chief Justice William Howard Taft, Congress appropriated money for the Supreme Court building in 1929. The five-story structure occupies a full square block across the street from the Capitol. Because the primary material in the impressive building is marble, it has been called a "marble palace." The aging of the Court's building and the need to house a staff that had grown considerably led to a major renovation project that was completed in 2011.

The building houses all the Court's facilities. Formal sessions are held in the courtroom on the first floor. Behind the courtroom is the conference room, where the justices meet to decide cases. Also near the courtroom are the chambers that contain offices for the associate justices and their staffs. The chief justice's chambers are attached to the conference room.

In 2010 the Court closed its main public entrance at the top of the stairs in the front of the building, citing security concerns. The symbolism of that closure led to considerable criticism, including an unusual statement by Justice Stephen Breyer opposing the closure, which Ruth Bader Ginsburg joined.[5] A federal statute that broadly prohibits political demonstrations and protests on the Court's grounds was held to violate the First Amendment by a federal district judge in 2013. The Court quickly adopted a regulation that limits demonstrations on its grounds, a regulation that has not yet been tested in court.[6]

Personnel: The Justices

Under the Constitution, Supreme Court justices are nominated by the president and confirmed by the Senate. By long-established Senate practice, a simple majority is required for confirmation. The Constitution says that justices will hold office "during good behavior"—that is, for life unless they relinquish their posts voluntarily or they are removed through impeachment proceedings. Beyond these basic rules, questions such as the number of justices, their qualifications, and their duties have been settled by federal statutes and by tradition.

The Constitution says nothing about the number of justices. The Judiciary Act of 1789 provided for six justices. Subsequent statutes changed the number successively to five, six, seven, nine, ten, seven, and nine. The changes were made in part to accommodate the justices' duties in the lower federal courts, in part to serve partisan and policy goals of the president and Congress. The most recent change to nine members was made in 1869, and any further changes in size seem quite unlikely.

As of 2015, each associate justice receives an annual salary of $246,800, and the chief justice receives $258,100. The justices gained raises of more than $30,000 in 2014 after a lower court ruled in favor of six federal judges who challenged congressional action that blocked cost-of-living adjustments to judicial salaries.[7] Justices are limited to about $27,000 in outside income from activities such as teaching, but there are no limits on income from books. Clarence Thomas earned about $1.5 million for his memoirs, and as of 2014 Sonia Sotomayor had earned about $3 million. Antonin Scalia earned several hundred thousand dollars for two books about interpretation of the law between 2007 and 2014. Some of the current justices, including John Roberts and Stephen Breyer, were wealthy when they came to the Court. Thomas and Sotomayor were far from wealthy, and their book earnings improved their financial status enormously.[8]

The primary duty of the justices is to participate in the collective decisions of the Court: determining which cases to hear, deciding cases, and writing and contributing to opinions. Ordinarily, the Court's decisions are made by all nine members, but exceptions occur. At times the Court has only eight members because a justice has left the Court and a replacement has not been appointed. A justice's illness may leave the Court temporarily shorthanded, or a justice may decide not to participate in a case because of a perceived conflict of interest. Under federal law, judges should withdraw from cases—recuse themselves—when a decision would affect their self-interest substantially or their impartiality "might reasonably be questioned."[9] The Court leaves this decision entirely to the individual justice.

Justices seldom explain the reasons for their recusals, but those reasons often can be discerned. The most common reason is a financial interest in a case—usually a result of a justice's investments. Some justices have sold stocks to enable them to participate in cases from which they would otherwise have had to recuse. Other recusals result when a justice was involved in a case in a prior position, such as a lower-court judgeship. Elena Kagan recused from about one-third of the cases during her first term on the Court because her office had worked on those cases when she was U.S. solicitor general.

Controversies about justices' recusal decisions have arisen in recent years, spurred primarily by public statements by justices about matters related to pending or future cases and by interactions between justices and people who have an interest in the outcome of a case.[10] Litigants and others who care about particular cases have sought recusals on those grounds. Justice Scalia agreed to recuse in one case in which he had criticized the lower court's decision in a speech,[11] but he has resisted other efforts to secure his recusal. When oral argument was about to begin in one case in which his recusal had been requested, Scalia stood up as if he were about to absent himself from the argument, but then he smiled and sat back down.[12] Outside groups pressured two justices to recuse from *National Federation of Independent Business v. Sebelius* (2012), in which the health care law enacted by Congress in 2010 was challenged on constitutional grounds. Conservative groups argued that Justice Kagan had dealt with the issue as solicitor general, and liberal groups argued that Justice Thomas's wife had been heavily involved in opposition to the law. Both justices resisted this pressure and participated in the case.

The Court may have a tie vote when only eight justices participate in a decision. A tie vote affirms the lower-court decision. If the tie applies to the whole decision, the votes of individual justices are not announced and no opinions are written. Similarly, the lower-court decision in a case is affirmed if the Court cannot reach a quorum of six members. This situation has occurred a few times in recent years, most often because litigants named most of the justices as defendants in their lawsuits.

In addition to their participation in collective decisions, the justices make some decisions individually as circuit justices. The United States has always been divided into federal judicial circuits. Originally, most appeals within a circuit were heard by ad hoc courts composed of a federal trial judge and two members of the Supreme Court who were assigned to that area as circuit justices. The circuit duties were arduous, especially at a time when travel was difficult. Some justices even suffered ill health from what was called circuit riding. Actions by Congress and by the justices themselves gradually reduced the extent of their circuit riding, and this duty ended altogether when Congress created the courts of appeals in 1891.

The justices today retain some duties as circuit justices, with each justice assigned to one or more circuits. As circuit justices they deal with applications for special action, such as a request to stay a lower-court decision (prevent it from taking effect) until the Court decides whether to hear the case. Such an application generally must go first to the circuit justice. That justice may rule on the application as an individual or refer the case to the whole

Court. If the circuit justice rejects an application, it can then be made to a second justice. That justice ordinarily refers it to the whole Court.

Probably the most common subject of stay requests is the death penalty. The Court is confronted with numerous requests to stay executions or vacate (remove) stays of execution, many of which come near the scheduled execution time. The Court grants only a small proportion of requests for stays of execution. Because five votes are required for a stay but only four votes to hear a case, it is possible that a prisoner will be executed even though the Court would have heard his case. Indeed, that happened in 2015 to a man who was one of four prisoners challenging the mix of drugs used for executions in Oklahoma. His application for a stay of execution was denied by a 5–4 vote, he was executed later that day, and eight days later the Court agreed to hear the case with the three remaining prisoners.[13]

Stays in other kinds of cases sometimes involve significant policy issues. In 2014 the Court acted on stay requests involving abortion, immigration, same-sex marriage, and administration of elections. The Court's action in several of these cases drew dissenting opinions.

All but one of the nine justices are equal in formal power. The exception is the chief justice, who is the formal leader of the Court. The chief justice presides over the Court's public sessions and conferences and assigns the Court's opinion whenever the chief voted with the majority. The chief also supervises administration of the Court with the assistance of committees.

By tradition, the junior justice, the one with the least seniority, sits on the Court's cafeteria committee. A 2010 review in the *Washington Post* gave the cafeteria a grade of F and concluded that "this food should be unconstitutional."[14] Joining the Court and the committee later that year, Justice Kagan got a frozen yogurt machine installed in the cafeteria. Chief Justice Roberts said that "no one can remember" such a significant achievement for the justice on the committee.[15] In 2013 the Court reportedly changed the management of its cafeteria, perhaps in an effort to improve its grade; Kagan's role in that decision is not known.

The chief justice appoints judges to administrative committees and some specialized courts. In 2013 one of those courts, the Foreign Intelligence Surveillance Court, garnered attention because of revelations about its formerly secret decisions expanding the federal government's power to engage in electronic surveillance for national security purposes. Roberts's appointment role was discussed during that episode because the great majority of the district judges whom he had assigned to the Surveillance Court for part-time duty were Republican appointees like Roberts himself, and some members of Congress proposed to limit or eliminate the chief justice's assignment power for that court.[16]

The job of Supreme Court justice brings with it both satisfactions and burdens. The extent of the burdens is a matter of disagreement. Some observers see the justices' workload as relatively light. They point to the relatively small number of cases that the Court now hears, the excellent support that the justices get from their law clerks, and the time that the justices are able to spend in activities outside the Court. One law professor, exaggerating for emphasis, said that in many ways "it's the cushiest job in the world."[17]

In contrast, justices often refer to the time their work requires, especially the volume of material they must read in the cases that come to the Court. At least some justices spend very long hours on the job. But in the current era, because justices typically stay on the Court until they reach an advanced age, the satisfactions of serving as a justice appear to outweigh the burdens of the job by a substantial margin.

Personnel: Law Clerks and Other Support Staff

A staff of about 460 people, serving in several units, supports the justices. Most of the staff members carry out custodial and police functions under the supervision of the marshal of the Court. The clerk of the Court handles the clerical processing of all the cases that come to the Court. The reporter of decisions supervises preparation of the official record of the Court's decisions, the *United States Reports*. The librarian is in charge of the libraries in the Supreme Court building. The Court's public information office responds to inquiries and distributes information about the Court.

Of all the members of the support staff, the law clerks have the most direct effect on the Court's decisions.[18] Associate justices may employ four

David Hume Kennerly/Getty Images

Justice Stephen Breyer with two of his law clerks. The Court's law clerks work directly with their justice in the process of reaching decisions.

clerks each, the chief justice five (though the chief generally hires only four). Clerks usually work with a justice for only one year. The typical clerk is a recent, high-ranked graduate of a prestigious law school. The clerks who served in the 2010–2014 terms came from two dozen law schools, but nearly half had gone to Harvard or Yale.[19] The great majority had clerked in a federal court of appeals before coming to the Supreme Court, and some had spent a short time in legal practice after their service in a court of appeals. Justices, especially those who are most conservative, tend to draw clerks from court of appeals judges who share the justices' ideological positions.[20]

Clerks typically spend much of their time on the petitions for hearings by the Court, reading the petitions and the lower-court records and summarizing them for the justices. Clerks also work on cases that have been accepted for decision. This work includes analysis of case materials and issues, discussions of cases with their justices, and drafting opinions. Justice Alito reported that his clerks "always do a draft for me," Justice Scalia said that "I almost never do the first draft,"[21] and all the other current justices have similar practices. Justice Kagan said that clerks also "wander around the building and find out a lot about what other people are thinking," and one reason is to help justices develop positions in cases that will win support from their colleagues.[22]

The extent of law clerks' influence over the Court's decisions is a matter of considerable interest and wide disagreement.[23] Observers who depict the clerks as quite powerful probably underestimate the justices' ability to maintain control over their decisions. Still, the jobs that justices give to their clerks ensure significant influence. Drafting opinions, for instance, allows clerks to shape the content of those opinions, whether or not they seek to do so. The same is true of the other work that clerks do.

After leaving the Court, law clerks take a variety of career paths, with private practice the most common. Clerks completing their term at the Court are prized by large law firms, especially those that handle Supreme Court cases, and firms offer them "signing bonuses" of as much as $300,000 in addition to high salaries.[24] Many former clerks go on to distinguished careers. Some justices were once law clerks, including John Roberts, Stephen Breyer, and Elena Kagan on the current Court.

The Court and the Outside World

Among people who care about politics or the law, the Supreme Court is the object of considerable fascination. There are often long lines of people who seek the limited numbers of seats available in the courtroom for oral argument sessions, and some people make money holding places in line for others.[25] At the end of the Court's annual term, when announcements of major decisions are expected, thousands of people watch the feed of information on SCOTUSblog to learn of the Court's rulings as quickly as possible. The lawyers and other people who subscribe to a journal called *The Green Bag* prize the bobbleheads of justices that the journal issues to its readers.

Responding to this interest, the news media devote considerable attention to the Court. Some of its decisions receive extensive coverage in newspapers, television broadcasts, and blogs. The justices are satirized in stories and cartoons, and their activities are extensively chronicled. To take one

Sarah L. Voisin/*Washington Post* via Getty Images

Edward Gero as Justice Antonin Scalia in The Originalist, *a play about Justice Scalia that premiered in Washington, D.C., in 2015. The staging of the play and its excellent ticket sales reflect the widespread interest in the Court and the justices.*

example, the parking tickets issued to two cars that had delivered and accompanied Justice Scalia to a Philadelphia speaking engagement were reported in the news.[26] Beyond the news media, individual justices and the Court as a whole have been the subjects of a series of books for a general audience over the years, and in recent years there has been a theatrical play about one of the Court's decisions, a play about Scalia, and an opera about Scalia and Justice Ginsburg (both serious opera fans themselves). In 2015 it was announced that Natalie Portman would play Ginsburg in a movie about her years as a lawyer litigating against sex discrimination.

Despite the high level of interest in the Court, both the Court as an institution and individual justices traditionally kept out of the public eye. For instance, justices seldom gave public interviews, and the Court's oral arguments and other formal proceedings were accessible only to those who attended them in person. This paucity of information may have been part of an effort to win favorable public attitudes toward the Court by fostering the impression that the Court stands apart from ordinary politics.[27]

The Court and the justices were never completely isolated from the world outside the Court, and they have become more open to that world in recent years.[28] The Court now provides a good deal of information about its work through its website. Transcripts of oral arguments are available on the same day as the arguments. Audio recordings are released a few days later and occasionally on the same day.

However, the Court has refused so far to allow oral arguments to be televised, despite pressure from Congress and widespread public support for televised arguments. At least some of the justices may want to avoid becoming too recognizable. They may also fear that lawyers (or their own colleagues) will grandstand for the cameras. One commentator, asked for his explanation, said that "they don't want to be made fun of on *The Daily Show*."[29] In 2014 John Oliver of HBO's *Last Week Tonight* got around the lack of televised arguments by staging part of the argument in one case with dogs representing the justices and lawyers while the audio of the argument played. Justice Ginsburg reported that "I thought it was hilarious."[30]

Justices have long been active within the legal community, participating in programs at law schools and speaking before groups of lawyers and judges. This continues to be true today, and justices travel a good deal to make these appearances. One common activity is teaching at summer law school programs outside the United States.

What has changed in the recent past is the justices' willingness to interact with people outside the legal system. Interviews with the news media are now common, and justices often speak before nonlegal groups. The justices who are book authors have made appearances to publicize their books, and Antonin Scalia and Sonia Sotomayor have been quite active in book promotion. Some justices take advantage of their celebrity to participate in activities they enjoy, such as throwing out the first pitch at Major League Baseball games, as Sotomayor, Samuel Alito, and John Paul Stevens have done. The high level of outside activity for some justices is symbolized by their occasional absences from public Court sessions on days when the Court does not hold oral argument but announces decisions.

In their appearances before legal and public groups, the justices sometimes express their views about issues of legal and public policy. Scalia does so most frequently, and Ginsburg has become increasingly willing to do so in recent years. These commentaries sometimes include defenses or criticisms of recent decisions by the Court, and occasionally justices express opinions that are relevant to potential future cases. One example was Ginsburg's negative comment on a Texas abortion law in a 2014 interview.[31] As noted earlier, some of those expressions have led to calls for justices to recuse themselves from the relevant cases. Justices sometimes have public and private interactions with groups that have policy agendas, such as their appearances at events sponsored by the conservative Federalist Society and the liberal American Constitution Society.

Justices differ in the extent to which they act as public figures. Among the current justices, Scalia and Sotomayor have been the most willing to take on that role. Sotomayor received attention as the first justice from the Latino community, and she has attracted additional attention with her best-selling memoir and her frequent appearances at public events and in the mass media. In 2013 she appeared on *60 Minutes, The View, Today, The Daily Show,* and *The Colbert Report*.[32] A year after she joined the Court, she estimated that what a friend called "her celebrity" took up about 40 percent of her time.[33] In contrast, some other justices are more reticent about taking on public roles. At the extreme was David Souter, who retired from the Court in 2009. Souter seemed to seek complete anonymity. He kept his distance from the news media and made few appearances at events outside the Court.

Among the public as a whole, knowledge of the Court and the justices is relatively limited. Still, most people who respond to public opinion surveys express positive or negative judgments about the Court. By most measures, the public's attitudes toward the Court today are considerably less positive than they were in the 1980s and 1990s. This trend concerns people who are sympathetic to the Court, largely because of the widespread belief that public support is important to the Court's success in getting its decisions carried out. The sources of this trend are uncertain, but the main driving force is probably a broader negativity in attitudes toward government. Chief Justice Roberts said of the Court's approval ratings in 2012 that "I think we're low because people's view of government is low."[34] As Roberts pointed out, the Court still does well in comparison with other institutions, and the gap between the Court and Congress in public approval is quite substantial.

The Court's Schedule

The Court has a regular annual schedule.[35] It holds one term each year, lasting from the first Monday in October until the beginning of the succeeding term a year later. The term is designated by the year in which it begins: The 2015 term began in October 2015. (However, the clerk's office treats a term as ending when the Court finishes its work in June.) The Court does nearly all its collective work from late September to late June. This work begins when the justices meet to act on the petitions for hearings that have accumulated during the summer and ends when the Court has issued decisions in all the cases it heard during the term.

Most of the term is divided into sittings of about two weeks, when the Court holds sessions to hear oral arguments in cases and to announce decisions in cases that were argued earlier in the term, and recesses of two weeks or longer. In May and June the Court hears no arguments but holds one or more sessions nearly every week to announce decisions. It issues few decisions early in the term because of the time required after oral arguments to write opinions and reach final positions, and about one-third of all decisions are issued in June. The justices scramble to meet the internal deadline of June 1st to circulate drafts of all majority opinions to their colleagues and to reach final decisions by the end of June. The scramble is especially frenetic for cases argued in April and for the most consequential and controversial cases. It is not surprising that a high proportion of all the Court's major decisions are announced in the last few days of the Court's term. This was true of the 2015 rulings on the 2010 health care law sponsored by President Obama and on same-sex marriage.[36]

When the Court has reached and announced decisions in all the cases it heard during the term, the summer recess begins. Cases that the Court accepted for hearing but that were not argued during the term are carried over to the next term. In summer the justices generally spend time away from Washington but continue their work on the petitions for hearings that arrive at the Court. During that time the Court and individual circuit justices respond to applications for special action. When the justices meet at the end of summer to dispose of the accumulated petitions, the annual cycle begins again.

The schedule of weekly activities, like the annual schedule, is fairly regular. During sittings, the Court generally holds sessions on Monday through Wednesday for two weeks and on Monday of the next week. The sessions begin at ten o'clock in the morning. Oral arguments usually are held during each session except on the last Monday of the sitting. They may be preceded by several types of business. On Mondays the Court announces the filing of its order list, which reports the Court's decisions on petitions for hearing and other actions taken at its conference the preceding Friday. On Tuesdays, as well as the last Monday of the sitting, justices announce their opinions in any cases the Court has resolved. In May and June, however, opinions may be announced on any day of the week.

The oral arguments consume most of the time during sessions. The usual practice is to allot one hour for arguments in a case. On most argument days the Court hears two cases.

During sittings, the Court holds two conferences each week. The Wednesday afternoon conference is devoted to discussion of the cases that were argued on Monday. In a longer conference on Friday the justices discuss the cases argued on Tuesday and Wednesday, along with petitions for certiorari and other matters the Court must decide. In May and June, after oral arguments have ended for the year, the Court has weekly conferences on Thursdays.

The Court also holds a conference on the last Friday of each recess to deal with the continuing flow of business. The remainder of the justices' time during recess periods is devoted to their individual work: study of petitions for hearing and cases scheduled for argument, writing of opinions, and reaction to other justices' opinions. This work continues during the sittings.

The Court's History

This book is concerned primarily with the Supreme Court at present and in the recent past, but I frequently refer to the Court's history to provide perspective on the current Court. Thus, an overview of that history will provide background for later chapters. Even a brief overview makes clear the links between the Court's own history and that of the nation as a whole. The Court has played a role in American political development, and it has been shaped by the development of other political institutions.

The Court from 1790 to 1865

The Constitution established the Supreme Court, but the Constitution says much less about the Court than about Congress and the president. The Judiciary Act of 1789, which set up the federal court system, granted the Court broad but ambiguous powers.

The Court started slowly, deciding only about fifty cases and making few significant decisions between 1790 and 1799.[37] Several people rejected offers to serve on the Court, and two justices—including Chief Justice John Jay—resigned to take more attractive positions in state government. The Court's fortunes improved considerably under John Marshall, chief justice from 1801 to 1835. Marshall, appointed by President John Adams, dominated the Court to a degree that no other justice has matched. He used his position to strengthen the Court's standing and advance policies he favored.

The Court's most important assertion of power under Marshall was probably its decision in *Marbury v. Madison* (1803), in which the Court struck down a federal statute for the first time. In his opinion for the Court, Marshall argued that when a federal law is inconsistent with the Constitution, the Court must declare the law unconstitutional and refuse to enforce it. A few years later, the Court claimed the same power of judicial review over state acts.

The Court's aggressiveness brought denunciations and threats against the Court, including an effort by President Thomas Jefferson to have Congress remove at least one justice through impeachment. But Marshall's skill in minimizing confrontations helped protect the Court from a successful attack. The other branches of government and the general public gradually accepted the powers that he claimed for the Court.

This acceptance was tested by the Court's decision in *Scott v. Sandford* (1857), generally known as the *Dred Scott* case. Prior to that decision, the Court had overturned only one federal statute, the minor law involved in *Marbury v. Madison*. In *Dred Scott,* however, Marshall's successor, Roger Taney (1836–1864), wrote the Court's opinion holding that Congress had exceeded its constitutional powers when it prohibited slavery in some territories. That decision was intended to resolve the legal controversy over slavery. Instead, the level of controversy increased, and the Court was vilified in the North. The Court's prestige suffered greatly, but its basic powers survived without serious challenge.[38]

In using the Court's powers, the Marshall and Taney Courts addressed major issues of public policy. They gave particular attention to federalism, the legal relationship between the national government and the states. Under Marshall, the Court gave strong support to national powers. Marshall wanted to restrict state policies where they interfered with activities of the national government, especially its power to regulate commerce among the states. The Taney Court was not as favorable to the national government, but Taney and his colleagues did little to reverse the Marshall Court's general expansion of federal power. As a result, the constitutional power of the federal government remained strong; the Court had permanently altered the lines between the national government and the state governments.

The Court from 1865 to 1937

After the Civil War, the Court began to focus its attention on government regulation of the economy. By the late nineteenth century, all levels of government were adopting new laws to regulate business activities. Among them were the federal antitrust laws, state regulations of railroad practices, and federal and state laws regulating employment conditions. Inevitably, much of this legislation was challenged in the courts on constitutional grounds.

The Supreme Court upheld a great many government policies regulating business in this period, but it gradually became less friendly toward those policies. That position was reflected in the development of constitutional doctrines limiting government power to control business activities. Those doctrines were used with increasing frequency to attack regulatory legislation, and in the 1920s the Supreme Court struck down more than 130 regulatory laws as unconstitutional.[39]

In the 1930s the Supreme Court's attacks on economic regulation brought it into serious conflict with the other branches. President Franklin Roosevelt's New Deal program to combat the Great Depression included sweeping statutes to control the economy, measures that enjoyed widespread support. In a series of decisions in 1935 and 1936, the Court struck down several of these statutes, including laws broadly regulating industry and agriculture. Most of these decisions were by 6–3 and 5–4 margins.[40]

Roosevelt responded in 1937 by proposing legislation under which an extra justice could be added to the Court for every sitting justice over the age of seventy who had served at least ten years, up to a maximum of six extra justices. If the legislation were enacted, Roosevelt could appoint six new justices, thereby packing the Court with justices favorable to his programs. While this plan was being debated in Congress, however, the Court weakened the impetus behind it. In several decisions in 1937, the Court reversed direction and upheld New Deal legislation and similar state laws by narrow margins.[41] Many observers have concluded that this shift was a deliberate effort by one or two moderate justices to mend the Court's contentious relationship with the other branches.[42] In any event, the Court-packing plan died.

The Court from 1937 to 1969

During the congressional debate in 1937, one of the justices who had frequently voted to strike down New Deal laws retired. Several other justices left the Court in the next few years, giving Roosevelt the ideological control of the Court that he had sought through the Court-packing legislation. The new Court created by his appointments fully accepted New Deal regulation of the economy, giving very broad interpretations to the constitutional powers to tax and to regulate interstate commerce. And in the decades that followed, the Court continued to uphold major economic policies of the federal government.

Because of the Court's consistent position on issues of economic regulation, that field gradually became less central to its role. Instead, the Court increasingly focused on civil liberties. By the mid-1960s, the Court was giving the most attention to interpretation of legal protections for freedom of expression and freedom of religion, for the procedural rights of criminal defendants and other people, and for equal treatment of disadvantaged groups.

During this period, the Court's overall support for civil liberties varied. That support peaked in the 1960s, the latter part of the period when Earl Warren was chief justice (1953–1969). The Court's policies during that period are often identified with Warren, but other liberal justices played roles of equal or greater importance: Roosevelt appointees Hugo Black and William Douglas and Eisenhower appointee William Brennan.

The most prominent decision of the Warren Court was *Brown v. Board of Education* (1954), in which the Court ordered desegregation of school systems that assigned students to separate schools by race. The Court supported the rights of African Americans in several other areas as well. During the 1960s the Court expanded the rights of criminal defendants in state cases. It issued landmark decisions on the right to counsel (*Gideon v. Wainwright*, 1963), police search and seizure practices (*Mapp v. Ohio*, 1961), and the questioning of suspects (*Miranda v. Arizona*, 1966). The Court supported freedom of expression by expanding First Amendment rights, especially on issues relating to obscenity and libel. In a line of cases beginning with *Baker v. Carr* (1962), the Court required that legislative districts be equal in population.

The Court from 1969 to the Present

When Earl Warren retired in 1969, he was succeeded as chief justice by Warren Burger, President Nixon's first Court appointee. In 1970 and 1971 Nixon made three more appointments. The Court's membership changed much more slowly after that. But each new member until 1993 was appointed by a conservative Republican president—one by Gerald Ford, three by Ronald Reagan, and two by George H. W. Bush. In 1986 Reagan named Nixon appointee William Rehnquist, the Court's most conservative justice, to succeed Warren Burger as chief justice. Each president serving since then—Bill Clinton, George W. Bush, and Barack Obama—has made two appointments. In 2005 Bush appointed John Roberts as chief justice to succeed Rehnquist.

The Republican appointments from 1969 through 1991 gradually made the Court more conservative. Even though four of the six appointments since then have come from Democratic presidents, the net effect of personnel changes since 1991 has been to move the Court a bit more to the right.

This ideological change is reflected in the Court's civil liberties policies, to a greater degree on some issues than on others. Perhaps the most decisive shift has come on issues of criminal procedure. The Court has not directly overturned any of the Warren Court's landmark decisions expanding defendants' rights, but it has cut back on the reach of decisions such as *Mapp* and *Miranda*. The Rehnquist and Roberts Courts generally have given narrow interpretations to federal statutes prohibiting discrimination. However, the Burger Court acted decisively to expand protections against sex discrimination under the Constitution, and the Rehnquist and Roberts Courts have made major rulings against legal discrimination based on sexual orientation. Those decisions culminated in the Court's decision in *Obergefell v. Hodges* (2015), which struck down state prohibitions on same-sex marriage.

Especially under Chief Justice Roberts, the Court has expanded civil liberties that conservatives tend to favor. A series of decisions from 1976 through 2014 limited government regulation of political campaign funding on the basis of the First Amendment.[43] In 2008 the Court held for the first time that the Second Amendment protected the right to individual gun ownership from federal abridgment, and two years later the Court ruled that this right applied to state governments as well.[44]

The Court has also shifted direction in economic policy. On the whole, its interpretations of federal statutes on environmental protection and labor-management relations have become more conservative. More broadly, its decisions have become more favorable to the business community. Since 1995 the Court has also narrowed congressional power to regulate the private sector and state governments in some respects.[45] In *National Federation of Independent Business v. Sebelius* (2012), the Court upheld the heart of President Obama's health care law on the basis of the federal taxing power. But this decision also held that the law could not be justified on the basis of the power to regulate interstate commerce, and it narrowed the power of the federal government to withhold money from states that did not sign on to federal programs.

The absence of a more decisive shift in the Court's policies since 1969 has disappointed some conservative observers of the Court. Still, those policies have moved considerably to the right, underlining the impact of the Court's membership on its work. Because of that impact the selection of justices is a crucial process—a process that the next chapter examines.

NOTES

1. These decisions were *National Federation of Independent Business v. Sebelius* (2012) and *King v. Burwell* (2015).
2. These decisions were *United States v. Nixon* (1974) and *Bush v. Gore* (2000).
3. Alexis de Tocqueville, *Democracy in America*, 2 vols., trans. Henry Reeve, rev. Francis Bowen (New York: Knopf, 1945), 1: 280.
4. The history of the case is summarized in the Court's 2015 decision, *Kansas v. Nebraska*.
5. *Statement Concerning the Supreme Court's Front Entrance*, 176 L. Ed. 2d i (2010).
6. Lyle Denniston, "New Protest Ban for the Plaza," SCOTUSblog, June 13, 2013, http://www.scotusblog.com/2013/06/new-protest-ban-for-the-plaza. The district court decision was *Hodge v. Talkin* (D.D.C. 2013).
7. *Beer v. United States* (Fed. Cir. 2012).
8. The justices' annual financial disclosure reports list the (very) approximate values of their financial assets at the end of each calendar year. They also list the justices' outside income, including book royalties. The reports for the justices since 2002 are posted at https://www.opensecrets.org/pfds.
9. 28 U.S.C. § 455.
10. James M. Sample, "Supreme Court Recusal: From Marbury to the Modern Day," *Georgetown Journal of Legal Ethics* 95 (Winter 2013): 95–151.
11. *Elk Grove v. Newdow* (2004).
12. Jess Bravin, *The Terror Courts: Rough Justice at Guantanamo Bay* (New Haven, Conn.: Yale University Press, 2013), 281.
13. *Warner v. Gross* (2015); *Glossip v. Gross* (2015). See Eric M. Freedman, "No Execution if Four Justices Object," *Hofstra Law Review* 43 (2015): 639–666.
14. Becky Krystal, "Supreme Court Cafeteria," *Washington Post*, July 14, 2010, E2.
15. Tony Mauro and Marcia Coyle, "Aside from Wal-Mart, Few Huge Cases at High Court," *National Law Journal*, December 26, 2011, 7.
16. Charlie Savage, "Roberts's Picks Reshaping Secret Surveillance Court," *New York Times*, July 26, 2013, A1, A13.
17. Devin Dwyer, "'Cushy' Job, or 'Isolated' Hell? Life as a Supreme Court Justice," *ABC News*, April 23, 2010, http://abcnews.go.com/Politics/Supreme_Court/life-supreme-court-cushy-job-justice/story?id=10449434.

18. On law clerks and justices, see Todd C. Peppers and Artemus Ward, eds., *In Chambers: Stories of Supreme Court Law Clerks and Their Justices* (Charlottesville: University of Virginia Press, 2012).
19. This figure was calculated from information sheets provided by the Supreme Court.
20. See Lawrence Baum, "Hiring Supreme Court Law Clerks: Probing the Ideological Linkage between Judges and Justices," *Marquette Law Review* 98 (Fall 2014): 333–360.
21. Brian Lamb, Susan Swain, and Mark Farkas, eds., *The Supreme Court: A C-Span Book Featuring the Justices in Their Own Words* (New York: PublicAffairs, 2010), 155; Jennifer Senior, "In Conversation: Antonin Scalia," *New York Magazine,* October 2013, 80.
22. "Kagan Offers a View of a Justice's Working Life," Harvard Law School, September 26, 2012, http://news.harvard.edu/gazette/story/newsplus/kagan-offers-a-view-of-a-justices-working-life.
23. Todd C. Peppers and Christopher Zorn, "Law Clerk Influence on Supreme Court Decision Making: An Empirical Assessment," *DePaul Law Review* 58 (2008): 410–427.
24. David Lat, "It's Official: Supreme Court Clerkship Bonuses Hit a New High," *Above the Law* blog, August 15, 2013, http://abovethelaw.com/2013/08/its-official-supreme-court-clerkship-bonuses-hit-a-new-high/#more-264505.
25. Adam Liptak, "Seeking Justice? Try the Courtroom, Not the Line Outside," *New York Times,* April 16, 2013, A13.
26. Miriam Hill, "Justice, Philadelphia Style: Scalia Gets Two Parking Tickets," *Philadelphia Inquirer,* October 17, 2012, B1.
27. Barbara A. Perry, *The Priestly Tribe: The Supreme Court's Image in the American Mind* (Westport, Conn.: Praeger, 1999).
28. Richard Davis, *Justices and Journalists: The U.S. Supreme Court and the Media* (New York: Cambridge University Press, 2011), 170–186.
29. Noah Rothman, "CNN's Jeffrey Toobin: Supreme Court Afraid of *The Daily Show,*" *Mediaite,* February 24, 2014, http://www.mediaite.com/tv/cnns-jeffrey-toobin-supreme-court-afraid-of-the-daily-show.
30. Jess Bravin, "Justice Ginsburg Was Very Amused by John Oliver's Doggy Supreme Court," *Wall Street Journal,* October 28, 2014, http://blogs.wsj.com/law/2014/10/28/justice-ginsburg-was-very-amused-by-john-olivers-doggy-supreme-court.
31. Jeffrey Rosen, "RBG Presides," *New Republic,* October 13, 2014, 22.
32. Tal Kopan, "The Not-so-Reclusive Justices," *Politico,* June 28, 2013, http://www.politico.com/story/2013/06/supreme-court-justices-public-appearances-93583.html.
33. Frederic Block, *Disrobed: An Inside Look at the Life and Work of a Federal Trial Judge* (Eagan, Minn.: West Publishing, 2012), 186.
34. Nichole Zhao, "Chief Justice Speaks at Rice," *The Rice Thresher,* October 19, 2012, http://www.ricethresher.org/article_16232aeb-468f-5d5f-b237-a997446e3d0e.html.
35. The Court's schedule is described in Stephen M. Shapiro, Kenneth S. Geller, Timothy S. Bishop, Edward A. Hartnett, and Dan Himmelfarb, *Supreme Court Practice,* 10th ed. (Arlington, Va.: Bloomberg BNA, 2013), 11–16.
36. The decisions were *King v. Burwell* (2015) and *Obergefell v. Hodges* (2015).

37. See William R. Casto, *The Supreme Court in the Early Republic: The Chief Justiceships of John Jay and Oliver Ellsworth* (Columbia: University of South Carolina Press, 1995). For another perspective, see Scott Douglas Gerber, ed., *Seriatim: The Supreme Court before John Marshall* (New York: New York University Press, 1998).

38. Robert G. McCloskey, *The American Supreme Court*, 6th ed., rev. Sanford Levinson (Chicago: University of Chicago Press, 2010), 64–66.

39. This figure was calculated from information in Congressional Research Service, *The Constitution of the United States of America: Analysis and Interpretation* (Washington, D.C.: Government Printing Office, 2014), 2283–2573.

40. The cases included *Carter v. Carter Coal Co.* (1936); *United States v. Butler* (1936); and *Schechter Poultry Corp. v. United States* (1935).

41. The cases included *National Labor Relations Board v. Jones & Laughlin Steel Corp.* (1937); *Steward Machine Co. v. Davis* (1937); and *West Coast Hotel Co. v. Parrish* (1937).

42. William G. Ross, *The Chief Justiceship of Charles Evans Hughes, 1930–1941* (Columbia: University of South Carolina Press, 2007), ix–xi and chap. 4.

43. The most important decisions were *Buckley v. Valeo* (1976) and *Citizens United v. Federal Election Commission* (2010); the most recent decision is *McCutcheon v. Federal Election Commission* (2014).

44. *District of Columbia v. Heller* (2008); *McDonald v. City of Chicago* (2010).

45. See *United States v. Morrison* (2000) and *Gonzales v. Raich* (2005).

Chapter 2

The Justices

In 2013 and 2014, a series of liberal commentators suggested in print that it would be a good idea for Justice Ruth Bader Ginsburg to retire in the near future. Why would these commentators want a justice to leave the Court when they heartily agreed with most of the votes she cast and the opinions she wrote? They feared that if the Senate gained a Republican majority in the 2014 elections, it would be difficult for President Obama to get a strong liberal nominee—or perhaps any nominee—confirmed in the two years that followed. And if Ginsburg waited until 2017 or later to retire, a Republican president might be in office to move the Court to the right by appointing Ginsburg's successor.

This episode underlines the importance of the Supreme Court's membership. To a great extent, the Court's policies are a product of who the justices are, and even a single justice can make considerable difference. For that reason, decisions by justices about leaving the Court and decisions by the president and Senate about nominating and confirming new justices are quite important.

As of mid-2015, presidents have made 153 nominations to the Supreme Court, and 112 justices have served on it. Four candidates were nominated and confirmed twice, and eight declined appointments or died before beginning service on the Court. Twenty-nine did not secure Senate confirmation; a few of these nominees dropped out before the Senate could consider them.[1]

Table 2-1 lists the thirty-three nominations to the Court since 1953 and the twenty-six justices chosen since that time. This chapter focuses on that period and primarily on the past few decades. In this chapter's three sections I discuss the selection of justices, the attributes of the people who are selected, and how and why justices leave the Court.

TABLE 2-1
Nominations to the Supreme Court since 1953

Name	Nominating president	Justice replaced	Years served
Earl Warren (CJ)	Eisenhower	Vinson	1953–1969
John Harlan	Eisenhower	Jackson	1955–1971
William Brennan	Eisenhower	Minton	1956–1990
Charles Whittaker	Eisenhower	Reed	1957–1962
Potter Stewart	Eisenhower	Burton	1958–1981
Byron White	Kennedy	Whittaker	1962–1993
Arthur Goldberg	Kennedy	Frankfurter	1962–1965
Abe Fortas	Johnson	Goldberg	1965–1969
Thurgood Marshall	Johnson	Clark	1967–1991
Abe Fortas (CJ)	Johnson	(Warren)	Withdrew, 1968
Homer Thornberry	Johnson	(Fortas)	Moot, 1968
Warren Burger (CJ)	Nixon	Warren	1969–1986
Clement Haynsworth	Nixon	(Fortas)	Defeated, 1969
G. Harrold Carswell	Nixon	(Fortas)	Defeated, 1970
Harry Blackmun	Nixon	Fortas	1970–1994
Lewis Powell	Nixon	Black	1971–1987
William Rehnquist	Nixon	Harlan	1971–2005
John Paul Stevens	Ford	Douglas	1975–2010
Sandra Day O'Connor	Reagan	Stewart	1981–2006
William Rehnquist (CJ)	Reagan	Burger	1986–2005
Antonin Scalia	Reagan	Rehnquist	1986–
Robert Bork	Reagan	(Powell)	Defeated, 1987
Douglas Ginsburg	Reagan	(Powell)	Withdrew, 1987
Anthony Kennedy	Reagan	Powell	1988–
David Souter	G. H. W. Bush	Brennan	1990–2009
Clarence Thomas	G. H. W. Bush	Marshall	1991–
Ruth Bader Ginsburg	Clinton	White	1993–
Stephen Breyer	Clinton	Blackmun	1994–
John Roberts (CJ)	G. W. Bush	Rehnquist	2005–
Harriet Miers	G. W. Bush	(O'Connor)	Withdrew, 2005
Samuel Alito	G. W. Bush	O'Connor	2006–
Sonia Sotomayor	Obama	Souter	2009–
Elena Kagan	Obama	Stevens	2010–

Note: CJ = chief justice. Fortas and Rehnquist were associate justices when nominated as chief justice. Roberts was originally nominated to replace O'Connor, then was nominated for chief justice after Rehnquist's death.

Withdrew = Nomination or planned nomination was withdrawn. The Fortas nomination was withdrawn after a vote to end a filibuster failed. Douglas Ginsburg withdrew before he was formally nominated.

Moot = When Fortas withdrew as nominee for chief justice, the Thornberry nomination to take Fortas's position as associate justice became moot.

Defeated = Senate voted against confirmation.

The Selection of Justices

The formal rules for selection of Supreme Court justices are simple. When a vacancy occurs, the president makes a nomination. The nomination must then be confirmed by the Senate, with a simple majority of participating senators required for confirmation. When the chief justice's position is vacant, the president has two options: to nominate a sitting justice to that position and also nominate a new associate justice or to nominate a person as chief justice from outside the Court. Presidents usually take the latter course, as President George W. Bush did when he selected John Roberts to succeed William Rehnquist in 2005. But President Ronald Reagan elevated Rehnquist from associate justice to chief justice after Warren Burger retired in 1986.

The actual process of selection is more complicated than the formal rules suggest. The decisions of presidents and senators are shaped by individuals and groups with a strong interest in these decisions, and the process of nomination and confirmation can be long and convoluted. I will discuss the roles of unofficial participants in the process and then consider how the president and the Senate reach their decisions.

Unofficial Participants

Because Supreme Court appointments are so important, many people seek to influence the president and the Senate. When a vacancy occurs, presidents and other administration officials may hear from a wide array of individuals and groups. So do senators who are deciding whether to support a nominee's confirmation. The most important of these individuals and groups fall into three categories: the legal community, other interest groups, and people who seek nominations for themselves.

The Legal Community. Lawyers have a particular interest in the Court's membership, and their views about potential justices may carry special weight. As the largest and most prominent organization of lawyers, the American Bar Association (ABA) occupies an important position. An ABA committee investigates presidential nominees who await confirmation and evaluates them as "well-qualified," "qualified," or "not qualified."

Some Republican senators believe that the ABA committee is biased against conservative nominees and give little weight to its judgment. Still, the committee's level of enthusiasm for a nominee can affect the confirmation process. (It has never rated a Supreme Court nominee as "not qualified.") A unanimous rating of "well-qualified," which most nominees receive, assists a nominee in winning Senate approval. By the same token, when four committee members rated Robert Bork as "not qualified" in 1987 and two gave that rating to Clarence Thomas in 1991, the nominees' prospects for confirmation were weakened. Those negative ratings of two conservative Republicans—one of them (Bork) a prestigious legal scholar—fostered the perception of bias in the ABA committee's decisions.

Other legal groups and individual lawyers also participate in the selection process. Law professors and other prominent attorneys often announce their evaluations of nominees the Senate is considering. For Republican presidents, the conservative Federalist Society of lawyers serves as a key source of advice. Seven of Samuel Alito's current and past colleagues on the federal Court of Appeals for the Third Circuit testified on his behalf in the Judiciary Committee after his nomination by President George W. Bush. Elena Kagan was solicitor general—head of the office that represents the federal government in the Supreme Court—when President Obama nominated her to the Court. Each of her predecessors in that office going back to 1985 joined a letter supporting her confirmation.

Supreme Court justices sometimes participate in the selection process, most often by recommending a potential nominee. Chief Justice Warren Burger went further. Appointed by Richard Nixon in 1969, he was active in suggesting names to fill other vacancies during the Nixon administration. He played a crucial role in the nomination of his longtime friend Harry Blackmun. Some years later, Burger lobbied the Reagan administration on behalf of Sandra Day O'Connor.[2]

Other Interest Groups. Many interest groups have a stake in Supreme Court decisions, so groups often seek to influence the selection of justices. The level of group activity has grown substantially in the past half century, and it now pervades both the nomination and confirmation stages of the selection process.

Interest groups would most like to influence the president's nomination decision. The groups that actually exert influence at this stage are typically the ones that are politically important to the president. Democratic presidents usually give some weight to the views of labor and civil rights groups. Republican presidents usually pay attention to groups that take conservative positions on social issues such as abortion.

The influence of these core groups was underlined in 2005, after President Bush nominated White House counsel Harriet Miers to succeed Sandra Day O'Connor. Many conservatives were uncertain that Miers held views similar to their own, and some groups and individuals mounted a strong campaign against her. After their campaign secured Miers's withdrawal, President Bush chose Samuel Alito, who was popular with conservative groups.

Once a nomination is announced, groups often work for or against Senate confirmation. Significant interest group activity was limited and sporadic until the late 1960s.[3] Its higher level since then reflects growth in the number of interest groups and the intensity of group activity, greater awareness that nominations to the Court are important, and group leaders' increased understanding of how to influence the confirmation process. Ideological groups have also found that opposition to controversial nominees is a good way to generate interest in their causes and monetary contributions from their supporters.

Groups that opposed specific nominees achieved noteworthy successes between 1968 and 1970. Conservative groups helped to defeat Abe Fortas, nominated for elevation to chief justice by President Lyndon Johnson in 1968, and labor and civil rights groups helped to secure the defeats of Richard Nixon's nominees Clement Haynsworth and G. Harrold Carswell. President Reagan's nomination of Robert Bork in 1987 gave rise to an unprecedented level of group activity, and the strong mobilization by liberal groups was one key to Bork's defeat in the Senate.

Since the Bork nomination, interest groups have played active roles in response to every Supreme Court nomination. Group activity increases with the perception that a nominee would shift the ideological balance in the Court substantially and that a nominee might be vulnerable to defeat. Both conditions existed with President George H. W. Bush's nomination of Clarence Thomas in 1991, and that nomination produced a heated battle between competing groups. But even when these conditions are lacking, there are always some groups that mount campaigns against nominees. That was true of Elena Kagan, whose nomination aroused opposition from groups such as Americans United for Life and the National Rifle Association. As one commentator described it, groups' opposition to Kagan "is an appeal to their bases, to keep them energized."[4]

Candidates for the Court. Some Supreme Court nominees had never thought of themselves as potential justices. President George W. Bush has reported that Harriet Miers "was surprised—more like shocked" when Bush asked about her interest in a nomination.[5] Some prospective nominees withdraw from consideration, and some turn down nominations. Former president Bill Clinton reported in 2012 that Governor Mario Cuomo of New York had declined a Clinton nomination to the Court.[6] Even some lawyers who accept nominations do so reluctantly. But for many lawyers, the Supreme Court is a long-standing dream, so they would (and do) accept nominations readily.

Some people conduct concerted private campaigns for Supreme Court nominations. William Howard Taft became chief justice in 1921 after years of efforts to position himself for that appointment. As an ex-president he had a great deal of influence, and one commentator described Taft as "virtually appointing himself" chief justice.[7] More often, prospective nominees engage in quieter campaigns to enhance their chances. Ruth Bader

Ginsburg reported that a law clerk told her some kind of campaign was necessary if she were to have a chance of elevation to the Supreme Court, and her husband Martin Ginsburg "became my campaign manager" and organized a campaign of letters on his wife's behalf.[8]

There is circumstantial evidence that some judges on the courts of appeals campaign in a different way, taking positions in cases that they hope will enhance their chances of a Supreme Court nomination.[9] In an era when potential nominees' records are scrutinized closely, even

AP Photo/Ed Bailey, File

Justice Ruth Bader Ginsburg with her husband Martin Ginsburg in 2003. As then-Judge Ginsburg's "campaign manager," Martin Ginsburg helped her become a strong candidate for the Supreme Court nomination that she received from President Bill Clinton in 1993.

one "wrong" vote in a case can jeopardize promotion. Retired justice John Paul Stevens speculated that a very well-regarded Republican court of appeals judge had lost his chance for a Supreme Court nomination when he voted to uphold the requirement in President Obama's health care plan that certain individuals purchase health insurance.[10]

Nominees participate actively in the confirmation process. They visit senators, provide voluminous written materials to the Senate Judiciary Committee, and testify before the committee at its hearings on confirmation. Nominees now meet with the great majority of senators. After a long series of such meetings, in which many senators asked whether she had ever fired a gun or gone hunting, a weary Elena Kagan told one senator that "if you were to invite me hunting, I would really love to go." After observing what she called "this look of total horror" on the senator's face, Kagan said, "I didn't really mean to invite myself, but I'll tell you what, if I am lucky enough to be confirmed, I will ask Justice Scalia to take me hunting"—which he has done several times.[11]

Because nominees' testimony receives so much attention, it has become a key to confirmation. Its importance is reflected in the elaborate preparations that nominees go through, which often include practice hearings. The questions that senators ask nominees range widely, but one important aim is to ascertain a nominee's views about the issues that the Supreme Court addresses.[12] Senators who seek to defeat a nominee try to get the nominee to take positions that could arouse opposition. But well-prepared nominees can usually overcome those efforts. They turn back questions about matters such as abortion or the death penalty on the ground—largely legitimate—that they do not want to "prejudge" issues that might come before the Court. They can limit criticism for being unresponsive by addressing questions about issues on which they know their answers will be popular or uncontroversial. As one senator said during the hearing on Samuel Alito, a hearing is "a subtle minuet, with the nominee answering as many questions as he thinks are necessary in order to be confirmed."[13]

In a 1995 article, law professor Elena Kagan strongly criticized nominees for their evasions and senators for failing to press nominees harder, and she said that confirmation hearings had become "a vapid and hollow charade."[14] But at her own confirmation hearing fifteen years later, she said that she had been wrong when she wrote that article, and she was as cautious as other recent nominees. Whatever she may have thought about the confirmation process, Kagan had little reason to abandon a strategy that had proved successful for other nominees.

Nominees do differ somewhat in their approaches, based in part on the concerns that have been raised about them. John Roberts impressed senators with his expertise and personality, and he adroitly avoided the traps that some Democratic committee members sought to lay for him. Alito was not quite as effective in putting forth a positive image, but he too avoided traps that were related to his reputation as a strong conservative. One commentator said, "John Roberts charmed his way through the proceedings. Sam Alito has chosen to simply bore his way through."[15] Sonia Sotomayor faced questions from Republican senators about decisions and out-of-court statements she had made that they saw as potentially damaging to her. She was cautious in her testimony but sought to address the concerns that Republicans raised. Her testimony did not satisfy her critics, but she did not say anything that attracted additional criticism.

The President's Decision

For the president, a Supreme Court vacancy provides a valuable opportunity to influence the Court's direction, and presidents seek to make the most of these opportunities. But the individuals and groups for whom nominations are important can subject the president to heavy and conflicting pressures, and the pressures have grown stronger in recent years.[16]

Presidents differ in their personal involvement in the selection process. Bill Clinton, George W. Bush, and Barack Obama played a more active role in the process than did their predecessors Ronald Reagan and George H. W. Bush. Obama, a former constitutional law professor with a strong interest in the Court, has been especially active. Obama interviewed several prospective nominees before selecting Sonia Sotomayor and Elena Kagan, and he met with Senate leaders from both parties prior to the Kagan nomination.

Still, all presidents delegate most of the search process to other officials in the executive branch. In recent administrations the process has been centered in the Office of the White House Counsel.[17] Obama's search for a nominee in 2009 involved intense activity within his administration. Staff in the counsel's office and Vice President Biden's office, among others, worked to identify and gather information on prospective nominees, and they enlisted people within and outside the administration to do extensive research on the candidates. Staff members and Biden himself interviewed candidates.

Administrations in the current era typically do a good deal of preparatory work even before a vacancy in the Court actually arises. In the George W. Bush administration, White House officials interviewed prospective nominees in 2001—four years before there was a vacancy to fill.[18] Once a vacancy occurs, occasionally a president fixes on a single candidate for nomination. When Chief Justice Rehnquist died, President Bush quickly chose John Roberts for that position; he had already nominated Roberts to succeed Justice O'Connor. More often, administrations create a short list and then work to identify the best candidate from that list. President Obama chose Elena Kagan from a group of finalists that included three judges on the federal courts of appeals.[19] This process allows presidents and other officials to work systematically through the advantages and disadvantages of choosing different names from the list. But uncertainties about potential nominees and shifting conditions often introduce an element of chaos to the process. That was true of the George W. Bush nominations and, even more, those made by President Clinton.

Administrations differ in the mix of criteria that presidents and their advisers use in choosing nominees. The possible criteria fall into several categories: the "objective" qualifications of potential nominees, their policy preferences, rewards to political and personal associates, and building political support. Cutting across these criteria and helping to determine their use is the reality that the Senate decides whether to confirm a nominee.

"Objective" Qualifications. Presidents have strong incentives to select Supreme Court nominees who have demonstrated high levels of legal competence and adherence to ethical standards. Most presidents respect the Court. Further, highly competent justices are in the best position to influence their colleagues. Finally, serious questions about a candidate's competence or ethical behavior work against Senate confirmation.

Because presidents care about competence, only in a few cases has a nominee's capacity to serve on the Court been seriously questioned. One of those was Nixon's nominee G. Harrold Carswell, who was denied confirmation. Perceptions that Harriet Miers had only limited knowledge of constitutional law were one source of the opposition that ultimately led her to withdraw as a nominee.

The ethical behavior of several nominees has been questioned. Opponents of Abe Fortas (when nominated to be chief justice), Clement Haynsworth, Stephen Breyer, and Samuel Alito pointed to what they saw as financial conflicts of interest. Fortas was also criticized for continuing to consult with President Johnson while serving as an associate justice. The charges against Fortas and Haynsworth helped prevent their confirmation. After Douglas Ginsburg was announced as a Reagan nominee, a disclosure about his past use of marijuana led to his withdrawal from consideration. An allegation that Clarence Thomas had sexually harassed an assistant while he was a federal administrator resulted in a special set of Senate hearings on the charge and put his confirmation in jeopardy.

To minimize the possibility of such embarrassments, administrations today give close scrutiny to the competence and ethics of potential nominees. Although these criteria eliminate some people from consideration, enough candidates survive to give presidents a wide range of choices for a nomination.

Policy Preferences. By policy preferences I mean an individual's attitudes toward policy issues. These criteria have always been a consideration in the selection of Supreme Court justices. In the current era every president gives considerable weight to the policy preferences of prospective nominees because of the Court's prominence as a policymaker and because interest groups associated with both parties care so much about the Court's direction.

But presidents continue to differ in how much they focus on nominees' policy views. Ronald Reagan, who wanted to change the Court's direction, gave this consideration some emphasis. Policy considerations were even more important to George W. Bush, in part because he and other conservatives were unhappy that a string of appointments by his Republican predecessors had changed the Court less than they had hoped. In contrast, Bill Clinton was less concerned with the policy views of his prospective nominees. Memoranda by people helping Clinton in 1993 described Stephen Breyer as moderate or even moderately conservative on some issues, but Clinton nonetheless nominated Breyer to the Court a year later.[20]

This criterion can create a dilemma for presidents. Interest groups and political activists associated with the two parties tend to favor nominees with strong ideological views—liberal Democrats or conservative Republicans. Most presidents themselves have similar preferences. But a nominee who is perceived as relatively extreme may be vulnerable to defeat in the Senate, because interest groups on the other side are more likely to mobilize against such a nominee and more senators will perceive the nominee as ideologically unacceptable. Presidents have responded to this dilemma in different ways, depending in part on their willingness to get into conflicts over the selection of nominees. President Obama chose Sonia Sotomayor and Elena Kagan over other candidates who seemed more liberal, in part to minimize problems in the confirmation process.

Presidents who want to put like-minded people on the Supreme Court need to ascertain that their nominees really are like-minded. This is one reason why every nominee since 1986 except for Kagan and Harriet Miers has come from a federal court of appeals. If a judge has a long record of judicial votes and opinions on issues of federal law, as Sotomayor and Samuel Alito did, presidents and their advisers can be fairly confident about the kinds of positions the judge would take on many issues as a justice.

Some nominees do not have these long records. Miers and Kagan had never served as judges. Sandra Day O'Connor had served only on state courts, and most kinds of issues that come to the Supreme Court are uncommon in state courts. John Roberts, Clarence Thomas, and David Souter had only short service on federal courts of appeals—Souter so short that he had written no opinions. For candidates such as these, other sources of information can be consulted. In Miers's case, George W. Bush had a good sense of her views from their long association with each other. Sometimes presidents or their representatives ask prospective nominees directly about their views. According to one report, presidential advisers questioned John Roberts closely in order to ascertain the strength of his conservatism.[21]

Presidents concerned with confirmation of their nominees prefer a situation in which they have a clear sense of their nominees' views, but there is little public evidence of those views for opponents to attack. As George W. Bush said about Miers, "There's not a lot of opinions for people to look at."[22] But the lack of hard evidence that Miers was strongly conservative on judicial issues bothered members of the president's own party. In the case of David Souter, President George H. W. Bush had what he thought was good evidence of the nominee's conservatism from people who knew him, but Senate Democrats had little evidence of their own with which to raise questions about Souter. Souter was confirmed with little difficulty, but his record as a justice indicates that he was not nearly as conservative as Bush thought. That record has served as a cautionary tale for conservatives, and fear of another Souter helps explain the strong opposition to Miers.

Exceptions such as Souter get considerable attention, but most justices turn out to take ideological positions on the Court that are similar to their appointing presidents' own positions. Those who deviate from the appointing president generally fall into two categories. First, some were chosen by presidents who lacked a strong interest in choosing compatible justices or who were not careful about doing so. Gerald Ford selected John Paul Stevens without regard for his nominee's policy preferences, so the gap between Ford's conservatism and Stevens's liberalism is not surprising. According to a widely circulated story of uncertain accuracy, Dwight Eisenhower cited his appointees Earl Warren and William Brennan as the two mistakes he had made as president.[23] But as California governor, Warren had shown signs of the liberalism he later manifested as chief justice, and Brennan's liberalism was apparent from his record as a state judge.

Second, some justices shift their ideological positions after reaching the Court. Richard Nixon's one "failure" was Harry Blackmun, who had a distinctly conservative record in his early years on the Court but gradually adopted more liberal positions. Anthony Kennedy also may have shifted in a liberal direction after reaching the Court, albeit to a lesser degree. A conservative publication later referred to Kennedy as "surely Reagan's biggest disappointment."[24]

Political and Personal Reward. When George W. Bush nominated Harriet Miers to the Supreme Court in 2005, he had known Miers for a dozen years. In Texas she was his personal lawyer. She joined his presidential administration in 2001, serving in the White House as staff secretary, deputy chief of staff, and counsel to the president.

In choosing Miers, Bush took what had been a common approach for most of the Supreme Court's history. As of the late 1960s, about 60 percent of the nominees to the Court had known the nominating president personally.[25] With the exception of Dwight Eisenhower, all the presidents from Franklin Roosevelt through Lyndon Johnson selected primarily personal acquaintances.

Rewarding political associates seemed to be the main criterion for Harry Truman in choosing justices. One of those associates was Sherman Minton, a friend and former Senate colleague of Truman's, who was serving as a federal judge in Indiana when he learned that one of the justices had died. He quickly boarded a train to Washington, went to the White House, and asked Truman to nominate him for the vacancy. Truman immediately agreed, and Minton became a justice.[26]

Some appointments to the Court were direct rewards for political help. Eisenhower selected Earl Warren to serve as chief justice largely because of Warren's crucial support of Eisenhower at the 1952 Republican convention. As governor of California and leader of that state's delegation at the convention, Warren had provided Eisenhower the needed votes on a preliminary issue and thereby helped secure his nomination.

Of the more recent nominees, Miers certainly falls in the category of close associates. Elena Kagan may fit in that category as well. President

Obama met her when both taught at the University of Chicago Law School, kept in contact with her after that, and selected her as solicitor general after he was elected president. In announcing Kagan's nomination, Obama called her "my friend."[27] But Miers and Kagan stand alone among the people whom presidents have selected since 1968. Indeed, few nominees in that period have had any contact with the president before being considered for the Court. Obama first met Sonia Sotomayor a few days before choosing her as his nominee in 2009.[28]

Perhaps the main reason for the decline in the selection of personal acquaintances is that such nominees are vulnerable to charges of "cronyism." That charge was made in 1968 when President Johnson nominated Justice Abe Fortas for elevation to chief justice and nominated Judge Homer Thornberry to succeed Fortas as associate justice; both Fortas and Thornberry were close to Johnson. The charge played a small role in building opposition to Fortas and Thornberry in the Senate. Ultimately, Fortas's confirmation was blocked by a filibuster, and Thornberry's nomination thus became moot. Miers's nomination was also attacked as a case of cronyism, and that charge was one factor in the pressures that led to her withdrawal.

One element of political reward has remained strong, however: About 90 percent of all nominees to the Court—and all those chosen since 1975—have been members of the president's party. One reason is that lawyers who share the president's policy views are more likely to come from the same party, especially in the current era of partisan polarization. But there is also a widespread feeling that such an attractive prize should go to one of the party faithful.

Building Political Support. Nominations can be made to reward people who helped the president in the past, but they can also be used to seek political benefits in the future. Most often, presidents select justices with certain attributes in order to appeal to leaders and voters who share those attributes.

Geography and religion were important criteria for selecting justices in some past eras, but their role in nominations has nearly disappeared. The decline of interest in maintaining geographical diversity is symbolized by the fact that four of the current justices grew up in New York City. Similarly, the decline of religion as a consideration is symbolized by the fact that the current Court includes no Protestants, even though they constitute a clear majority of people in the country who have religious affiliations.

In contrast, representation by race, gender, and ethnicity has become quite important. President George H. W. Bush's nomination of Clarence Thomas to succeed Thurgood Marshall reflected the pressure he felt to maintain black representation on the Court. President Reagan felt even greater pressure to choose the first female justice, and he responded by selecting Sandra Day O'Connor as his first nominee. The nominations of Harriet Miers, Sonia Sotomayor, and Elena Kagan also reflected an interest in putting women on the Court. Notably, Miers and Sotomayor were selected from sets of finalists who were all female. Barack Obama's choice of Sotomayor over the other finalists was heavily influenced by a desire to select the first Hispanic justice, largely to please an important group in the electorate. Indeed, in 2012 Obama's reelection campaign issued a video that featured Latina women praising his appointment of Sotomayor.

Summary. Presidents use several criteria to choose Supreme Court nominees. The importance of these considerations changes over time and varies from one nomination to another.

The Court's importance has powerful effects on these criteria. First, it leads presidents and their representatives to weigh all the criteria more carefully than they generally do in nominating judges to lower courts. Second, it leads to an emphasis on competence and policy preferences rather than the "political" considerations of reward and support building. If Supreme Court justices are better jurists than the judges on lower federal courts, and if their policy preferences are more accurate reflections of their nominators' views, it is chiefly because presidents have a strong incentive to achieve those results.

Senate Confirmation

A president's nomination to the Court goes to the Senate for confirmation. The nomination is referred to the Judiciary Committee, which gathers extensive information on the nominee, holds hearings at which the nominee and other witnesses testify, and then votes its recommendation for Senate action. After this vote the nomination is referred to the floor, where it is debated and a confirmation vote taken.

Although a simple majority is needed for confirmation, a large minority of senators (under the current rules, forty-one) could block confirmation through a filibuster that uses extended debate to prevent a confirmation vote. That was the fate of Abe Fortas's nomination for chief justice in 1968. In 2006 some Democrats called for a filibuster against confirmation of Samuel Alito, but the Senate voted 75–25 to end debate and proceed to a vote.

The Senate's Role and Record. When the president nominates someone to any position, the presumption typically is in favor of confirmation. That presumption applies to the Supreme Court. But the Senate gives Supreme Court nominations close scrutiny, and confirmation is far from automatic.

Indeed, defeats of nominees are hardly rare. Through mid-2015 the Senate has refused to confirm twenty-six nominations to the Supreme Court, through either an adverse vote or inaction. These twenty-six cases constitute about one-sixth of the nominations that the Senate has considered. This proportion of defeats is the highest of any position to which the president makes appointments. For example, presidents have made far more nominations of cabinet members, but only nine have failed to win confirmation.

Presidents have been more successful with Supreme Court nominations in the twentieth century and the early twenty-first century than in the nineteenth. Since 1900 only five of the sixty-three nominations considered by the Senate have failed: Herbert Hoover's nomination of John Parker in 1930, Johnson's elevation of Abe Fortas to chief justice in 1968, Nixon's nominations of Clement Haynsworth in 1969 and G. Harrold Carswell in 1970 (both for the same vacancy), and Reagan's nomination of Robert Bork in 1987.

Even with a continuing high level of success for nominees, on the whole they have faced increased opposition in the past few decades because of two developments. First, the expansive interpretations of constitutional protections for civil liberties by the Warren Court in the 1960s increased senators' interest in the Court's policies and thus in its membership. Second, growing partisan and ideological polarization in American politics since around the 1980s has given senators who are not in the president's party stronger incentives to oppose nominees.

Those developments have led to closer scrutiny of nominees: The median time from nomination to confirmation vote was twenty-eight days between 1949 and 1980 and eighty-four days since then.[29] They are also reflected in the Senate confirmation votes shown in Table 2-2. Since 1967, not only have four nominees failed to win confirmation but several others have received substantial numbers of negative votes. Senators have been especially willing to vote against nominees in the past two decades. The last four nominees, selected by George W. Bush and Barack Obama, all received more than twenty negative votes. Of the 132 votes cast against those four nominees, only two came from members of the president's party.

Nominees and Situations. Nominees vary a great deal in the difficulty they face in the Senate, from those who face no opposition to those who fail to win the needed majority. This variation reflects the attributes of nominees and of the situations in which the Senate considers them.[30]

The attributes of nominees that affect confirmation the most are their perceived ideological positions and qualifications. Nominees who are thought to be highly liberal or highly conservative have greater difficulty than those who seem to be moderate. And nominees who seem less qualified than they should be also arouse opposition. The two attributes can

TABLE 2-2
Senate Votes on Supreme Court Nominations since 1949

Nominee	Year	Vote
Tom Clark	1949	73–8
Sherman Minton	1949	48–16
Earl Warren	1954	NRV
John Harlan	1955	71–11
William Brennan	1956	NRV
Charles Whittaker	1957	NRV
Potter Stewart	1959	70–17
Byron White	1962	NRV
Arthur Goldberg	1962	NRV
Abe Fortas	1965	NRV
Thurgood Marshall	1967	69–11
Abe Fortas[a]	1968	Withdrawn
Homer Thornberry	(1968)	No action
Warren Burger	1969	74–3
Clement Haynsworth	1969	45–55
G. Harrold Carswell	1970	45–51
Harry Blackmun	1970	94–0
Lewis Powell	1971	89–1
William Rehnquist	1971	68–26
John Paul Stevens	1975	98–0
Sandra Day O'Connor	1981	99–0
William Rehnquist[b]	1986	65–33
Antonin Scalia	1986	98–0
Robert Bork	1987	42–58
Douglas Ginsburg	(1987)	No action
Anthony Kennedy	1988	97–0
David Souter	1990	90–9
Clarence Thomas	1991	52–48
Ruth Bader Ginsburg	1993	96–3
Stephen Breyer	1994	87–9
John Roberts	2005	78–22
Harriet Miers	(2005)	No action
Samuel Alito	2006	58–42
Sonia Sotomayor	2009	68–31
Elena Kagan	2010	63–37

Source: David G. Savage, *Guide to the U.S. Supreme Court,* 5th ed. (Washington, DC.: Congressional Quarterly, 2010), 1253–1254; table updated by the author.

Note: NRV = no recorded vote.

a. Elevation to chief justice; nomination withdrawn after the Senate vote of 45–43 failed to end a filibuster against the nomination (two-thirds majority was required).

b. Elevation to chief justice

become intertwined, in that senators who are ideologically distant from a nominee often use doubts about a nominee's legal skills or ethical standards as a justification for opposing the nominee. But senators who are not distant from a nominee may also oppose confirmation because they conclude that the nominee's qualifications are deficient.

David Souter and Clarence Thomas illustrate the importance of personal attributes. The two were chosen by President George H. W. Bush in 1990 and 1991, with the Democrats holding majorities in the Senate. Each would replace a strongly liberal justice, so both seemed likely to change the Court's ideological tenor considerably. Souter won confirmation with only moderate difficulty, but Thomas's margin was only four votes. The difference can be explained primarily by two widespread perceptions: that Souter was a moderate conservative and Thomas a strong conservative and that Souter was well qualified but Thomas's qualifications might be questioned.

Several aspects of the situation at the time of nomination also affect the Senate's action. One is the president's political strength in the Senate. According to one count, presidents whose party holds a Senate majority have had 90 percent of their nominees confirmed, as against 61 percent for presidents who faced an opposition majority.[31] One reason for this difference is that senators of the majority party chair the Judiciary Committee and schedule votes on the floor. Another reason is that a Senate controlled by the opposition has more senators who are politically opposed to the president and who are ideologically distant from a nominee. For both reasons, George W. Bush and Barack Obama began with a significant advantage in making the last four appointments of justices because their nominations came when their party had a Senate majority.

Other factors affect the president's strength. Presidents with high public approval ratings have an advantage because strong public support deters opposition to their nominees. And nominations made late in a president's term are more vulnerable for several reasons: The president's popularity tends to decline over time, second-term presidents are "lame ducks" who will leave office shortly, and partisanship often increases. Only 54 percent of the nominees selected in the last year of a presidential term won confirmation.[32] No justice has left the Court in the last year of a term since 1968, primarily because justices recognize the controversy that often arises when nominations are made in that year.

A second aspect of the situation is the mobilization of support and opposition to the nominee. It makes a difference whether some senators decide to play an active role in mustering votes against a nominee and whether the administration mounts a strong effort to secure confirmation.[33] Outside government, a strong interest group campaign against a nomination can overcome the assumption that the nominee will be confirmed and thereby get senators to consider voting against confirmation. Such campaigns can also reduce public support for a nominee, and public opinion affects senators' votes for or against nominees.[34]

Finally, the perceived impact of a nomination helps to determine whether senators believe that efforts to defeat the nominee are worthwhile. In part, the intense scrutiny given to recent nominations reflects the increased prominence of the Supreme Court as a policymaker on controversial issues. Senators attach particular importance to a nomination if the nominee might change the Court's policies substantially—either because the nominee is much more liberal or conservative than the justice leaving the Court or because of a close ideological balance on the Court.

Antonin Scalia and Robert Bork, nominated by President Reagan in 1986 and 1987, illustrate the importance of the situation. Both were viewed as highly conservative, and both were considered well qualified for service on the Court. Scalia was confirmed unanimously, but Bork was defeated. One difference was that the Senate had a Republican majority in 1986 but a Democratic majority the next year. Another was that Scalia would replace another strong conservative but Bork would replace a moderate conservative on a Court that was closely divided between liberals and conservatives. Finally, in 1986, liberal senators and interest groups focused their efforts on defeating William Rehnquist's nomination for chief justice and largely ignored Scalia. In 1987, in contrast, liberals in and out of the Senate gave intense attention to Bork.

The factors that shape Senate action can be illustrated further by looking at two sets of nominations. The first includes the four nominees who failed to win confirmation in the past half century. The second includes the four nominees considered by the Senate since 2005, all of whom won confirmation.

The Defeats. From 1930 to 1967 a long series of Supreme Court nominees won confirmation. Then, in the period from 1968 to 1970, three nominees lost in the Senate. The first was Abe Fortas, a sitting justice whom President Johnson nominated to be chief justice in 1968. The Senate had a Democratic majority, but many of the Democrats were conservative, and Fortas's strong liberalism on the liberal Warren Court aroused conservative opposition. Further, some Republicans wanted to prevent Fortas's confirmation in order to reserve the vacancy for a new president—expected to be Republican—in 1969. These opponents pointed to two activities that raised doubts about Fortas's ethical fitness: his continued consultation with President Johnson about policy matters while serving on the Court and an arrangement by which he gave nine lectures at American University, in Washington, D.C., for a fee of $15,000 raised from businesses.

The Judiciary Committee approved Fortas's confirmation by a divided vote, but it ran into a filibuster on the Senate floor. A vote to end the filibuster fell fourteen votes short of the two-thirds majority then required; the opposition came almost entirely from Republicans and southern Democrats. President Johnson then withdrew the nomination at Fortas's request.

In 1969 Fortas resigned from the Court. President Nixon selected Clement Haynsworth, chief judge of a federal court of appeals, to replace him. Haynsworth was opposed by labor groups and the National

Association for the Advancement of Colored People (NAACP), both of which disliked his judicial record. Liberal senators, unhappy about that record themselves, sought revenge for Fortas's defeat as well. Haynsworth was also charged with unethical conduct: He had sat on two cases involving subsidiaries of companies in which he owned stock, and in another case he had bought the stock of a corporation in the interval between his court's decision in its favor and the announcement of that decision. These charges led to additional opposition from Senate moderates. Haynsworth ultimately was defeated by a 45–55 vote, with a large minority of Republicans voting against confirmation.

President Nixon then nominated another court of appeals judge, G. Harrold Carswell. After the fight over Haynsworth, most senators were inclined to support the next nominee. One senator predicted that any new Nixon nominee "will have no trouble getting confirmed unless he has committed murder—recently."[35] But Carswell drew opposition from civil rights groups for what they perceived as his hostility to their interests, and their cause gained strength from a series of revelations about the nominee that suggested active opposition to racial equality. Carswell was also criticized for an alleged lack of judicial competence. After escorting Carswell to talk with senators, one of Nixon's staffers reported to the president that "they think Carswell's a boob, a dummy. And what counter is there to that? He is."[36] The nomination was defeated by a 45–51 vote, with a lineup similar to the vote on Haynsworth.

Robert Bork's 1987 defeat differed from the three that preceded it in that no serious charges were made about Bork's competence or his ethical standards. But liberals were concerned about his strong conservatism on civil liberties issues and his potential to shift the Court's ideological balance. Senator Ted Kennedy and liberal interest groups worked hard to secure votes against Bork. Concern about Bork's views was intensified by his testimony before the Senate Judiciary Committee, in which he discussed in detail his positions on issues such as the right to privacy.

This growing concern, combined with the unprecedented level of interest group activity against Bork, made his defeat possible. Also important was President Reagan's political weakness: Not only did the Democrats control the Senate but Reagan's popularity inside and outside Congress had declined. Even so, a more effective campaign for Bork by the administration might have secured his confirmation. In any event, confirmation was denied by a 42–58 vote. All but eight senators voted along party lines; the overwhelming and unexpected opposition of southern Democrats made the difference in the outcome.

These four defeats, different though they were, have some things in common. In each instance, many senators were inclined to oppose the nominee on ideological grounds. All but Fortas faced a Senate controlled by the opposite party, and Fortas was confronted by a conservative majority.

And each nominee was weakened by a "smoking gun" that provided a basis for opposition: the ethical questions about Fortas and Haynsworth, the allegations of racism and incompetence against Carswell, and the charge that Bork was outside the mainstream in his views on judicial issues. The combination of these problems led to enough negative votes to prevent confirmation in each instance.

The Recent Confirmations. Between 1993 and 2010 the Senate voted on six nominations. All six nominees won confirmation, but their paths to victory differed considerably. President Clinton's nominees, Ruth Bader Ginsburg in 1993 and Stephen Breyer in 1994, faced some opposition but ultimately won confirmation by overwhelming votes. In contrast, the four nominees since 2005 were met with stronger opposition and large numbers of negative votes. Those four cases provide a sense of the current politics of confirmation.

George W. Bush's nominations of John Roberts and Samuel Alito in 2005 came at a time when polarization between the parties had reached a high level and there was considerable concern about the Supreme Court's future direction. As a result, it was likely that Senate Democrats would oppose a nominee who seemed to be a strong conservative. Yet interest groups allied with the Republican Party were adamant that the president choose strong conservatives, and the president's own inclination seemed to be the same. Bush had the advantage of a moderately large Republican majority in the Senate, increasing the chances of a favorable outcome for any nominee. Under the circumstances, he chose two nominees whose records suggested that they were quite conservative. (Bush also saw Harriet Miers as strongly conservative.)

Nothing like a smoking gun emerged for Roberts. Indeed, his testimony in the Judiciary Committee left most observers with a highly positive image of him. Ultimately, he was confirmed by a 78–22 vote, with all the negative votes coming from Democrats.

Like Roberts, Alito had demonstrated a high level of legal skills. But he was more vulnerable than Roberts because he had a more extensive record of strongly conservative positions. Some opponents thought they had a smoking gun in two statements he had made in 1985. In those statements Alito said that he was proud of his contributions to the Reagan administration's arguments that the "Constitution does not protect the right to an abortion" and implied that his goal was "the eventual overruling of *Roe v. Wade.*"[37] Alito was also criticized for participating as a judge in one case involving a mutual fund firm that held a substantial investment of his, despite a pledge to recuse himself from such cases when he was nominated to the court of appeals. Perhaps most important, Alito would replace moderate conservative Sandra Day O'Connor. Thus, unlike Roberts, who succeeded William Rehnquist, Alito could move the Court substantially to the right.

Alito Confirmation	
Y = 10 N = 6	
Biden (D)	N
Brownback (R)	Y
Coburn (R)	Y
Cornyn (R)	Y
DeWine (R)	Y
Durbin (D)	N
Feingold (D)	
Feinstein (D)	N
Graham (R)	Y
Grassley (R)	Y
Hatch (R)	Y
Kennedy (D)	N
Kohl (D)	N
Kyl (R)	Y
Leahy (D)	N
Schumer (D)	
Sessions (R)	Y
Specter (R)	Y

SEN. DIANNE FEINSTEIN
D-California

C-SPAN

Democratic senator Dianne Feinstein of California watching as the vote to confirm Samuel Alito to the Supreme Court is tallied up in 2006. The 42 votes cast against Alito's confirmation reflect the inclination of senators in the current era to vote against nominees chosen by presidents of the other party.

Most senators seemed to regard Alito's participation in the case that was related to his investment as inadvertent and inconsequential. In contrast, Alito's efforts to reassure senators that he was not an extreme conservative and that he would not necessarily vote to overturn *Roe* had limited success with Democrats. But it was clear early in the process that nearly all Republican senators would vote for him. As the minority party in the Senate, the Democrats could block Alito only with a successful filibuster, and many Democratic senators saw a filibuster as inappropriate or at least bad political strategy. After the vote to end debate, Alito won confirmation by a 58–42 margin. One Republican and all but four Democrats voted against him.

Sonia Sotomayor entered the confirmation process with the great advantage of a Democratic majority in the Senate and the additional advantage that her replacement of David Souter was unlikely to change the Court's overall ideological balance very much. Still, some Senate Republicans joined conservative interest groups in expressing strong opposition to Sotomayor. She had said in one talk, "I would hope that a wise Latina woman with the richness of her experiences would more often than not reach a better conclusion than a white male who hasn't lived that life."[38] Opponents argued that this passage and other statements and actions indicated a lack of impartiality on her part. They also charged that some of her positions in court of appeals decisions were unduly liberal and departed from good interpretations of the law.

None of these criticisms constituted the kind of smoking gun that might have attracted Democratic opposition to the nomination. Indeed, no Democratic senator voted against Sotomayor. But the great majority of Republicans—31 of 40—cast negative votes. Although those Republicans cited specific concerns about Sotomayor, their votes were primarily a product of ideological considerations: conservative senators and interest groups that were important to those senators saw the nominee as unduly liberal.

Elena Kagan benefited from the same Democratic majority as Sotomayor. And like Sotomayor, she would not change the ideological balance of the Court. Indeed, some liberals complained that she was probably more conservative than John Paul Stevens, the justice she would succeed.

Yet Kagan still faced widespread opposition from Senate Republicans and conservative interest groups. Opponents cited her lack of judicial experience and her limited experience as a practicing lawyer. Even in the absence of a prior judicial record, they found evidence of what they saw as strongly liberal views. Republicans were especially critical of her actions as dean at Harvard Law School that limited the access of military recruiters to law students because of the military's prohibition of service by openly gay and lesbian people. Ultimately, Kagan won even less Republican support than Sotomayor, with 36 of the 41 Republicans voting against her. That difference may have reflected the reluctance of a few Republicans to vote against the first Hispanic nominee to the Court.

The Current Picture. Even more than the increased concern with Supreme Court policy, the high level of political polarization in the current era has changed the confirmation process. This change is reflected in Justice Ginsburg's statement in 2011 that her work with the American Civil Liberties Union (ACLU) "would probably disqualify me" in the current era and Chief Justice Roberts's judgment in 2014 that neither Ginsburg nor Antonin Scalia "would have a chance" of confirmation today.[39] One way to summarize this change is that the attributes of nominees have become less important and certain attributes of the situation more important. All four nominees between 2005 and 2010 probably would have been uncontroversial as late as the early 1990s. Each seemed well qualified, and all but Samuel Alito seemed likely to leave the Court's ideological balance about the same. But each attracted strong criticism from the opposite party, and only John Roberts—the first of the four—won as many as ten votes from that party.

As the votes on the four recent nominees indicate, control of the Senate has become even more important than it was in past eras. None of these four nominees was ever in serious danger of defeat, because the president's party had a Senate majority in each instance. In an era of strong partisan polarization, senators nearly always vote to confirm nominees from their own party.[40] By the same token, a president whose party lacks a Senate majority may have considerable difficulty in winning confirmation for nominees, especially when a new justice has the potential to shift the Court's policies substantially. This reality explains the commentaries that urged Justice Ginsburg to retire before the congressional elections in 2014.

Who Is Selected

In some respects the people who have served as Supreme Court justices are a diverse group. But because of the workings of the selection process, certain kinds of people are far more likely to reach the Court than others. The attributes of the justices may be important symbolically; Justice Kagan has said that diversity in the justices' backgrounds "allows people to identify" with the Court.[41] Those backgrounds also affect the justices as decision makers. As Justice Sotomayor said, "Life experiences play a role in every judge's judging because we are creatures of our experience."[42]

Career Paths

The kinds of people who become justices can be understood largely in terms of the paths that people take to get to the Court. These paths have changed over time. In order to highlight that change, in this section I examine the set of thirty-seven justices appointed since 1937. Recent justices are of particular interest, and the box on pages 52–53 summarizes the careers of the justices who sat on the Court in 2015.[43]

The Legal Profession. The Constitution specifies no requirements for Supreme Court justices, so they need not be attorneys. In practice, however, this restriction has been absolute. Nearly everyone involved in the selection process assumes that only a person with legal training can serve effectively on the Court. If a president nominated a nonlawyer to the Court, this assumption—and the large number of lawyers in the Senate—almost surely would prevent confirmation.

Thus, holding a law degree constitutes the first and least flexible requirement for recruitment to the Court. Most of the justices who served during the first century of the Court's history followed what was then the standard practice, apprenticing under a practicing attorney. In several instances the practicing attorney was a leading member of the bar. James Byrnes (chosen in 1941) was the last justice to study law through apprenticeship; all the people appointed since then have taken what is now the nearly universal route of law school training. A high proportion of justices have graduated from prestigious schools.

High Positions. If legal education is a necessary first step in the paths to the Court, almost equally important as a last step is attaining a high position in government or the legal profession. Obscure private practitioners or state trial judges might be superbly qualified for the Court, but their qualifications would still be questioned because of their lowly positions. A high position in government or the legal profession also makes a person more visible to the president and to the officials who identify potential nominees.

At the time they were selected, the justices appointed since 1937 held positions of four types. They were judges, executive branch officials, elected officials, or well-respected leaders in the legal profession.

Nineteen of the justices appointed in this period were appellate judges at the time of selection. Seventeen sat on the federal courts of appeals. The other two (William Brennan and Sandra Day O'Connor) served on state courts. Six of the seventeen federal judges came from the District of Columbia circuit, which is especially visible to the president and other federal officials.

Eleven justices served in the federal executive branch, eight of them in the Justice Department. The other three justices served as chair of the Securities and Exchange Commission (William Douglas), secretary of the Treasury (Fred Vinson), and secretary of labor (Arthur Goldberg).

Of the other seven justices appointed since 1937, four held high elective office. Three were senators (Hugo Black, James Byrnes, and Harold Burton), and the fourth was the governor of California (Earl Warren). The other three held positions outside government. Each had attained extraordinary success and respect—as a legal scholar (Felix Frankfurter), a Washington lawyer (Abe Fortas), and a leader of the legal profession (Lewis Powell). Frankfurter and Fortas had also been informal presidential advisers.

The Steps Between. The people who have become Supreme Court justices took several routes from their legal education to the high positions that made them credible candidates for the Court. Frankfurter, Fortas, and Powell illustrate one simple route: entry into legal practice or academia, followed by a gradual rise to high standing in the legal profession. Some justices took a similar route through public office. Earl Warren held a series of appointive and elective offices, leading to his California governorship. Clarence Thomas and Samuel Alito each served in several nonelected government positions and then as a judge on a federal court of appeals.

Since 1975 the most common route to the Court has been through private practice or law teaching, often combined with some time in government, before appointment to a federal court of appeals. Antonin Scalia, Ruth Bader Ginsburg, and Stephen Breyer were law professors. Anthony Kennedy and John Roberts were in private practice. In a variant of that path, Sonia Sotomayor left private practice to become a federal district judge and was later elevated to a court of appeals. Before becoming judges, all six had held government positions or participated informally in the governmental process.

Justice O'Connor took a unique path to the Court. She spent time in private practice and government legal positions, with some career interruptions for family reasons, before becoming an Arizona state senator and majority leader of the senate. O'Connor left the legislature for a trial judgeship. Her promotion to the state court of appeals through a gubernatorial appointment put her in a position to be considered for the Supreme Court.

Changes in Paths. Even within the period since 1937, there has been a striking change in justices' pre-Court careers. Put simply, those careers have come to involve less politics and more law. As shown in Table 2-3, there is a substantial difference in those respects between the justices who were appointed between 1937 and 1968 and the justices chosen since then.

The twenty-one justices appointed to the Court between 1937 and 1968 were fairly typical of those selected in earlier periods. About half had judicial experience, nearly as many had held elective office, and more than a quarter had headed a federal administrative agency.

The sixteen justices who have arrived at the Court since 1969 are different. All but three have come directly from lower courts. Only Sandra Day O'Connor had ever held elective office. Only Clarence Thomas had headed a federal agency, and several had spent little or no time in government before winning judgeships. For these justices, the median proportion of their careers spent in what might be called the legal system—private practice, law school teaching, and the judiciary—was 85 percent. For the justices appointed between 1937 and 1968, the median was 67 percent.[44] The extent of this change was underlined in the period between 2006 and 2010, when all nine sitting justices had come to the Court from a federal court of appeals.

TABLE 2-3
Selected Career Experiences of Justices Appointed since 1937
(in percentages)

Years appointed	Experience during career		
	Elective office	Head of federal agency	Judgeship
1937–1968	43	29	48
1969–2015	7	7	81
	Position at appointment		
1937–1968	19	29	29
1969–2015	0	0	81

Source: Biographical Directory of Federal Judges, Federal Judicial Center, http://www.fjc.gov/history/home.nsf/page/judges.html.

Note: Federal agencies include cabinet departments and independent agencies. Heads of offices within departments (e.g., the Office of the Solicitor General in the Justice Department) are not counted.

Careers of the Supreme Court...

John G. Roberts Jr. (born 1955)
Law degree, Harvard University, 1979
Law clerk, U.S. Court of Appeals, 1979–1980
Law clerk, Supreme Court, 1980–1981
U.S. Justice Department, 1981–1982
Office of White House Counsel, 1982–1986
U.S. Office of the Solicitor General, 1989–1993
Private law practice, 1986–1989, 1993–2003
Judge, U.S. Court of Appeals, 2003–2005
Appointed chief justice, 2005

Antonin Scalia (born 1936)
Law degree, Harvard University, 1960
Private law practice, 1960–1967
Law school teaching, 1967–1971
Legal positions in federal government, 1971–1977
Law school teaching, 1977–1982
Judge, U.S. Court of Appeals, 1982–1986
Appointed to Supreme Court, 1986

Anthony M. Kennedy (born 1936)
Law degree, Harvard University, 1961
Private law practice, 1961–1975
Judge, U.S. Court of Appeals, 1975–1988
Appointed to Supreme Court, 1988

Clarence Thomas (born 1940)
Law degree, Yale University, 1974
Missouri attorney general's office, 1974–1977
Attorney for Monsanto Company, 1977–1979
Legislative assistant to a U.S. senator, 1979–1981
Assistant U.S. secretary of education, 1981–1982
Chair, U.S. Equal Employment Opportunity Commission,
   1982–1990
Judge, U.S. Court of Appeals, 1990–1991
Appointed to Supreme Court, 1991

Ruth Bader Ginsburg (born 1933)
Law degree, Columbia University, 1959
Law clerk, federal district court, 1959–1961
Law school research position, 1961–1963
Law school teaching, 1963–1980
Judge, U.S. Court of Appeals, 1980–1993
Appointed to Supreme Court, 1993

...Justices (2015)

Stephen G. Breyer (born 1938)
Law degree, Harvard University, 1964
Law clerk, Supreme Court, 1964–1965
U.S. Justice Department, 1965–1967
Law school teaching, 1967–1980
Staff, U.S. Senate Judiciary Committee, 1974–1975,
1979–1980
Judge, U.S. Court of Appeals, 1980–1994
Appointed to Supreme Court, 1994

Samuel A. Alito Jr. (born 1950)
Law degree, Yale University, 1975
Law clerk, U.S. Court of Appeals, 1976–1977
Assistant U.S. Attorney, 1977–1981
U.S. Office of the Solicitor General 1981–1985
U.S. Justice Department, 1985–1987
U.S. Attorney, 1987–1990
Judge, U.S. Court of Appeals, 1990–2006
Appointed to Supreme Court, 2006

Sonia Sotomayor (born 1954)
Law degree, Yale University, 1979
Assistant district attorney, 1979–1984
Private law practice, 1984–1992
Judge, U.S. District Court, 1992–1998
Judge, U.S. Court of Appeals, 1998–2009
Appointed to Supreme Court, 2009

Elena Kagan (born 1960)
Law degree, Harvard University, 1986
Law clerk, U.S. Court of Appeals, 1986–1987
Law clerk, Supreme Court, 1987–1988
Private law practice, 1989–1991
Law school teaching, 1991–1995
Positions in executive branch, 1995–1999
Law school teaching and administration, 1999–2009
U.S. Solicitor General, 2009–2010
Appointed to Supreme Court, 2010

Source: Biographical Directory of Federal Judges, Federal Judicial Center, http://www.fjc.gov/history/home.nsf/page/judges.html. All photos: Steve Petteway, Collection of the Supreme Court of the United States.

Note: With the exception of Justice Breyer's Senate staff service, only the primary position held by a future justice during each career stage is listed.

One reason for this change, perhaps the primary one, is that a prior judicial record helps presidents and their advisers to predict the positions that prospective nominees might take as justices. In an era in which most presidents care a great deal about the Court's direction, any help in making these predictions is valued. There may also be a growing feeling that service on a lower court helps to prepare a judge for the Supreme Court. Harriet Miers and Elena Kagan were criticized for the absence of that service.

The change in paths to the Court since 1968 may affect the justices' perspectives and their thinking about legal issues. Chief Justice Roberts raised one possibility in 2013, suggesting that justices with experience primarily in the other branches might focus more on the policy implications of cases than those whose experience is primarily in the judiciary.[45] Similarly, federal court of appeals judge Richard Posner suggested that the Court has "suffered from the narrowness of the pre-appointment careers of the current and recent Justices" in its handling of cases related to the political process.[46]

Other Attributes of the Justices

Career experience is only one important characteristic of the people who become justices. But other attributes can be understood partly in terms of the career paths that take people to the Court.

Age. Since 1937 most Supreme Court justices have been in their fifties at the time of their appointments and the rest in their forties or early sixties. William Douglas was the youngest appointee, at age forty; at the other end of the spectrum, Lewis Powell was sixty-four.

The ages of Court appointees reflect a balance between two considerations. On the one hand, lawyers need time to develop the record of achievement that makes them credible candidates for the Court. On the other hand, presidents would like their appointees to serve for many years in order to achieve the maximum impact on the Court. Thus, a candidate such as Clarence Thomas, forty-three when George H. W. Bush appointed him, can be especially attractive. Elena Kagan was fifty when Barack Obama nominated her to the Court in 2010. Almost surely, her relative youth compared with the other leading candidates worked in her favor.

Class, Race, and Sex. The Supreme Court's membership has diverged from the general population in regard to social class: Most justices grew up in families that were relatively well off. One study found that one-third of the justices were from the upper class and one-quarter were from the upper middle class. Less than one-quarter were from the lower middle class or below.[47]

The justices selected since the 1930s have been less of a high-status group than were their predecessors, and the current Court reflects that change. Of the justices who sat on the Court in 2015, Clarence Thomas's family was impoverished, and Sonia Sotomayor's family was lower middle class. The families of the other seven justices on the 2015 Court were divided about evenly between the middle class and upper middle class.

The historic predominance of higher-status backgrounds can be explained by the career paths that most justices take. First and most important, a justice must obtain a legal education. To do so is easiest for individuals of high status, because of the cost of law school and the college education that precedes it. Early in the Court's history, when most justices had apprenticed with an attorney, such advantaged people had the best opportunity to apprentice with leading lawyers.

Second, individuals of high status have a variety of advantages in their careers. Those who can afford to attend elite law schools, for instance, have the easiest time obtaining Supreme Court clerkships and positions in successful law firms. The partial deviation from this pattern since the 1930s reflects the increased availability of college and legal education as well as other social changes. Despite their limited financial resources, Sonia Sotomayor and Clarence Thomas were able to go to private colleges and then to Yale Law School.

Until 1967 all the justices were white men. This pattern is not difficult to understand. Because of various restrictions, women and members of racial minority groups long had enormous difficulty pursuing a legal education. As a result, few members of these groups passed the first barrier to selection. In addition, prejudice limited their ability to advance in the legal profession and in politics. Thus, very few individuals who were not white men could achieve the high positions that people generally must obtain to be considered for nomination to the Court.

Since 1967 four women (Sandra Day O'Connor, Ruth Bader Ginsburg, Sonia Sotomayor, and Elena Kagan), two African Americans (Thurgood Marshall and Clarence Thomas), and a Hispanic American (Sotomayor) have won appointments to the Court. These appointments reflect changes in society that made it less difficult for people other than white men to achieve high positions. They also reflect the growing willingness of presidents to consider women and members of racial minority groups as prospective nominees.

As the Court has moved away from the long-standing monopoly of white men on the Court, and as fewer justices have come from high-income families, how have these changes affected its policies? People who do not share the traditional attributes of justices might bring new perspectives to the Court, and these perspectives might influence the thinking of their colleagues. For instance, both Ruth Bader Ginsburg and Sandra Day

Corbis/AP Images

A class at Harvard Law School. All nine justices who were serving in 2015 went to law school at Harvard or Yale.

O'Connor have expressed their view that the presence of female justices affects the Court's collective judgments in some cases.[48]

On the other hand, justices with similar backgrounds or similar life experiences may develop very different points of view. Sonia Sotomayor and Clarence Thomas both benefited from affirmative action programs at universities, but they reached completely different conclusions about the desirability of those programs. And justices' social class origins might affect their views less than does the high professional status that they all achieved. This might help to explain why the justices with humble backgrounds have included conservatives such as Thomas and Warren Burger as well as liberals such as Sotomayor and Earl Warren.

In terms of race and sex, the current Court is the most diverse in history. It is not very diverse in some other respects. As Elena Kagan pointed out, today's Court is a "very coastal, urban and elite law school court."[49] The justices' educational backgrounds are especially striking. All nine of the 2015 justices graduated from private undergraduate schools, including five who went to Ivy League schools and two who studied at Stanford. And all nine justices went to law school at Harvard or Yale, though Ruth Bader Ginsburg transferred from Harvard to Columbia for her final year. In educational terms, then, today's Court is very much an elite group. This fact reflects the respect and career advantages gained by graduates of prestigious schools and perhaps the special aura attached to the Yale and Harvard Law Schools. Some commentators have expressed concern about what they see as the insularity of a Court that comes from such a narrow range of schools. As Justice Kagan said, "Know what our diversity is? Justice Ginsburg spent a year at Columbia."[50]

Partisan Political Activity. Even though today's justices spent the bulk of their pre-Court years in the legal system, most share with their predecessors a degree of involvement in partisan politics. Antonin Scalia, John Roberts, and Samuel Alito each held multiple positions in Republican administrations. Anthony Kennedy drafted a state ballot proposition for California governor Ronald Reagan. Clarence Thomas worked with John Danforth when Danforth was the Missouri attorney general and a U.S. senator, and Thomas later served in the Reagan and George H. W. Bush administrations. Stephen Breyer interrupted his service as a law professor twice to work with Democrats on the Senate Judiciary Committee.

This pattern reflects the criteria for selecting justices. Even when nominations to the Court are not used as political rewards, presidents look more favorably on people who have contributed to their party's success. Partisan activity also brings people to the attention of presidents, their staff members, and others who influence nomination decisions. Perhaps more important, it enables people to win the high government positions that make them credible candidates for the Court.

The Role of Chance. No one becomes a Supreme Court justice through an inevitable process. Rather, advancement from membership in the bar to a seat on the Court results from luck as much as anything else. This luck comes in two stages: achieving the high positions in government or law that make individuals possible candidates for the Court and then getting serious consideration for the Court and actually winning an appointment.

In that second stage, a potential justice gains enormously by belonging to a particular political party at the appropriate time. Every appointment to the Court between 1969 and 1992 was made by a Republican president. As a result, a whole generation of potential justices who were liberal Democrats had no chance to win appointments. Further, someone whose friend or associate achieves a powerful position becomes a far stronger candidate for a seat on the Court. Elena Kagan accomplished a great deal, culminating in her appointment as dean at the Harvard Law School. But if she had not known Barack Obama, there is little chance that she would have become solicitor general and then won a Supreme Court appointment.

More broadly, everyone appointed to the Court has benefited from a favorable series of circumstances. John Paul Stevens has reported that his pro bono volunteer services for a client led to favorable publicity that later helped him win a judicial appointment.[51] If William Rehnquist had retired during George W. Bush's first term rather than remaining on the Court, it is unlikely that John Roberts would have succeeded him as chief justice, because Roberts did not become a lower-court judge until 2003.[52]

This does not mean that the effects of presidential appointments to the Court are random. Presidents and their aides increasingly make systematic efforts to identify the nominees who serve their goals best. But it does mean that specific individuals achieve membership on the Court in large part through good fortune. As Justice Kagan said, "It's a lot of chance that the nine of us are there rather than nine other people."[53]

Leaving the Court

In the Supreme Court's first century, Congress sometimes increased the Court's size to allow new appointments of justices. Such legislation has become almost unthinkable. Today, new members come to the Court only when a sitting justice leaves.

Justices can leave the Court in three ways: through death, a voluntary decision, or external pressure.[54] In contrast with the nineteenth century, justices today seldom stay on the Court until they die. Before William Rehnquist's death in 2005, the last justice to die in office had been Robert Jackson in 1954. Thus, departures from the Court result primarily from voluntary choices and external pressure. Table 2-4 summarizes the reasons for departure since 1965.

Voluntary Departures

After its rocky start, the Supreme Court became a prestigious body with considerable influence on American life. As a result, justices are reluctant to leave the Court. In the past century, only a handful of justices have done so to take other positions or opportunities. The most recent was Arthur Goldberg, who resigned in 1965 to become U.S. ambassador to the United Nations.

Still, justices must decide whether and when to retire from the Court. Financial considerations once played an important part in those choices: several justices stayed on the Court, sometimes with serious infirmities, to keep receiving their salaries. Congress established a judicial pension in 1869, and it is now quite generous. Justices who have served as federal judges for at least ten years and who are at least sixty-five years old can retire and continue to receive the salary earned at the time of retirement if their age and years of service add up to eighty or more. Justices can also receive any salary increases granted to sitting justices if they are disabled or if they perform a certain amount of service for the federal courts—generally equal to one-quarter of full-time work.

Thereby freed from financial concerns, older justices weigh the satisfactions of remaining on the Court against the satisfactions of retirement and against concern about their capacity to handle their work. Some justices have remained on the Court after their health had

TABLE 2-4
Reasons for Leaving the Court since 1965

Year	Justice	Age	Primary reasons for leaving	Length of time from leaving until death
1965	Goldberg	56	Appointment as ambassador to the United Nations	24 years
1967	Clark	67	Son's appointment as attorney general	10 years
1969	Fortas	58	Pressures based on possible ethical violations	13 years
1969[a]	Warren	78[b]	Age	5 years
1971	Black	85	Age and ill health	1 month
1971	Harlan	72	Age and ill health	3 months
1975	Douglas	77	Age and ill health	4 years
1981	Stewart	66	Age	4 years
1986	Burger	78	Uncertain: age, demands of service on a federal commission may have been factors	9 years
1987	Powell	79	Age and health concerns	11 years
1990	Brennan	84	Age and ill health	7 years
1991	Marshall	83[b]	Age and ill health	2 years
1993	White	76[b]	Desire to allow another person to serve, possibly age	9 years
1994	Blackmun	85	Age	5 years
2005	Rehnquist	80	Death	Same time
2006[a]	O'Connor	75	Spouse's ill health	NA
2009	Souter	69	Desire to return to New Hampshire	NA
2010	Stevens	90[b]	Age	NA

Sources: Biographical sources, newspaper stories.

Note: NA = not applicable.

a. Warren originally announced the intent to leave the Court in 1968, O'Connor in 2005.

b. When they announced their intent to leave the Court, Warren was seventy-seven, Marshall eighty-two, White seventy-five, and Stevens eighty-nine.

weakened considerably. Writing in 2000, one scholar argued that since World War II, seven justices had stayed on the Court "years or months" too long, after a decline in their mental capacities.[55] William Rehnquist continued his service as chief justice in 2005 even after he was unable to fully participate in the Court's work because of cancer.

But most justices leave the Court when their infirmities become clear, and some do so while they are still in good health. It is noteworthy that Rehnquist was the only justice in the past half century to die in office. John Paul Stevens asked his colleague David Souter to let him know when he was no longer doing his job effectively. In early 2010, after Souter had retired, Stevens was troubled when he found himself stumbling over words for the first time while presenting his opinion in a case. That experience helped to move him toward retirement, which he announced three months later. Still, shortly after his retirement he said that he "may have jumped the gun a little bit" in leaving the Court.[56] Souter and Sandra Day O'Connor retired in the absence of health problems—Souter because of his preference for living in his native New Hampshire and O'Connor because of her husband's ill health.

The suggestions from liberal commentators that Justice Ginsburg retire in order to give President Obama a chance to appoint her successor raise the question of how much weight justices give to that consideration in deciding when to leave the Court. Some sitting and retired justices have indicated that they did take into account who would choose their successor, and indeed there is a tendency for justices to retire under presidents whose views are compatible with theirs. A friend of David Souter's reported that Souter told him in 2008, "If Obama wins, I'll be the first one to retire."[57] Indeed, Souter announced his retirement three months after Obama took office.

Ginsburg herself has said that "I think" the president's party is a factor "for all of us."[58] She also predicted in 2013 that a new Democratic president would be elected in 2016, a prediction that reduced any sense of urgency she might have about retiring before then.[59] In 2014 she added that, because of a potential filibuster by Senate Republicans, "If I resign any time this year," President Obama "could not successfully appoint anyone I would like to see in the court."[60]

One current justice gave very early notice of his retirement. In 1992, a year after he joined the Court, Clarence Thomas told two of his clerks that he would remain on the Court until 2034. He explained, "The liberals made my life miserable for 43 years, and I'm going to make their lives miserable for 43 years."[61]

Justices who enjoy good health after their retirement often remain active, and that is true of the three most recent retirees. David Souter has served frequently in the federal court of appeals in Boston, near his New Hampshire home. In the first five years after his 2009 retirement, he participated in more than 200 decisions.[62] Since his 2010 retirement, John Paul Stevens has written two books and some lengthy book reviews, and he has given a number of speeches and interviews. In 2014 he testified before a congressional committee in favor of a constitutional amendment to overturn several Supreme Court decisions striking down regulations of campaign finance on the basis of the First Amendment. Stevens has criticized several other Court decisions that were handed down before and after his retirement.

Sandra Day O'Connor has combined Souter's and Stevens's pursuits, sitting with all eleven regional courts of appeals and speaking on behalf of causes such as civic education and replacement of state judicial elections with appointment systems. Some commentators have argued that her combination of hearing cases and public advocacy was inappropriate, while others have defended her. In any event, her example—like that of Stevens and Souter—underlines the fact that many justices leave the Court while they still have the capacity to play active roles.

External Pressure

Although justices make their own decisions whether to resign or retire, Congress and the president can try to influence those decisions. The legislation creating attractive pension rights has had considerable effect. Some presidents have sought to secure the retirements of older justices in order to create vacancies that they can then fill. John Kennedy reportedly persuaded Felix Frankfurter to retire after ill health had decreased his effectiveness, but Thurgood Marshall bitterly resisted efforts by the Carter administration to get him to retire.

Presidents can offer other positions to younger justices in an effort to lure them away from the Court. Lyndon Johnson offered Arthur Goldberg the position of ambassador to the United Nations and then exerted intense personal pressure on Goldberg until he accepted that position. Byron White, however, rejected the idea of becoming FBI director when the Reagan administration sounded him out about it.

In contrast with those kinds of pressures, impeachment is beyond the justices' control. Under the Constitution, justices, like other federal officials, can be removed through impeachment proceedings for "treason, bribery, or other high crimes and misdemeanors."[63] President Thomas Jefferson actually sought to gain control of the largely Federalist (and anti-Jefferson) judiciary through the use of impeachment, and Congress did impeach and convict a federal district judge in 1803. Justice Samuel Chase made himself vulnerable to impeachment by participating in President John Adams's campaign for reelection in 1800 and by making some injudicious and partisan remarks to a Maryland grand jury in 1803. Chase was impeached, but the Senate acquitted him in 1805. His acquittal effectively ended Jefferson's plans to seek the impeachment of other justices.

No justice has been impeached since then, but the possible impeachment of two justices has been the subject of serious discussion. Several efforts were made to remove William Douglas (most seriously in 1969 and 1970), motivated by opposition to his strong liberalism. The reasons stated publicly by opponents were his financial connections with a foundation and his outside writings.[64] A special House committee failed to approve a resolution to impeach Douglas, however, and the resolution died in 1970.

Had Abe Fortas not resigned from the Court in 1969, he actually might have been removed by Congress.[65] Fortas had been criticized for his financial dealings at the time of his unsuccessful nomination as chief justice in 1968. A year later it was disclosed that he had a lifetime contract as a consultant to a foundation and had received money from the foundation at a time when the person who directed it was being prosecuted by the federal government. Under considerable pressure, Fortas resigned. The resignation came too quickly to determine how successful an impeachment effort would have been, but almost certainly it would have been serious.

The campaigns against Douglas and Fortas came primarily from the Nixon administration, which sought to replace the two liberals with more conservative justices. John Dean, a lawyer on Nixon's staff, later reported that Fortas's resignation led to "a small celebration in the attorney general's office," which "was capped with a call from the president, congratulating" Justice Department officials "on a job well done."[66] In contrast, according to Dean, the unsuccessful campaign against Douglas "created an intractable resolve by Douglas never to resign while Nixon was president."[67]

The Fortas episode seems unlikely to be repeated, in part because it reminded justices of the need to avoid questionable financial conduct. The occasional removal of federal judges through impeachment proceedings makes it clear that impeachment is a real option. But it is used only in cases with strong evidence of serious misdeeds, often involving allegations of corrupt behavior.

Thus, the timing of a justice's leaving the Court reflects primarily the justice's own inclinations, health, and longevity. Those who want to influence the Court's membership may have their say when a vacancy occurs, but they have little control over the creation of vacancies.

Conclusion

The recruitment of Supreme Court justices is a complex process. People do not rise to the Court in an orderly fashion. Rather, whether they become credible candidates for the Court and whether they actually win appointments depend on a wide range of circumstances. Indeed, something close to pure luck plays a powerful role in determining who becomes a justice.

The criteria that presidents use in choosing nominees and the balance of power between president and Senate have varied over the Court's history. The attributes of the people selected as justices have also varied. Justices today are relatively diverse in race, gender, and social class, but they are also a relatively narrow group in their educational and career backgrounds.

In the current era presidents choose nominees with close attention to their policy preferences, senators scrutinize nominees closely, interest groups seek to influence the selection of justices, and most sitting justices are reluctant to give up their positions. That is not surprising. All these participants recognize the Court's power and prestige, and they also perceive a strong link between the Court's membership and its decisions. That perception is well founded. In later chapters I will discuss how the identities of the justices shape the Court's positions on legal and policy issues.

NOTES

1. The four who were nominated and confirmed twice include three individuals elevated from associate justice to chief justice (Edward White, Harlan Stone, and William Rehnquist) and one (Charles Evans Hughes) who resigned from the Court and was later appointed chief justice. Douglas Ginsburg is counted as a nominee even though he withdrew from consideration in 1987, before he was officially nominated. Harriet Miers was nominated in 2005 but withdrew before the Senate could consider her nomination.

2. Joan Biskupic, *Sandra Day O'Connor* (New York: HarperCollins, 2005), 72–73. Burger's role in the Nixon nominations is discussed in John W. Dean, *The Rehnquist Choice* (New York: Free Press, 2001), 19, 52, 179–185.

3. This discussion is based in part on John Anthony Maltese, *The Selling of Supreme Court Nominees* (Baltimore, Md.: Johns Hopkins University Press, 1995); and Gregory A. Caldeira and John R. Wright, "Lobbying for Justice: The Rise of Organized Conflict in the Politics of Federal Judgeships," in *Contemplating Courts*, ed. Lee Epstein (Washington, D.C.: CQ Press, 1995), 44–71.

4. Mark Arsenault, "Groups Seek Forum by Fighting Kagan," *Boston Globe*, June 10, 2010, A1.

5. George W. Bush, *Decision Points* (New York: Crown Publishers, 2010), 100.

6. Joanna Molloy, "Bill Clinton Reveals for the First Time that Former New York Gov. Mario Cuomo Rejected Supreme Court Nomination," *New York Daily News*, June 6, 2012, http://www.nydailynews.com/news/politics/bill-clinton-reveals-time-new-york-gov-mario-cuomo-rejected-supreme-court-nomination-article-1.1090738.

7. Henry J. Abraham, *Justices, Presidents, and Senators: A History of U.S. Supreme Court Appointments from Washington to Bush II*, 5th ed. (Lanham, Md.: Rowman & Littlefield, 2008), 146.

8. Robert Barnes, "Stay or Go?" *Washington Post*, October 6, 2013, A9.

9. Jeffrey Budziak, "Blind Justice or Blind Ambition? The Influence of Promotion on Decision Making in the U.S. Courts of Appeals," *Justice System Journal* 34 (2013), 295–320; Ryan C. Black and Ryan J. Owens, "Courting the President: How Circuit Court Judges Alter Their Behavior for Promotion to the Supreme Court," *American Journal of Political Science*, forthcoming.

10. "Stevens on the Cost of Upholding the Health Care Law," *Wall Street Journal Law Blog*, November 16, 2011, http://blogs.wsj.com/law/2011/11/16/stevens-on-the-cost-of-upholding-the-health-care-law. The case was *Thomas More Law Center v. Obama* (6th Cir. 2011).

11. Garance Franke-Ruta, "Justice Kagan and Justice Scalia Are Hunting Buddies—Really," *Atlantic* online, June 30, 2013, http://www.theatlantic.com/politics/archive/2013/06/justice-kagan-and-justice-scalia-are-hunting-buddies-really/277401.

12. See Paul M. Collins Jr. and Lori A. Ringhand, *Supreme Court Confirmation Hearings and Constitutional Change* (New York: Cambridge University Press, 2013).

13. Richard Brust, "No More Kabuki Confirmations," *ABA Journal* 95 (October 2009): 39.

14. Elena Kagan, "Confirmation Messes, Old and New," *University of Chicago Law Review* 62 (Spring 1995): 941.

15. Dahlia Lithwick, "Confirmation Report," *Slate Magazine*, January 10, 2006, http://www.slate.com/articles/news_and_politics/jurisprudence/features/2006/confirmation_report/revenge_of_the_nerd.html.

16. The discussion of nomination decisions that follows draws much from Christine L. Nemacheck, *Strategic Selection: Presidential Nomination of Supreme Court Justices from Herbert Hoover through George W. Bush* (Charlottesville: University of Virginia Press, 2007); and David Alistair Yalof, *Pursuit of Justices: Presidential Politics and the Selection of Supreme Court Justices* (Chicago: University of Chicago Press, 1999).

17. Nemacheck, *Strategic Selection*, chap. 5; Sheldon Goldman, Elliot Slotnick, and Sara Schiavoni, "Obama's Judiciary at Midterm," *Judicature* 94 (May–June 2011): 275.

18. Brian Lamb, Susan Swain, and Mark Farkas, eds., *The Supreme Court: A C-Span Book Featuring the Justices in Their Own Words* (New York: Public Affairs), 160.

19. Nemacheck, *Strategic Selection*, chap. 3; Goldman, Slotnick, and Schiavoni, "Obama's Judiciary at Midterm," 277.

20. Robert Barnes, "Clinton Papers Illuminate the Selection Process," *Washington Post*, June 9, 2014, A13.

21. Steve Holland, "Bush Defends Pick for Supreme Court," *Toronto Star*, October 5, 2005, A11.

22. Fred Barnes, "Souter-Phobia," *Weekly Standard*, August 1, 2005, 11–12.

23. Alyssa Sepinwall, "The Making of a Presidential Myth" (letter), *Wall Street Journal*, September 4, 1990, A11; Tony Mauro, "Leak of Souter Keeps McGuigan in Plan," *Legal Times*, September 10, 1990, 11.

24. "Justice Anthony Kennedy: Surely Reagan's Biggest Disappointment," *Human Events*, May 31–June 7, 1990, 3.

25. Robert Scigliano, *The Supreme Court and the Presidency* (New York: Free Press, 1971), 95.

26. John Paul Stevens, *Five Chiefs: A Supreme Court Memoir* (New York: Little, Brown, 2011), 60–61.

27. White House Office of the Press Secretary, "Remarks by the President and Solicitor General Elena Kagan at the Nomination of Solicitor General Elena Kagan to the Supreme Court," May 10, 2010, http://www.whitehouse.gov.

28. Peter Baker and Jeff Zeleny, "Obama Nominates Hispanic Judge for Supreme Court," *New York Times*, May 27, 2009, A17.

29. These figures were calculated from data in R. Sam Garrett and Denis Steven Rutkus, *Speed of Presidential and Senate Actions on Supreme Court Nominations, 1900–2010* (Washington, D.C.: Congressional Research Service, 2010), 37–42, with the figures for the Kagan confirmation added.

30. See Lee Epstein, René Lindstädt, Jeffrey A. Segal, and Chad Westerland, "The Changing Dynamics of Senate Voting on Supreme Court Nominees," *Journal of Politics* 68 (May 2006): 296–307.

31. These percentages are based on figures in Jeffrey Segal, "Senate Confirmation of Supreme Court Justices: Partisan and Institutional Politics," *Journal of Politics* 49 (November 1987): 1008 (updated by the author).

32. Based on ibid., updated by the author. Nominations made during a president's fourth year but after the president's reelection are not included.
33. See Maltese, *Selling of Supreme Court Nominees.*
34. Jonathan P. Kastellec, Jeffrey R. Lax, and Justin H. Phillips, "Public Opinion and Senate Confirmation of Supreme Court Nominees," *Journal of Politics* 72 (July 2010): 767–784.
35. "Here Comes the Judge," *Newsweek,* February 2, 1970, 19.
36. Richard Reeves, *President Nixon: Alone in the White House* (New York: Simon & Schuster, 2001), 161.
37. Ronald Brownstein, "Alito's Remarks on Roe May Not Be Fighting Words," *Los Angeles Times,* December 12, 2005, A11.
38. Sonia Sotomayor, "A Latina Judge's Voice," *Berkeley La Raza Law Journal* 13 (2002): 92.
39. Jamie Stengle, "Ruth Bader Ginsburg Speaks at SMU," *Deseret News* (Salt Lake City), August 29, 2011, http://www.deseretnews.com/article/700174796/Ruth-Bader-Ginsburg-speaks-at-SMU.html; Brent Martin, "Chief Justice Roberts: Scalia, Ginsburg Wouldn't be Confirmed Today," Nebraska Radio Network, September 19, 2014, http://nebraskaradionetwork.com/2014/09/19/chief-justice-roberts-scalia-ginsburg-wouldnt-be-confirmed-today-audio.
40. Scott Basinger and Maxwell Mak, "The Changing Politics of Supreme Court Confirmations," *American Politics Research* 40 (July 2012): 737–763.
41. Ed Enoch, "U.S. Supreme Court Justice Elena Kagan Speaks About Diversity," *Tuscaloosa News,* October 4, 2013, http://www.tuscaloosanews.com/article/20131004/NEWS/131009860.
42. Samiha Shafy, "Supreme Court Justice Sotomayor: 'Sometimes You Have to Do the Unexpected,'" *Spiegel Online International,* April 2, 2014, http://www.spiegel.de/international/world/interview-with-supreme-court-justice-sonia-sotomayor-a-961986.html.
43. This discussion of justices' backgrounds is based in part on John R. Schmidhauser, *Judges and Justices: The Federal Appellate Judiciary* (Boston, Mass.: Little, Brown, 1979), 41–100.
44. These proportions are based on biographies in the *Biographical Directory of Federal Judges,* compiled by the Federal Judicial Center, http://www.fjc.gov/history/home.nsf/page/judges.html.
45. Linda Greenhouse, "Justices on the Job," *New York Times Opinionator,* July 24, 2013, http://opinionator.blogs.nytimes.com/2013/07/24/justices-on-the-job/?_php=true&_type=blogs&_r=0.
46. Richard A. Posner, *Reflections on Judging* (Cambridge, Mass.: Harvard University Press, 2013), 52–53.
47. Lee Epstein, Jeffrey A. Segal, Harold J. Spaeth, and Thomas G. Walker, *The Supreme Court Compendium,* 5th ed. (Washington, D.C.: CQ Press, 2012), 296–303.
48. Bradley Blackburn, "Justices Ruth Bader Ginsburg and Sandra Day O'Connor on Life and the Supreme Court," *ABC News,* October 26, 2010, http://abcnews.go.com.
49. Enoch, "Justice Kagan Speaks About Diversity."
50. Bruce Vielmetti, "Visiting MU, Justice Kagan Tells of Hunting with Scalia," *Milwaukee Journal Sentinel,* April 3, 2012, http://www.jsonline.com/news/milwaukee/visiting-mu-justice-kagan-tells-of-hunting-with-scalia-e84rus1-146048325.html. See Patrick J. Glen, "Harvard and Yale Ascendant: The Legal Education of the Justices from Holmes to Kagan," *UCLA Law Review Discourse* 58 (2010): 129–154.

51. Richard C. Reuben, "Justice Stevens: I Benefited from Pro Bono Work," *Los Angeles Daily Journal*, August 11, 1992, 11. See Kenneth A. Manaster, *Illinois Justice: The Scandal of 1969 and the Rise of John Paul Stevens* (Chicago: University of Chicago Press, 2001).

52. See Jan Crawford Greenburg, *Supreme Conflict: The Inside Story of the Struggle for Control of the United States Supreme Court* (New York: Penguin Press, 2007), 242–243.

53. Colleen Walsh, "Associate Justice Elena Kagan Provides Peek into Supreme Court's Everyday Workings," *Harvard Gazette*, September 4, 2014, http://news.harvard.edu/gazette/story/2014/09/court-sense.

54. This discussion of resignation and retirement draws on David N. Atkinson, *Leaving the Bench: Supreme Court Justices at the End* (Lawrence: University Press of Kansas, 1999); and Artemus Ward, *Deciding to Leave: The Politics of Retirement from the United States Supreme Court* (Albany: State University of New York Press, 2003).

55. David J. Garrow, "Mental Decrepitude on the U.S. Supreme Court: The Historical Case for a 28th Amendment," *University of Chicago Law Review* 67 (Fall 2000): 1085.

56. Interview with John Paul Stevens, "Inside E Street," AARP television program, July 5, 2011, http://www.aarp.org/health/longevity/info-07-2011/video-john-paul-stevens-conversation-on-longevity.html.

57. Robert Barnes, "Souter Reportedly Planning to Retire from High Court," *Washington Post*, May 1, 2009, A1.

58. Jeffrey Toobin, "Heavyweight: How Ruth Bader Ginsburg has Moved the Supreme Court," *New Yorker*, March 11, 2013, 47.

59. Robert Barnes, "The Question Facing Ruth Bader Ginsburg: Stay or Go," *Washington Post*, October 4, 2013, http://www.washingtonpost.com/lifestyle/magazine/the-question-facing-ruth-bader-ginsburg-stay-or-go/2013/10/04/4d789e28-1574-11e3-a2ec-b47e45e6f8ef_story.html.

60. Jessica Weisberg, "Reigning Supreme," *Elle*, October 2014, 362.

61. Neil A. Lewis, "2 Years After His Bruising Hearing, Justice Thomas Still Shows the Hurt," *New York Times*, November 27, 1993, 6.

62. Information on participation in cases by Justices Souter and O'Connor was drawn from the LexisNexis archive of court of appeals decisions.

63. U.S. Constitution, art. 2, § 4.

64. John Ehrlichman, *Witness to Power: The Nixon Years* (New York: Simon & Schuster, 1982), 122.

65. Laura Kalman, *Abe Fortas: A Biography* (New Haven, Conn.: Yale University Press, 1990), 359–376; Bruce Allen Murphy, *Fortas: The Rise and Ruin of a Supreme Court Justice* (New York: Morrow, 1988).

66. Dean, *Rehnquist Choice*, 11.

67. Ibid., 26.

Chapter 3

The Cases

In the term that ended in June 2014, the Supreme Court issued 72 full decisions. The cases that the Court put on its agenda and then decided were a very small proportion of all the court cases and potential cases that might have resulted in decisions by the Court. This chapter examines the process of agenda setting that produces those rare events. In the first stage of that process, people make a series of decisions that bring their cases to the Supreme Court. In the second stage, the Court selects from those cases the few—currently about 1 in 100—that it will fully consider and decide. With the exception of a few special sets of cases, when the Court agrees to hear a case it does so formally by granting a writ of certiorari to call the case up from a lower court.

Several sets of people and institutions help set the Court's agenda. In the first stage, litigants file cases and bring them through the legal system to the Court. Most of these litigants are represented by lawyers in at least part of this process, and some receive direct or indirect help from interest groups. The Court itself plays no direct part at this stage. But people's expectations about how the Court might respond to their case affect their decision whether to bring it to the Court, and justices sometimes use their opinions to encourage certain kinds of cases. In *Whitman v. United States* (2014), for instance, Justice Scalia wrote a short opinion to say that if a litigant brought the Court a case raising a particular issue in an appropriate form, "I will be receptive to" hearing the case.[1]

In the second stage, the justices are the sole decision makers. But their choices may be influenced by the litigants, lawyers, and interest groups that participate in cases. For their part, the other branches of the federal government structure both stages by setting the Court's jurisdiction and writing other rules that affect cases, and they participate directly in many cases.

The first two sections of this chapter examine the two stages of agenda setting in the Court. In the first section, I consider how and why cases are brought to the Court. In the second, I discuss how and why the justices choose certain cases to decide on the merits by ruling on the legal issues in those cases. In the final section, I consider why the Court's agenda is as small as it is.

Reaching the Court: Litigants, Attorneys, and Interest Groups

Litigants, their attorneys, and interest groups are all important in determining which cases get to the Supreme Court, and I will examine the role of each in turn. The federal government is the most frequent and most distinctive participant in Supreme Court cases, and its role deserves separate consideration.

Litigants

Every case that comes to the Supreme Court has at least one formal party, or litigant, on each side. For a case to reach the Court, one or more of the parties must initiate the litigation and move it upward through the court system.

Litigants in the Court are diverse. Among those who petition the Court to hear cases, the great majority are individuals. Most of these individuals are criminal defendants; the others occupy a variety of roles. Among respondents—the litigants who are on the other side from petitioners— the largest category consists of governments and government agencies at all levels. Individuals are respondents in many cases. Businesses frequently appear as petitioners or respondents. Other kinds of organizations, such as nonprofit groups and labor unions, are parties in some Court cases.

One key question about litigants is why they become involved in court cases and carry those cases to the Supreme Court. We can think of litigants' motives as falling into two categories: advancing a direct personal or organizational interest, and seeking to shape public policy. Cases in which the first motive is dominant can be called ordinary litigation, while those in which the second motive is dominant can be called political litigation.

I use the term *ordinary litigation* because the overwhelming majority of court cases are motivated by direct self-interest. For instance, plaintiffs file personal injury suits because they hope to receive money through a court verdict or an out-of-court settlement. Indeed, the great majority of cases brought to the Supreme Court are essentially ordinary litigation. Most are criminal cases in which a convicted defendant wants to get out of prison or to stay out. Other cases involve efforts by individuals to obtain monetary benefits from government agencies or monetary damages from private entities. Some cases come from business corporations that have a significant economic stake in a dispute with other businesses or with a government body.

One example of ordinary litigation in the Supreme Court is *POM Wonderful v. Coca-Cola Company* (2014). The POM Wonderful company sells pomegranate juice and blends of juices, including one with pomegranate and blueberry juices. In 2007, Coca-Cola's Minute Maid division began to sell a blend of five juices in a container whose label emphasized the pomegranate and blueberry components, although those two ingredients constituted one-half of 1 percent of the contents. Because POM Wonderful seemed to be losing sales to the Minute Maid product, the company sued Coca-Cola in 2008 under the federal Lanham Act, which allows lawsuits for unfair competition based on false or misleading product descriptions. A federal court of appeals concluded that a different federal statute—the Food, Drug, and Cosmetic Act—had the effect of ruling out such lawsuits when they involved labeling of food and beverages. The Supreme Court reversed the court of appeals decision, ruling in favor of POM Wonderful. The Court's decision established a legal principle that could have broad effects, but the officials at POM Wonderful who brought the lawsuit were concerned simply with their own competitive position.

In political litigation, the most common goal is gaining a judicial decision that favors the litigant's policy goals. Litigants with that purpose usually care more about the legal rules that the Court issues than about simply winning the case.

The proportion of cases that can be classified as fully or partly political increases with each step upward in the judicial system, so political litigation is most common in the Supreme Court. This pattern is not accidental. Ordinary litigation usually ends at an early stage, because the parties find it advantageous to settle their dispute or even to accept defeat rather than to fight on. In contrast, political litigants often want to get a case to the highest court, where a victory may establish a national policy they favor. In addition, political litigation sometimes attracts the support of interest groups that help to shoulder the costs and other burdens of carrying a case through the judicial system. And political litigation is especially common among the cases that the Court agrees to hear, because political cases are more likely than ordinary litigation to contain broad legal issues that interest the justices.

Rules of legal standing require that a litigant have a direct stake in a case. So even when lawyers or interest groups orchestrate a case on the basis of their policy goals, they must bring the case in the name of one or more people who would be affected by the outcome. As a result, what looks like political litigation from the perspective of lawyers and interest groups might have a large element of ordinary litigation from the point of view of the litigants they support or recruit.

Still, some litigants care more about the policy issues in a case than about their own personal stakes. Edward Blum, who heads a group called the Project on Fair Representation, has sought out litigants to challenge affirmative action programs in college admissions—even advertising for litigants on websites. In *Fisher v. University of Texas* (2013), the litigant was Abigail Fisher, the daughter of an old friend of Blum's, who had not been admitted to the university as an undergraduate. Fisher said that she "assumed that whatever would come of it would take a really long time. It would be for others."[2] Indeed, Fisher graduated from Louisiana State University a year before the Supreme Court ruled in her favor by holding that a lower court had not used the right legal standard in analyzing the case. (Fisher probably had a continuing legal stake in the case, in part because of the application fee she had paid to the University of Texas; the Supreme Court did not address that question.)

Some cases cannot easily be labeled as ordinary or political litigation, because the litigants have mixed motives. That appears to be true, for instance, of some litigants who have challenged restrictions on campaign funding and government involvement in religion. In cases brought by government agencies, ordinary and political elements may be difficult to separate: prosecutors file criminal cases to advance the specific mission of their agencies, but that mission is linked to the broader policy goal of attacking crime.

Some litigants help to publicize their causes before and after the Supreme Court's decision. This was true of Edith Windsor, who successfully challenged the statute prohibiting the federal government from recognizing same-sex marriages in *United States v. Windsor* (2013).[3] Mary Beth Tinker, one of the public school students who won a landmark First Amendment case in *Tinker v. Des Moines* (1969), has been an advocate for freedom of expression and launched a national "Tinker Tour" "to promote youth voices, free speech and a free press" in 2013.[4] Other litigants stay in the background, largely unnoticed even as their cases shape legal policy on major issues.

Mary Beth Tinker with her brother John in 1968 and at her home in Washington, D.C., in 2013. In 1969 the Supreme Court overturned the school suspensions of the Tinkers and Christopher Eckhardt for wearing antiwar armbands. She later served as an advocate for the rights of young people, including freedom of expression.

Supreme Court litigants that are organizations sometimes play active roles in decisions about their cases. That is not often true of individuals, and under some conditions their lawyers might make decisions that do not fully serve their clients' interests.[5] But even lawyers who litigate on behalf of causes typically give close attention to their clients' needs. This was true of Ruth Bader Ginsburg when she was bringing cases to the Supreme Court to challenge sex discrimination in the law. She has reported that "I've kept up over the years with all" of her former clients in those cases. One of those clients was Stephen Wiesenfeld, who sought and won survivors' benefits in 1975 to help him raise his son Jason after his wife died in childbirth. Ginsburg presided at Jason's wedding in 1998 and at Stephen's remarriage at the age of seventy-one in 2014.[6]

Attorneys

Cases that get to the Supreme Court usually have high stakes for the litigants, and the Court's decisions often have major effects on national policy. For this reason, we would expect litigants to be represented by lawyers who have considerable expertise in handling cases in the Court.

For most of the twentieth century, however, this was generally not true. The lawyers in the Office of the Solicitor General in the Justice Department regularly wrote briefs and presented oral arguments in the Court, so they quickly became both experienced and expert. A few interest groups, such as the NAACP Legal Defense Fund, took enough cases to the Court that their lawyers also became experts. But most cases were brought to the Court and argued before it by attorneys who had little or no experience in Supreme Court litigation.

That situation has changed a good deal since the 1980s. As a group, lawyers in the solicitor general's office continue to stand out for the numbers of cases they handle in the Court, and those who remain in the office for most of their careers amass very large numbers of oral arguments: through the 2013 term, by one count, Edwin Kneedler had argued 121 cases and Michael Dreeben 90.[7] But increasingly, parties other than the federal government are also represented by experienced Supreme Court litigators.

For the most part, these lawyers are in private law firms that have Supreme Court cases as one of their major areas of practice. Many of the lawyers in these firms who handle cases in the Court had prior experience in the solicitor general's office, as law clerks in the Court, or both. The most striking exception is Tom Goldstein, who built up a Supreme Court practice without either form of experience and while he was working out of his home rather than in a large law firm. Since 1999, he has argued more than thirty cases in the Court.

Other experienced lawyers come from state governments. States are parties in a good many Supreme Court cases, but traditionally they were represented by lawyers with little experience in the Court, including elected attorney generals. According to Justice Scalia, some of the attorney generals "were just disasters."[8] Seeking to improve their performance, about two-thirds of the states have followed the example of the federal government and created their own solicitor generals' offices.[9] Ted Cruz, a U.S. senator from Texas and a candidate for the 2016 Republican presidential nomination, served as Texas solicitor general from 2003 to 2008 and presented eight oral arguments in the Court during that time.

Table 3-1 shows how the experience of lawyers in the Court has grown since the early 1990s. Leaving aside the lawyers in the federal solicitor general's office, the proportion of oral arguments in the Court that were presented by lawyers who argued other cases over a five-year period jumped from one-quarter in the 1993 term to one-half in the 2013 term. But as these figures suggest, advocates who appear before the Court only on rare occasions—often a single time over their careers—have hardly disappeared.

Who are these one-time advocates? As in the past, most of them become involved in a case early in its history and continue to represent their client in the Supreme Court. In *Burrage v. United States* (2014), for instance, the petitioner was an indigent criminal defendant. Angela Campbell, part of a four-lawyer firm in Des Moines, had represented the defendant at trial in federal district court and then in his unsuccessful appeal in the court

TABLE 3-1

Numbers of Oral Arguments over a Five-Term Period by Lawyers Arguing Cases in the 1993 and 2013 Terms (Lawyers for Federal Government Excluded)

Number of arguments	1993 (Percentage)	2013 (Percentage)
1	74.7	48.0
2	15.3	13.6
3–5	4.0	13.6
6–10	4.7	12.0
11–15	0.0	5.6
16–25	1.3	7.2

Note: For lawyers who argued cases in 1993, the five-term period is 1989–1993; for lawyers who argued cases in 2013, the period is 2009–2013. Lawyers who argued multiple cases in 1993 or 2013 are counted each time they argued a case. Thus, the 7.2 percent in the lower-right cell of the table means that, leaving aside arguments by lawyers for the federal government, 7.2 percent of the oral arguments in the 2013 term were made by lawyers who had 16–25 arguments in the 2009–2013 terms.

of appeals. After writing the petition for certiorari and collaborating on the brief on the merits for Burrage, she presented the oral argument for him. Two months later, the Court ruled unanimously for her client.[10]

There are differences in skills even among the lawyers who have substantial experience in the Court, but on the whole those who participate frequently in cases are effective advocates. The growing role of specialists from law firms has contributed to a general improvement in the quality of advocacy in the Court, a development that Justice Samuel Alito and retired justice John Paul Stevens have noted.[11]

Some lawyers who appear before the Court for the first time do a poor job. In a 2012 case a reporter concluded that a lawyer in the New Orleans district attorney's office had "found ways to botch virtually every point."[12] But many first-time advocates in the Court are effective. Speaking about oral argument, Justice Antonin Scalia has said that "I'm often amazed at how good some of these people from nowhere are—court appointed counsel from Podunk."[13]

Todd Crespi

Angela Campbell, an Iowa attorney, presenting oral argument in the Supreme Court in November 2013. Arguing before the Court for the first time, Campbell won a unanimous decision for her client in Burrage v. United States *(2014).*

Also amazing are the occasional nonlawyers who write their own petitions for certiorari and secure hearings from the Court. One example was the Arkansas prisoner whose petition led to the Court's decision favoring his religious freedom claim in *Holt v. Hobbs* (2015). Even more amazing was the work of Shon Hopwood, who was serving a ten-year sentence in a federal prison for bank robbery when a fellow inmate asked Hopwood to write a petition for certiorari to the Supreme Court on his behalf.[14] Lacking any legal training, Hopwood won a grant of certiorari. A distinguished Supreme Court advocate said that "it was probably one of the best cert. petitions I have ever read," and he agreed to take on the case after it was accepted only if Hopwood would help him. They won in a unanimous decision. After his release from prison, Hopwood eventually went to law school at the University of Washington. In 2014 he began a law clerkship with a federal court of appeals judge.

It is uncertain how much effect good or bad advocacy has on Supreme Court decisions. But the quality of lawyers' work undoubtedly has considerable effect at the certiorari stage, because the justices and their clerks are heavily dependent on the briefs they receive from the parties. In the small number of cases they accept, the justices have more sources of information and more time to consider cases, and they often come to cases with strong predispositions. One commentator noted that "even the best lawyer can't convince a majority of the justices to take a position they're allergic to."[15]

In the legal system as a whole, a relationship exists between the wealth of an individual or institution and the quality of the legal services available to that party. To a degree, this is true of the Supreme Court. The experienced Supreme Court advocates in private practice are most readily available to large corporations and other prosperous organizations that can afford their substantial fees. Further, because their firms regularly represent businesses, many of these lawyers will not represent consumers or employees in conflicts with businesses.[16]

But several mechanisms improve the position of people who lack wealth. First, the Court appoints an attorney to represent any indigent litigant whose case it accepts, if that litigant does not already have a lawyer, and many of those attorneys are highly skilled. Further, Supreme Court cases are both scarce and attractive to lawyers. For that reason, Supreme Court specialists sometimes offer their services at no cost to litigants whose cases have been accepted by the Court and even to litigants who have not yet asked the Court to hear their cases. Meanwhile, several prestigious law schools have established clinics to handle Supreme Court cases for no charge, and they too seek out cases. These clinics, sometimes affiliated with law firms that have Supreme Court specialists, can provide high-quality legal services.[17] As Tom Goldstein said, "There is plenty of good lawyering to go around."[18] Still, as a group, those litigants who can afford to hire the most experienced advocates have an advantage over those who cannot.

The last nonlawyer who presented oral argument in his own case in the Court did so in 1978 (he won in a unanimous decision), and after that the Court regularly prohibited specific litigants from following his example when they sought to do so.[19] In 2013 the Court adopted a blanket rule limiting oral argument to lawyers. Attorneys are eligible to participate in cases if they join the Supreme Court bar, for which the most important requirement is that they have been admitted to practice in a state for at least the past three years. Lawyers who cannot meet this requirement, however, usually are allowed to argue cases they have brought to the Court. Lawyers join the Supreme Court bar primarily for the prestige. An average of nearly 4,000 lawyers join each year, and the great majority will never participate in a Supreme Court case.[20]

Interest Groups

Leaders of interest groups must decide how to allocate their time, effort, and money. Groups vary considerably in how much attention they give to the Supreme Court. One key consideration is the relevance of the Court's work to a group's goals. A group that is concerned with civil liberties issues, such as the American Civil Liberties Union (ACLU), necessarily devotes a good deal of its work to litigation, including Supreme Court cases. Another consideration is the Court's likely receptiveness to a group's arguments. It is not surprising that conservative groups have become more active in the Court as it has become increasingly conservative, while liberal groups sometimes try to keep issues out of the Court because the prospects are unfavorable.

The primary goal of interest groups is to shape government policy, such as Supreme Court decisions. But group leaders are also concerned with maintenance of the group itself, and they may use their involvement with the Court as a means to attract members or financial contributions. As a result of these two goals, a great deal of interest group activity is devoted to the Court.

The Array of Groups in the Court. Interest group activity aimed at the Supreme Court has increased dramatically in the past half century. One indication of that growth is the higher level of group participation in the process of selecting justices. Another is the increasing numbers of amicus curiae briefs, which are submitted by individuals and organizations in cases in which they are not parties. In cases with oral arguments the Court received an average of 0.63 briefs per case in the 1956–1965 terms and 11.62 briefs per case in the 2013 term.[21] One reason for this growth is that the number of active interest groups and the level of their activity have increased considerably. Another is that the apparent success of some groups in shaping the Supreme Court's policies has encouraged other groups to seek similar success.

Hundreds of interest groups now participate in Supreme Court cases in some way. Among them are nearly all the groups that are most active in Congress and the executive branch. The box on page 76 provides a sampling of this participation by listing some of the groups that submitted amicus briefs in the 2014 term.

A Sampling of Groups Submitting Amicus Curiae Briefs to the Supreme Court in the 2014 Term

Economic Groups: Business and Occupational

AFL-CIO
American Dental Association
Google, Inc.
National Association of Criminal Defense Lawyers
National Association of Manufacturers
National Retail Federation

Noneconomic Interests

AARP
Anti-Defamation League
Gun Owners Foundation
National Congress of American Indians

Ideological and Issue Groups

Americans United for Separation of Church and State
Cato Institute
Public Citizen, Inc.
Washington Legal Foundation

Governments and Governmental Groups

Federation of State Boards of Physical Therapy
National Governors Association
National League of Cities
State of Wisconsin
U.S. Senate

The groups that participate in Supreme Court cases can be placed in four broad categories. The first is economic: individual businesses, trade associations, professional groups, labor unions, and farm groups. Much of the Court's work affects the interests of these groups, on issues that range from employment discrimination to regulation of product safety. The business community is especially well represented in the Court. Individual businesses frequently are parties to cases, and businesses and business groups regularly submit amicus briefs.

The most prominent economic group in the Supreme Court is the National Chamber Litigation Center, the litigation arm of the U.S. Chamber of Commerce.[22] The Center is very active as an amicus, and it stands out among nongovernmental groups for the frequency with which it files amicus briefs at the certiorari stage. The Chamber sometimes acts directly as a litigant, as it did in a 2014 case involving federal regulation of greenhouse gas emissions.[23] The Center also holds moot courts to prepare lawyers representing business interests for their arguments in the Court.

In the second category are groups that represent segments of the population defined by something other than economics. Most of these groups are based on personal attributes such as race, gender, age, and sexual orientation. The prototype for these groups is the NAACP Legal Defense and Educational Fund (sometimes called the NAACP Legal Defense Fund or simply the Fund). The Fund initially focused its efforts on voting rights and school desegregation. It later turned to other areas such as employment and criminal justice, giving special attention to the death penalty. The Fund's successes in the Supreme Court encouraged the creation of organizations that were concerned with discrimination on grounds other than race, groups that proliferated from the 1960s onward. It also served as a model for groups in other fields such as Earthjustice, which litigates on environmental issues.[24]

The groups in the third category represent broad ideological positions or more specific issue positions rather than the interests of a specific segment of society. Here, the prototype is the ACLU.[25] Established in 1920 to protect civil liberties, the ACLU involves itself in nearly every area of civil liberties law. The ACLU also has created special projects to undertake concerted litigation campaigns in specific areas of concern, such as women's rights, capital punishment, and national security. Among the other groups that work to achieve liberal policy goals are the Constitutional Accountability Center, which litigates on a wide range of issues, and the Planned Parenthood Federation of America, for which abortion is a major concern.

Issue and ideological groups that favor conservative positions were slower to involve themselves in litigation, but many such groups are now active. Some focus primarily on economic issues. The Institute for Justice, for instance, litigates against government regulation of economic activity and government action to take private property. Others give primary attention to civil liberties issues. The most prominent activity of the Center for Individual Rights is a long-term campaign against affirmative action programs. Several litigating groups, such as the American Center for Law and Justice, represent conservative religious interests.

The final category consists of governments and groups of government officials. Governments regularly appear as interest groups in the Court. The federal government is a special case, discussed later in this section. State and local governments often come to the Court as litigants. In addition, they frequently file amicus briefs. It has become standard practice for many or most states to join in a brief to emphasize their strong, shared interest in a case. But states sometimes line up on both sides, either because their interests diverge (as they do on greenhouse gas emissions) or because they have different ideological orientations (as they do on same-sex marriage). Because of joint briefs, individual states can participate in large numbers of cases. Over a four-year period, for instance, Ohio participated in fifty-three amicus briefs.[26]

Forms of Group Activity. As the discussion so far suggests, interest groups can attempt to influence the Court in multiple ways. First, they can try to exert influence from outside the litigation process. As described in Chapter 2, some groups participate unofficially in the nomination and confirmation of justices. Groups can also lobby the Court indirectly through marches and demonstrations or by seeking favorable coverage for their positions in the news media or legal publications. Occasionally, groups try to bolster their positions on legal issues by sponsoring empirical research on questions such as the extent of racial discrimination in use of the death penalty.

Second, groups can enter cases by submitting amicus briefs.[27] With the consent of the parties to a case or the Court, any person or organization may submit an amicus brief to supplement the arguments of the parties. (Legal representatives of governments do not need to obtain consent.) Most of the time, the parties agree to the submission of amicus briefs on both sides. When the Court's consent is needed, it seldom is denied. Amicus briefs can be submitted on whether a case should be heard or, after a case is accepted for hearing, directly on the merits.

Amicus briefs are submitted in only a small minority of cases at the case selection stage. They are far more common in cases that the Court has accepted for consideration on the merits. Interest groups are the most frequent submitters of amicus briefs, though governments and individual businesses are also active participants in amicus activity. In the 2013 term amicus briefs were submitted in 96 percent of the cases in which the Court held oral argument, 82 percent of the cases had at least five briefs, and 39 percent had at least ten briefs.[28] In cases that affect the interests of a broad range of interest groups, the Court sometimes receives massive numbers of briefs—about 130 in the challenges to "Obamacare" that the Court addressed in 2012, about 140 in the 2015 challenge to state prohibitions of same-sex marriage.[29] And because groups or individuals regularly join in submitting a brief, the number of participants is considerably larger than the number of briefs.

Amicus briefs are popular for several reasons. First, although the costs of preparing them are substantial, they are considerably cheaper than taking a more direct role in litigation. Second, writing and submitting an amicus brief is straightforward, so that any group with the needed financial resources can do so. Finally, many lawyers and other people believe that amicus briefs influence the Court's decisions. For this reason, groups whose interests or concerns are implicated by a case regularly weigh in, and parties to cases often encourage or even orchestrate supportive briefs.

Direct participation in litigation is the third form of group activity in the Court. If a group has legal standing, it can initiate a case in its own name. The Association of American Railroads, the American Lung Association, the Southeastern Legal Foundation, and the U.S. Chamber of Commerce were among the interest groups that were parties in the cases that the Court decided in its 2013 and 2014 terms.

More often, a group sponsors a case on behalf of another party— sometimes a litigant that the group has recruited. A group sponsor provides legal services to the litigant, bears other costs, and directs the course of the case. Sponsorship can be difficult to carry out, so relatively few groups undertake full sponsorship of cases. But sometimes groups engage in limited sponsorship of cases that have already been initiated, helping to bear the financial costs and supplying legal services and advice.

Some interest groups establish long-term litigation strategies in which they seek to shape legal policy over time. These campaigns face serious challenges due to the costs of litigation, the difficulty of controlling which cases are brought to court, and the potential for defeats that sidetrack a campaign. But when groups are skilled and their goals align with the Supreme Court's disposition, they sometimes win major victories. The NAACP Legal Defense Fund successfully attacked racial segregation in education in a series of cases that culminated in *Brown v. Board of Education* (1954). The ACLU's Women's Rights Project won most of the cases it brought to the Supreme Court in the 1970s, a time when the Court began to look skeptically at government practices that treated women and men differently. More recently, conservative groups such as the Chamber of Commerce and organizations that oppose affirmative action have achieved significant successes.

The range of activities that interest groups can use to shape Supreme Court policy is illustrated by the legal campaign against the federal health care law of 2010 that President Obama had sponsored.[30] Even as Congress was debating the law in 2009, opponents began to develop arguments that Congress lacked the power to require some individuals to buy health insurance or pay a monetary penalty. The Republican attorney general of

Virginia brought one lawsuit challenging the mandate to purchase insurance shortly after the law was enacted, and many other states with Republican attorney generals or governors eventually joined in a second lawsuit that Florida initiated at about the same time. The National Federation of Independent Business joined the Florida lawsuit, along with two of its members, to ensure that there were parties with legal standing in the case. The federation also provided the bulk of the legal costs for Florida and the other plaintiffs in the lawsuit. Other lawsuits were filed against the law.

Before and after the lawsuits were filed, legal scholars, Republican leaders, and other conservatives aired and refined their arguments against the mandate in publications, speeches, and a prominent legal blog. Opponents of the health care law submitted amicus briefs to lower courts that heard challenges to the mandate. Through all this activity, they helped overcome initial skepticism about their arguments. After the Supreme Court agreed to hear the Florida case, efforts to make the case against the law continued in a large number of amicus briefs, public demonstrations, and other forms. Ultimately, the Court ruled by a 5–4 vote that Congress could not justify the mandate on the basis of the commerce power, but Chief Justice Roberts's opinion justifying it on the basis of the taxation power allowed that provision and the bulk of the law to stand.

Having suffered this defeat, groups that opposed the health care law pressed challenges to the law and to the rules established for its operation on other grounds. Most important, they argued that the wording of the statute allowed the federal government to subsidize health insurance only in the states in which the state governments had set up health care "exchanges" or programs under the law and not in the states in which the federal government had set up the programs. If their argument was successful, it would effectively prevent the heart of the health care law from operating in two-thirds of the states. The Supreme Court heard a case raising this argument, and its decision in *King v. Burwell* (2015) saved the health care law once again. But even before the Court heard arguments in that case, the Republican-controlled House of Representatives filed a new lawsuit challenging two major features of the Obama administration's implementation of the health care law.

The Significance of Interest Groups. Interest groups can influence whether the Supreme Court accepts a case as well as the Court's rulings in the cases it does accept. Influence at those two stages is discussed later in this chapter and in Chapter 4. Here, I consider their effect on whether cases get to the Court in the first place. In this respect, cases may be placed in three categories.

The largest category contains the cases that come to the Court without any participation by interest groups. The issues in these cases are too narrow to interest any group. They reach the Court because the parties and attorneys have strong incentives to seek a Supreme Court hearing and sufficient resources to finance the litigation. Indigent criminal defendants who face significant prison terms have the needed incentive, and they need not pay lawyers' fees or other expenses to get a case to the Court.

The second category consists of cases that would have reached the Court without any interest group involvement but in which groups are involved in some way. An interest group may assist one of the parties by providing attorneys' services or financing, or it may submit an amicus brief supporting a petition for hearing.

The third category includes cases that would not reach the Court without group sponsorship. There are many important legal questions in civil liberties that no individual litigant would take to the Supreme Court without help. For example, most of the individuals whose cases the ACLU takes could not have gone to court in the first place without the group's assistance.

Because group sponsorship of cases in the Court is relatively rare, only a small proportion of cases brought to the Court fall into this third category. But groups are most likely to provide full or partial sponsorship for cases that have a good chance to be heard by the Court and to produce major legal rulings. Indeed, much of the Court's support for legal protections for civil liberties over the past century was made possible by interest group action.[31]

The Federal Government as Litigant

Of all the litigants in the Supreme Court, the federal government appears most frequently. It is a party in a large minority of the cases brought to the Court for consideration. It participates as a party or an amicus in most cases that are actually argued before the Court—about 85 percent in the 2013 term. As a result of its frequent participation, the federal government is the most important interest group in the Court.

In turn, the group of about twenty lawyers in the Office of the Solicitor General in the Justice Department has more impact on the Court than any other set of attorneys. With assistance from other lawyers in the Justice Department, lawyers in the Solicitor General's office represent the federal government in the Supreme Court. They decide whether to bring federal government cases to the Court; only a few federal agencies can take cases to the Court without the solicitor general's approval. They also do the bulk of the government's legal work in Supreme Court cases, including petitions for hearings, the writing of briefs, and oral arguments.

The solicitor general's office occupies a complicated position. On the one hand, it represents the president and the executive branch, functioning as their law firm. In this role, the office helps to carry out the president's policies. But the office also has a unique relationship with the Supreme Court, one in which it serves as an adviser as well as an advocate. As Richard Pacelle put it, the solicitor general's office straddles the line "between law and politics."[32]

The office's unique relationship with the Court rests on the fact that it represents a unique litigant. For one thing, the executive branch and the Supreme Court are both part of the federal government. And because the executive branch is involved in so many potential and actual Supreme Court cases, the solicitor general has the opportunity to build a mutually advantageous relationship with the Court.

One way the solicitor general does so is by exercising self-restraint in requesting that the Court hear cases. The federal government asked the Court to hear thirteen cases in the 2013 term, a very small percentage of all the cases it had lost in the courts of appeals. In contrast, the government's opponents file thousands of petitions each term. When she was serving as solicitor general, Elena Kagan said that she regularly turned down requests by other federal officials to bring cases to the Court, "because I say the Court won't take it, our credibility is on the line, the Court will wonder why on earth we're filing this cert. petition."[33]

The solicitor general's office also seeks to maintain credibility by taking a more neutral stance than other litigants. In 2012, for instance, the office argued that the Court should not hear a case brought against the government by a prison inmate, but it also alerted the justices to an issue that the inmate had not raised. The Court accepted the case on the basis of that issue, and Solicitor General Donald Verrilli then informed the Court that he thought the lower-court decision favoring the government on that issue was wrong. Ultimately, the Court ruled unanimously for Verrilli's position and against the government.[34] In contrast with the office's image as relatively impartial, however, in recent years critics have charged that the office made misleading statements to the Court in support of its positions in some cases.[35]

Another step that the office takes to maintain its standing with the Court is to adhere to the position that a prior administration has taken in a case even though the new administration has a different point of view. Chief Justice Roberts has indicated that when the solicitor general departs from that policy, its credibility suffers.[36] And with occasional exceptions, the office defends all federal laws against constitutional challenges, whether or not the president agrees with those laws. One exception was the decision by the Obama administration not to defend the Defense of Marriage Act (DOMA), which prohibited the federal government from recognizing same-sex marriages. In that case, the solicitor general's office actually filed a brief advocating that the law be struck down.[37] Senate Republicans substituted for the executive branch as defenders of DOMA in the Court. Ultimately, the Court accepted the administration's position, declaring the law unconstitutional in *United States v. Windsor* (2013).

For their part, the justices have given the solicitor general's office a unique role. The Court frequently "invites" (in reality, orders) the solicitor general to file amicus briefs in cases that do not affect the federal government directly, because the justices are interested in the government's views.[38] In the 2013 term the solicitor general's office filed amicus briefs with recommendations about eighteen petitions for hearings, all of them at the Court's invitation. And the solicitor general often participates in oral argument as amicus by invitation or its own request, as it did in 36 cases—a little more than half of all cases with oral argument—in the 2013 term. With the occasional exception of state governments, other organizations seldom receive that privilege.

The office's special relationship with the Court leads to a degree of independence from the president and the attorney general, who understand the value of maintaining that relationship. But the solicitor general usually is someone who shares the president's general point of view about legal policy. Further, the office operates in a climate created by the president and the attorney general. These superiors occasionally intervene in the office's handling of specific cases, typically cases that involve major policy issues.

The impact of a presidential administration on the solicitor general's choices varies with the situation.[39] There are certain positions that the office would take regardless of who the president is. When the solicitor general participates as amicus, the office necessarily supports government interests. Thus, when the office acts as an amicus in a state criminal case, it almost always supports the prosecution even in a Democratic administration. In many other cases the solicitor general chooses a position without regard to the liberalism or conservatism of the administration. But there are some cases—primarily those involving contentious issues in civil rights and civil liberties—in which the ideological coloration of the administration affects the solicitor general's position.

Adding all this together, the solicitor general has considerable independence from the president, an independence that helps to make the office an effective advocate in the Court. However, that independence is most limited on issues that presidents and their administrations care the most about. And in some administrations the office has reflected the president's positions and priorities to more than the usual degree.

Deciding What to Hear: The Court's Role

In its 2013 term the Supreme Court considered more than 7,000 petitions for hearings. The Court granted certiorari and full consideration in only seventy-four cases.[40] Of the thousands of other petitions, the overwhelming majority were simply denied, allowing the lower-court decision to become final. Many of these cases had high stakes for the people who petitioned the Court, and some raised important legal and policy issues. Nonetheless, the Court chose not to hear them. In selecting a few dozen cases from the thousands brought to them, the justices determined which legal claims and policy questions they would address.

Options

In screening petitions for hearings, the Court makes choices that are more complicated than simply accepting and rejecting individual cases. To begin with, petitions are not always considered in isolation from one another. The justices may accept a case to clarify or expand on an earlier decision in the same policy area. They may accept multiple cases that raise the same issue in order to address that issue more fully than a single case would allow them to do. They may reject a case because they are looking for a more suitable case on the same issue.

When the Court does accept a case, it does not necessarily adopt the set of legal questions that was presented in the petition for hearing. In the cases that the Court accepted for argument and decided in the 2001–2013 terms, it eliminated one or more questions in 17 percent of the cases it heard and added questions 5 percent of the time.[41] Occasionally, the Court's opinion addresses a question that was not in the set that the Court indicated it would address, and such an action sometimes provokes a dissent from justices who see it as inappropriate.

According to one account, there was a serious conflict within the Court in *Citizens United v. Federal Election Commission* (2010), which was argued to the Court on a narrow issue involving regulation of campaign finance. After oral argument, the Court's five conservative justices united behind an opinion by Justice Anthony Kennedy that addressed a much broader issue and substantially limited government power to regulate campaign finance. Justice David Souter then wrote a strong draft dissent protesting the majority's action. Chief Justice Roberts responded by proposing that the case be reargued on the basis of the broader question that Kennedy's opinion had decided, the reargument was held, and the five conservative justices joined an opinion by Kennedy reaching the same result as the one that Souter had protested several months earlier.[42]

In accepting a case the Court also determines what kind of consideration the case will receive. It may give the case full consideration, which means that the Court receives a new set of briefs on the merits from the parties and holds oral argument, then issues a decision on the merits with a full opinion explaining the decision. Alternatively, it may give the case summary consideration. This usually means that the case is decided without new briefs or oral argument; the Court relies on the materials that the parties have already submitted.

In most summary decisions, typically several dozen each term, the Supreme Court issues a one-sentence GVR order—that is, granting certiorari, vacating the lower-court decision, and remanding the case to that court for reconsideration. The great majority of GVR orders are issued because some event after the lower-court decision—usually a recent Supreme Court decision—is relevant to the case. GVR orders leave the lower court with considerable discretion to reach their own judgment, and in one 2014 decision Justice Alito wrote a concurring opinion to influence how a federal court of appeals used that discretion.[43]

In other summary decisions, the Court actually reaches a decision on the merits and issues an opinion of several paragraphs or even several pages. This opinion typically is labeled per curiam, meaning "by the Court," rather than being signed by a justice, but it has the same legal force as a signed opinion. Such decisions are usually reversals of lower-court decisions, and most come in criminal cases.

Finally, the Court sometimes issues summary decisions in the appeals from three-judge federal district courts that it is required to decide. *Bluman v. Federal Election Commission* (2012) involved a First Amendment challenge to a federal statutory provision that prohibited political campaign donations by people who are not U.S. citizens and who are not lawful permanent residents of the United States. The three-judge court upheld the provision. When the case was appealed to the Supreme Court, it received considerable attention because some people thought the Court would use it as a vehicle to continue its process of limiting federal power to regulate campaign finance. But the Court simply issued a two-word decision: "Judgment affirmed."

Even after accepting a case, the Court occasionally avoids a decision by issuing what is called a DIG, or "dismissed as improvidently granted," as it did three times in its 2013 term. A DIG usually occurs when the parties' briefs on the merits or the oral arguments suggest to the justices that the case is inappropriate for a decision. But one of the DIGs in the 2013 term came after the Court took the unusual step of asking the Oklahoma Supreme Court to clarify the meaning of a state abortion law that the Oklahoma court had struck down. After receiving the clarification, the Supreme Court decided to dismiss the case.[44] Like GVRs, DIGs seem routine, but both sometimes draw heated dissents from justices who think they are inappropriate in a particular case.

Screening Procedures

The Court screens petitions for hearing through a series of procedures, which are made more complex by two distinctions. The first distinction is between the certiorari cases, over which the Court's jurisdiction is discretionary, and the cases labeled appeals, which the Court is required to decide. Few appeals reach the Court. As the *Bluman* case illustrates, the Court has the option of deciding appeals without holding oral argument or issuing full opinions. The second distinction, between paid cases and paupers' cases, requires more extensive discussion.

Paid Cases and Paupers' Cases. In recent years only about one-fifth of the requests for hearings that arrive at the Supreme Court have been paid cases, for which the petitioner pays the Court's filing fee of $300. The remaining cases are brought in forma pauperis by indigent people, for whom the fee is waived and requirements for the format of litigants' written materials are relaxed. The great majority of the paupers' petitions (also called "unpaid") are brought by federal and state prisoners. (A person responding to a petition may also be given pauper status.)

Criminal defendants who have had counsel provided to them in the lower courts because of their low incomes are automatically entitled to bring paupers' cases in the Supreme Court. Other litigants must submit an affidavit supporting their motion for leave to file as paupers. The Court has never developed precise rules for when a litigant can claim pauper status. However, it denies many litigants the right to proceed as paupers in particular cases on the grounds that they are not truly paupers or that their petitions are frivolous or malicious. The Court also issues a general denial of pauper status in noncriminal cases to some litigants who have filed large numbers of paupers' petitions.

A very small proportion of paupers' petitions are accepted for full decisions on the merits—0.16 percent in the 2010–2013 terms, compared with 4.6 percent of the paid cases in the same period. The low acceptance rate reflects the lack of inherent merit in many of these cases and the fact that many litigants have to draft petitions without a lawyer's assistance. It may also be that the justices and law clerks look less closely at paupers' petitions than at the paid petitions. There is some evidence that, all else being equal, the Court is less likely to accept a pauper's petition than a paid petition.[45] Because there are so many paupers' petitions, even the small proportion that are accepted add up to a significant number of cases—an average of ten a term in the 2010–2013 terms.

The great majority of these accepted paupers' cases are criminal, and they constitute an important part of the Court's work on issues of criminal procedure. In 2014 the Court accepted a pauper's petition in a civil case, filed without a lawyer. But by then the petitioner had disappeared; the clerk's office of the Court could not get in contact with him, and he failed to file his brief on the merits. The Court then dismissed the case, two months after accepting it. A month after that dismissal, the petitioner reappeared, now represented by a leading Supreme Court advocate. Explaining that he had been unaware that his case was accepted because he had been away from home and out of touch, he petitioned the Court to reinstate his case by granting a rehearing. The Court rejected that petition without comment.[46]

Prescreening: The Discuss List. Under its "rule of four," the Court grants a writ of certiorari and hears a case on the merits if at least four justices vote at conference to grant the writ. But petitions for hearings are considered at conference only if they are put on the Court's "discuss list." The chief justice creates the discuss list, but other justices can and do add cases to it. Cases left off the discuss list are denied hearings automatically. Justice Kennedy reported in 2013 that the Court puts about 500 cases on the discuss list each year—less than one in ten of the cases brought to it.[47]

The discuss list procedure serves to limit the Court's workload. But this procedure also reflects a belief that most petitions do not require collective consideration because they are such poor candidates for acceptance. It is easy to reject petitions that raise only narrow issues or make weak legal claims.

Action in Conference. In conference the chief justice or the justice who added a case to the discuss list opens consideration of the case. In order of seniority, from senior to junior, the justices then speak and usually announce their votes. If the discussion does not make the justices' positions clear, a formal vote is taken, also in order of seniority. Despite the prescreening of cases, a large majority of the petitions considered in conference are denied.

Most cases receive only brief discussion in conference. Some cases get more consideration, which sometimes extends beyond the initial discussion. In conference any justice can ask that a case be "distributed" once again for a later conference. This step might be taken to obtain additional information in the case. A justice also might ask for another distribution in order to circulate an opinion dissenting from the Court's tentative denial of a hearing and thereby try to change the Court's decision. Most cases that the Court accepted for its 2014 term were considered at multiple conferences, and the justices now may be giving a second look to cases they are inclined to accept in order to make sure that these cases are appropriate for decisions by the Court.[48]

When it accepts a case, the Court also decides whether to allow oral argument or to decide the case summarily on the basis of the written materials. Four votes are required for oral argument. With GVRs and other summary decisions, typically certiorari is granted and the disposition of the case is determined at the same conference, so the two stages of decision in effect become one.

The Court does not issue opinions to explain its acceptance or rejection of cases. Nor are individual votes announced. But justices occasionally record their dissents from denials of petitions for hearings, usually accompanied by dissenting opinions. There were six cases with such dissents in the 2013 term, including one death penalty case in which Justice Sonia Sotomayor wrote a seventeen-page opinion.[49] Sometimes justices write opinions to explain their votes not to grant certiorari, as they did in four cases in the 2013 term.

The Clerks' Role. One of the law clerks' primary functions is to scrutinize requests for hearings. As of 2015, all the justices except Samuel Alito are part of the "cert. (for certiorari) pool." Petitions and other materials on each case are divided among the clerks for the justices in the pool. The clerk who has responsibility for a case writes a memorandum, one that typically includes a summary of the case and a recommendation that the petition be granted or denied.

Because there are so many petitions, and because pool memos are the most extensive source of information about them, recommendations in the memos surely have some impact on the justices' certiorari votes. Indeed, one study provides evidence of this impact, though it found that the influence of memos varies with attributes of the case and other circumstances.[50] One broad effect may be to reduce the number of cases that the Court hears. On the whole, clerks who write pool memos are cautious about recommending that the Court hear a case. One reason is that they know such recommendations will be scrutinized more closely than recommendations to deny. And it would be embarrassing for a clerk to suggest that the Court take a case and have the Court do so, only to have the case disposed of with a DIG later because the clerk had missed an important fact.[51]

Two factors limit the impact of the pool on certiorari decisions. First, the great majority of petitions would elicit a denial from any justice or clerk. Justice Stephen Breyer has said that of the approximately 150 petitions that the Court receives each week, "there are only about 10 or 12 that are even possible, that anyone would think of considering for granting."[52] Second, the justices, with help from their own clerks, undertake some independent review of cases. It is noteworthy that in a substantial proportion of the cases that the Court hears, the pool memo did not recommend that the Court accept the case.[53]

Criteria for Decision

In deciding whether to accept or deny petitions, the justices look for cases whose attributes make them desirable to hear. The Court's Rule 10 lists some of those attributes, which are based on the Court's role in enhancing the certainty and consistency of the law. Rule 10 indicates that the

Court is more interested in hearing cases if they contain important issues of federal law that the Court has not yet decided, if there is conflict between lower courts on an important legal question or conflict between a lower court's decision and the Supreme Court's prior decisions, or if a federal court of appeals has drastically departed "from the accepted and usual course of judicial proceedings" or allowed a lower court to do so.

The presence of these attributes does increase the chances that a case will be accepted, but the list in Rule 10 suggests a conception of the Court's function and of its members' interests that is unrealistically narrow. The Court's pattern of screening decisions and evidence from other sources indicate the significance of several types of considerations.

Technical Criteria. The Court will reject a petition for hearing if it fails to meet certain technical requirements. Some of these requirements are specific to the Court. For example, paid petitions must comply with the Court's Rule 33, which establishes requirements on matters such as the size of print and margins used, type of paper, format and color of the cover, and maximum length.

The Court also imposes the same kinds of technical requirements that other courts apply. One specific requirement is that petitions for hearing be filed within ninety days after judgment is entered in the lower court, unless the time has been extended in advance. The Court consistently refuses to allow the filing of petitions that are brought after the deadline.

More fundamental are the requirements of jurisdiction and standing. The Court cannot accept a case for hearing that clearly falls outside its jurisdiction. For example, the Court could not hear a state case in which the petitioner had raised no issues of federal law in the state courts.

The rule of standing holds that a court may not hear a case unless the party bringing the case is properly before it. The most important element of standing is the requirement that a party in a case have a real and direct legal stake in its outcome. This requirement precludes hypothetical cases, cases brought on behalf of another person, "friendly suits" between parties that are not really adversaries, and cases that have become "moot" (in effect, hypothetical) because the parties can no longer be affected by the outcome.

Because of the mootness rule, the Court generally must dismiss a case if the parties have reached a settlement or if the only party on one side has died. In 2015, for instance, the Court dismissed *Toca v. Louisiana,* which involved two issues in criminal law. A month after the Court accepted the case and one day after his lawyers filed their brief in the case, the defendant reached a bargain with prosecutors that freed him from prison. As a result, the issue in the case became moot.

When something like that happens, the Court temporarily loses the chance to address the issue in question. But another case raising the same issue is likely to come to the Court later on. In 2011 and 2013, the Court accepted cases on a key issue in interpreting the federal fair housing statute. The Court had to dismiss both cases because of settlements between the parties—settlements motivated in part by the efforts of civil rights advocates to avoid what they anticipated would be an unfavorable decision by the Court. But the Court accepted a third case in 2014. Because this case was *not* settled, the Court finally could rule on the issue in question in 2015, surprising most observers by deciding that people could bring discrimination cases under the statute that were based on differential effects of housing practices on racial groups rather than on intentional discrimination.[54] This episode illustrates both the Court's dependence on litigants for cases and the extent of the justices' ability to shape their agenda.

Conflict between Courts. In 2013 and 2014, there was a series of rulings by federal district judges that state prohibitions on same-sex marriage were unconstitutional. In the summer of 2014, three courts of appeals affirmed those rulings. Several states whose laws were struck down by the three courts of appeals asked the Supreme Court to hear their cases. Few issues affect and interest so many people, yet the Court decided in October 2014 not to hear these cases.

The Court's decision not to intervene had the effect of increasing substantially the number of states in which same-sex marriage was allowed, and new lower-court decisions continued to add to that number. As some people saw it, the justices had chosen to step aside and let the movement toward acceptance of same-sex marriage proceed without their further involvement in the issue. But then, in January 2015, the Court accepted a new set of cases on the issue. Why did the Court belatedly decide to intervene?

The answer seems clear: The new set of cases involved a court of appeals ruling that prohibitions of same-sex marriage were *not* unconstitutional. That ruling created a conflict between courts of appeals on the issue. And as Justice Ginsburg had predicted the preceding September, it was the development of a conflict that created "some urgency" about addressing the issue in the Court.[55]

If this was an extraordinary issue, it illustrated the more general reality that Rule 10 suggests: Conflict among lower courts is an important criterion for acceptance of cases. The existence of a clear legal conflict—typically between federal courts of appeals—increases enormously the chances that a case will be accepted.[56] When the Court's opinion indicates why a case was accepted, by far the most common reason is the existence of a conflict between lower courts.

This does not mean that the Court accepts every case involving conflict between courts. There are simply too many of those cases for the Court to hear all of them. Rule 10 emphasizes the importance of the issue on which a conflict has arisen as a criterion for the Court, and that criterion undoubtedly affects the justices' choices of which conflict cases to hear. Yet the Court occasionally accepts a case to resolve a conflict on a seemingly minor issue, and it sometimes turns down cases involving conflicts on major issues.

Importance of the Issues. Of all the cases in which litigants petition for a writ of certiorari, the great majority involve narrow issues. Frequently, the "questions presented" at the beginning of the petition ask only whether the case was wrongly decided. Those cases are easy to turn away because the justices see no point in allocating part of the

AP Photo/Evan Vucci, File

Judge Jeffrey Sutton of the federal Court of Appeals for the Sixth Circuit in Cincinnati. Judge Sutton wrote that court's opinion upholding state prohibitions of same-sex marriage in November 2014. This decision created a conflict on that issue between courts of appeals, a conflict that gave the Supreme Court a strong reason to accept cases on the issue.

limited space on their agenda to cases in which a decision would have little effect beyond the immediate parties. Rather, the best way for the Court to maximize its impact is to decide the cases that raise the most important policy questions.

Importance is a more subjective matter than conflict between courts, so different justices may assess the importance of a case quite differently. In general, justices look for cases in which a decision would have a broad effect on courts, government, or society as a whole. In some of the cases that meet this criterion, the issues are dramatic. In others, the issues are dry and technical but nonetheless important. Chief Justice William Rehnquist noted in 2003 that the Court heard a steady stream of cases under the federal Employee Retirement Income Security Act (ERISA). "The thing that stands out about them is that they're dreary," he said, and the Court takes such cases as a matter of "duty, not choice."[57] Since Rehnquist offered that judgment the justices have heard another dozen ERISA cases, presumably without any great enthusiasm.

Just as the Court rejects some cases that involve conflicts between lower courts, it also rejects some important cases. One reason for such denials is the same reason why the Court does not resolve all conflicts between lower courts: The number of cases with significant issues is considerably larger than the number the Court is willing and able to hear. Justices sometimes have more specific reasons to vote against hearing such cases. To take two examples, they may agree with the lower-court decision or may want to delay before tackling a difficult issue.

Policy Preferences. Rule 10 does not mention justices' personal conceptions of good policy as a criterion for accepting or rejecting cases, but those conceptions have considerable effect on the Court's choices. Because the Court's agenda largely determines the scope of its work as a policymaker, members of the Court inevitably use the agenda-setting process to advance their own policy goals.

Justices can act on their policy goals primarily in two ways. First, they may vote to hear cases because they disagree with the lower-court decision they are reviewing: Tentatively concluding that the lower court established an undesirable policy, they want to correct it. Second, they may act strategically by voting to hear a case when they think the Court would reach a decision they favor on policy grounds if it decided the case on the merits and voting against certiorari when they think the Court would produce what they consider to be bad policy. For either approach, the limits on the number of cases that the Court hears require justices to be selective. For instance, if they strongly disagree with a lower-court decision but think that the case has only narrow policy implications, they are likely to pass it by. (In some cases of this type, the Court issues a summary decision reversing the lower-court decision without getting additional briefs or holding oral argument.)

The justices' use of the first approach is made clear by the Court's decisions on the merits. The Court overturns the lower court altogether or in part in more than two-thirds of its decisions. The comparable rate for the federal courts of appeals, which lack the Court's power to screen the cases brought to it, is under 10 percent.[58] One reason for the Court's reversal rate is that it accepts so many cases in order to resolve conflicts between lower courts; in those cases, there is something like a 50–50 chance that the Court will overturn the decision it reviews. Even so, the reversal rate could not be nearly as high as it is if the justices were not inclined to hear cases when they have doubts about the validity of the lower court's decision.

The justices sometimes use the second, strategic approach as well. Elena Kagan has said that when she was a law clerk for Justice Thurgood Marshall, she and her fellow clerks would "channel" Marshall in their memos and say that "here are the cases which the Court is likely to do good things with from your perspective, and here are the ones where they are not."[59] In a 2012 case, Stephen Breyer directly acknowledged this consideration in an opinion joined by the other three liberal justices. Breyer said that he would have voted to give full consideration to a case involving regulation of campaign finance, except that he did not "see a significant possibility" that the Court would reconsider what he saw as a bad policy.[60]

However, it is uncertain how often the justices act strategically in their certiorari votes. Justices probably concentrate their strategic calculations on the relatively small proportion of petitions that are good candidates for acceptance on other grounds. They may also be more inclined to take the Court's prospective decisions into account when they are part of the Court's ideological minority, because members of the minority have the most reason to worry about what the Court might decide.

These two ways of acting on policy goals are likely to have the greatest impact when they reinforce each other. If a case is a good candidate for acceptance on other grounds, justices who disagree with a lower-court decision and who think that the Court would agree with them on the merits have good reason to vote for certiorari.

Identities of the Participants. Every petition for certiorari involves at least two competing parties. In most paid cases and many paupers' cases, the petitioner is represented by a lawyer. And in some cases, the petitioner is supported by one or more interest groups in amicus briefs. The identities of those participants might have an impact on the Court's decisions whether to grant certiorari.

One participant, the federal government, stands out for its success in winning hearings from the Court. In the 2012 and 2013 terms the Court accepted about 70 percent of the government's requests to hear cases.[61] That success rate is enormously high in comparison with the low overall rate of success for petitioners.

Some possible sources of this level of success relate to the unique role of the solicitor general's office in the Court. Justices may view petitions from the federal government more favorably than those from other parties because the solicitor general's selectivity in filing petitions gives greater credibility to the petitions it does file. Justices may also act on their gratitude that this selectivity reduces their workloads. Selectivity improves the office's success rate in another way. Its lawyers can choose the cases that are most likely to be accepted, and almost any litigant who could be so selective would enjoy a relatively high winning percentage at the certiorari stage.

Another advantage of the solicitor general is the expertise that attorneys in the office develop through their frequent participation in Supreme Court cases. As a result, the government can do more than most other litigants to make cases appear worthy of acceptance. Still another possibility is that the justices defer to the executive branch as a coordinate branch of government.

It is difficult to determine the validity of these various possibilities, though it seems likely that all play some role in the solicitor general's success as a petitioner. Undoubtedly, the office's selectivity makes considerable difference. It is also noteworthy that when the Court asks the solicitor general to submit an amicus brief on the question of whether to hear a case, the office's recommendation seems to have considerable impact on the Court's decision.[62] This impact suggests that the solicitor general's special status in the Court contributes to its success.

Although no other set of lawyers can match the solicitor general's success, the lawyers in private practice who frequently appear in the Court and lawyers in firms with Supreme Court specializations also do well. One study found that a set of "elite" lawyers did far better than other lawyers in getting petitions from businesses accepted by the Court, and they did enormously better in getting petitions from individuals accepted.[63] To a degree, this success probably reflects a tendency for elite lawyers to take cases that are relatively strong. But their skills and their reputations also make a difference. Justice Kennedy has said that "we look at the names of counsel for lawyers we trust."[64] And justices are reluctant to take a case in which the poor quality of the certiorari petition suggests that the case will be argued badly. Justice Clarence Thomas reports that "any number of people will vote against a cert petition if they think the lawyering is bad."[65]

Amicus briefs on behalf of petitioners improve the chances that a petition will be accepted. As one leading Supreme Court advocate has pointed out, an amicus brief indicates the significance of a case beyond the parties themselves.[66] And specific interest groups may have special credibility with some justices because they regularly submit high-quality briefs or because the justices respect the groups themselves. But the impact of amicus briefs advocating that a case be heard has declined since the 1960s, perhaps because these briefs have become more common and thus less meaningful.[67]

Problematic Cases and Issues. Sometimes the Court chooses not to hear a case in order to avoid a problem. Justices may vote against hearing a case because they want to await more decisions on the issue in the lower courts—decisions that may refine the issue or give the justices a better chance to assess it. And sometimes they see a case as a "bad vehicle" for resolution of an issue because of the factual circumstances or the presence of other issues that complicate the case. In 2014, for instance, the Court denied certiorari in a trio of cases that appeared to provide conservative justices a good opportunity to continue a line of decisions limiting class action suits by consumers and employees. But the facts of the cases seemed unfavorable to the companies that were defendants in these lawsuits, and the Court's conservatives may have decided to await more suitable cases.[68]

Another possible concern is that resolving a particular issue might embroil the Court in controversy. The justices often are willing to address such issues. One striking example is *Bush v. Gore* (2000), in which the Court accepted a case in which its decision resolved the outcome of the presidential election that year. In 2013, retired justice Sandra Day O'Connor expressed her concern about the effect of the case on the Court's reputation. "Maybe," she mused, "the court should have said, 'We're not going to take it, goodbye.'"[69] At times, however, the justices have seemed to duck issues because they were worried about potential reactions to the Court's decision.

The Court's mixed response to controversial issues is illustrated by its approach to government regulation of abortion and firearms. In both areas the Court has reached landmark decisions despite heated disagreement in government and society about the issues the Court chose to decide. But after its 2008 holding that individuals have gun rights under the Second Amendment and its 2010 decision that those rights applied at the state level, over the next four years the Court turned down all the cases in which specific gun regulations were challenged. Similarly, since its 1992 decision that modified the constitutional standard for regulations of abortion, the Court has accepted few cases involving the application of that standard to particular forms of regulation.[70] In each area, the justices may have wanted to give the Court some distance from the divisive questions that these follow-up cases raised.

Summary. When Supreme Court justices vote on petitions for hearings by the Court, they act on a complex set of considerations. Inevitably, justices with different goals and perspectives respond differently to petitions. Some give a higher priority to resolving lower-court conflicts than others. Justices assess the importance of cases in various ways. And they act on quite different sets of policy preferences.

It follows that the Court's selection of cases to decide fully, like everything else it does, is affected by its membership at any given time. The great majority of petitions are unlikely to be accepted no matter who is on the Court. But the composition of the cases the Supreme Court actually accepts in a term strongly reflects the identities of the justices who serve during that term.

Setting the Size of the Agenda

In the 2010–2013 terms the Supreme Court accepted an average of 80 petitions for certiorari each term—less than half the average in the first half of the 1980s. The average number of cases in which the Court heard oral arguments and reached decisions with full opinions dropped by slightly more than half, from 156 to 77.[71] These decreases are all the more striking because the number of petitions that litigants brought to the Court nearly doubled over that time. Why have those trends run in opposite directions?

An answer to that question requires some historical perspective. The number of cases brought to the Court went up dramatically over the years in a trend that culminated in the 1960s. That growth seemed to have several sources. Outside the Court these sources included an apparent increase in "rights consciousness," which led people to bring more legal claims; the development of interest groups that assisted litigants in carrying cases through the courts; and the massive growth in activities of the federal government, which produced new laws and legal questions. The Court itself contributed to the growth in its caseload. Most important, its positive responses to claims that government actions violated civil liberties encouraged people who felt that their rights had been violated to bring cases to the Court.

By the 1970s some observers of the Court and some justices argued that the larger number of cases had created problems for the Court and for federal law. For the Court the perceived problem was that the justices' ability to do their work well was compromised by the increased volume of work. For federal law the concern was that the Court was accepting a smaller proportion of petitions as their numbers grew, so important issues were going unresolved. But proposals to remedy these problems, including the creation of a new court to help the Supreme Court with its work, did not succeed.

After a period of relative stability in the number of cases brought to the Court, a new period of rapid growth began in the late 1980s and continued through the 2006 term. This second period of growth was quite different from the earlier one. As Figure 3-1 shows, it was limited to paupers' petitions. The number of paid petitions per term has been relatively stable since the early 1970s, and it has actually declined by more than 20 percent since the late 1990s. In contrast, the number of paupers' petitions, which hovered around 2,000 per term from the late 1960s to the mid-1980s, grew to a high of about 7,100 in the 2006 term, before declining by more than 1,000 since that time.

The great majority of paupers' petitions come from prisoners. The number of adults in prison more than quadrupled between 1980 and 2000.[72] This trend accounts for most if not all of the increase in paupers' cases.

The pattern of growth in the Court's caseload over the last two decades helps to explain why the Court is not hearing more cases than it did in the mid-1980s. Paupers' petitions are always accepted at relatively low rates, and a Court that has become less sympathetic to claims by prisoners

FIGURE 3-1
Paid and Paupers' Cases Filed in the Supreme Court per Term, by Five-Year Averages, 1964–2013 Terms

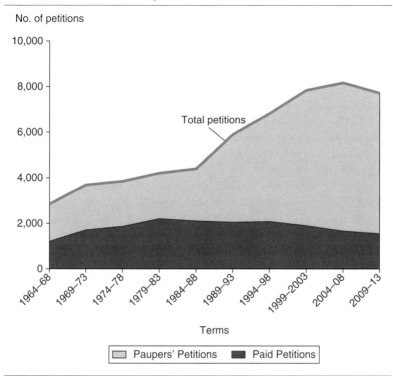

Sources: Gerhard Casper and Richard A. Posner, *The Workload of the Supreme Court* (Chicago: American Bar Foundation, 1976), 34; "Statistical Recap of Supreme Court's Workload during Last Three Terms," *United States Law Week,* various years; "Statistics" in the Supreme Court's *Journal,* various years.

undoubtedly finds fewer of those petitions worthy. But why would the Court hear only half as many cases as it did before?

Commentators and the justices themselves have offered several answers that lie outside the Court.[73] Congress in 1988 greatly narrowed the types of cases that are classified as appeals (rather than petitions for certiorari), which the Court is required to decide, and the Court now hears twenty to thirty fewer appeals each term than it did before 1988. The number of conflicts between lower courts in their rulings on legal questions may have declined, and the justices and their clerks may be scrutinizing petitioners' claims of conflicts more carefully. In recent years the solicitor general's office, with its high rate of success in winning hearings for its petitions, has been bringing fewer cases to the Court. And perhaps Congress is enacting fewer major laws that require interpretation.

Other possible answers lie within the Court. On the whole, the justices who joined the Court in the late 1980s and early 1990s were less inclined to vote for certiorari than the justices they succeeded.[74] Some observers think that the justices simply like having fewer cases to decide, to free up some of their time. And once the decline occurred, the justices became accustomed to a smaller number of decisions each term, so it might be difficult for them to adjust to a reversal of the decline. Even though justices occasionally say that the Court should hear more cases than the seventy to eighty per term that has become the standard number, such an increase has not yet occurred.

Although the validity of specific explanations can be debated, it seems clear that the decline in the number of cases that the Court decides reflects multiple factors. Overall, the justices themselves are probably a more important factor than conditions outside the Court.[75] The biggest cuts in the number of cases accepted came long before the number of paid petitions and petitions from the solicitor general declined. And even if there are fewer major statutes and fewer conflicts between lower courts than there were in the past, there is no shortage of cases that the Court reasonably could decide.

Certainly the difficulty of gaining a hearing in the Supreme Court has increased. In its 1985 term the Court accepted for full consideration about 1 in 12 of the paid petitions filed with it. In the 2013 term that rate was 1 in 24. For paupers' petitions the decline was precipitous, from an already low 1 in 108 in 1985 to a very low 1 in 747 in 2013. Given the worsening odds and the significant costs of filing paid petitions for those who use lawyers' services, it is not surprising that the number of paid petitions have declined since the late 1990s.

Conclusion

Like other courts, the Supreme Court can decide only the cases that come to it. For that reason, people and institutions outside the Court have great influence on the Court's agenda. Ultimately, however, the Court determines which cases it hears. From the wide variety of legal and policy questions brought to the Court, the justices can choose the few they will address fully. They can also choose which issues in a case they will decide. And the justices help determine which cases are brought to them by indicating with their opinions what kinds of legal claims they view favorably.

The Court is sometimes criticized for its choices of cases to hear and turn aside, and in recent years it has also been criticized for the small number of cases it accepts each term. Whatever the validity of these criticisms may be, the justices employ their agenda-setting powers rather well to serve their purposes. They accept and reject cases on the basis of individual and collective goals such as avoiding troublesome issues, resolving conflicts in the interpretation of federal law, and establishing policies that the justices favor. The justices' selection of cases for full decisions helps them shape the Court's role as a policymaker. They also use that process to limit their workloads.

After the Court selects the cases to hear, of course, it decides those cases. In the next chapter I will examine the Court's decision-making process and the forces that shape its choices.

NOTES

1. *Whitman v. United States*, 190 L. Ed. 2d 381, 383 (2014).
2. Joan Biskupic, "Special Report: Behind U.S. Race Cases, a Little-Known Recruiter," *Reuters*, December 4, 2012, http://www.reuters.com/article/2012/12/04/us-usa-court-casemaker-idUSBRE8B30V220121204. The website advertising is described in Adam Liptak, "Unofficial Enforcer of Ruling on Race in College Admissions," *New York Times*, April 8, 2014, A16.
3. Ariel Levy, "The Perfect Wife," *New Yorker*, September 30, 2013, 54–63.
4. "About the Tinker Tour," Tinker Tour USA, http://tinkertourusa.org/about/tinkertour.
5. See Aaron Fang, "The Ethics of Opposing Certiorari Before the Supreme Court," *Harvard Journal of Law and Public Policy* 35 (Summer 2012): 933–990.
6. Robert Barnes, "Justice Ginsburg Takes This Former Client's Wedding to Heart," *Washington Post*, May 26, 2014, A15. The case was *Weinberger v. Wiesenfeld* (1975).
7. These figures are updated from Kedar S. Bhatia, "Top Supreme Court Advocates of the Twentieth-First Century," *Journal of Law* 2 (2012): 570.
8. Jennifer Senior, "In Conversation: Antonin Scalia," *New York Magazine*, October 14, 2013, 80.
9. See Banks Miller, "Describing the State Solicitors General," *Judicature* 93 (May–June 2010): 238–246.
10. See Grant Rodgers, "Taking Case Before U.S. Supreme Court Takes Lots of Work," *Des Moines Register*, November 9, 2013.
11. Tony Mauro, "After a Year on the Court, Alito Holds Forth," *Legal Times*, February 12, 2007, 12; Bryan A. Garner, "John Paul Stevens," *Scribes Journal of Legal Writing* 13 (2010): 45.
12. Lyle Denniston, "Argument Recap: Disaster at the Lectern," SCOTUSblog, November 8, 2011, http://www.scotusblog.com/2011/11/argument-recap-disaster-at-the-lectern. The case was *Smith v. Cain* (2012).
13. Brent Kendall, "Getting on Scalia's Good Side," *Daily Journal* Newswire Article, May 12, 2008, http://pda-appellateblog.blogspot.com/2008_05_01_archive.html#4396419852952598031.
14. Shon Hopwood, *My Story of Robbing Banks, Winning Supreme Court Cases, and Finding Redemption* (New York: Crown Publishers, 2012). The quotation is from

Adam Liptak, "As a Criminal, Mediocre; as a Jailhouse Lawyer, an Advocate Unmatched," *New York Times*, February 9, 2010, A12. The case was *Fellers v. United States* (2004).

15. Emily Bazelon, "Reversal of Fortune," *Slate*, July 5, 2012, http://www.slate .com/articles/news_and_politics/jurisprudence/2012/07/paul_clement_is_ considered_the_best_supreme_court_attorney_but_he_lost_the_two_ biggest_case_of_the_last_supreme_court_term_.html.

16. Joan Biskupic, Janet Roberts, and John Shiffman, "Special Report: The Echo Chamber," *Reuters*, December 8, 2014, http://www.reuters.com/investigates/ special-report/scotus.

17. Jeffrey L. Fisher, "A Clinic's Place in the Supreme Court Bar," *Stanford Law Review* 65 (January 2013): 137–201.

18. Tom Goldstein, "The Supreme Court as a Tool of Business," SCOTUSblog, January 6, 2015, http://www.scotusblog.com/2015/01/the-supreme-court-bar-as-a-tool-of-business.

19. Jessica Gresko, "Only Lawyers Now Can Argue before Supreme Court," Associated Press, July 1, 2013. The 1978 case was *Securities and Exchange Commission v. Sloan* (1978).

20. Jessica Gresko, "For Lawyers, the Supreme Court Bar Is a Vanity Trip," Associated Press, March 21, 2013.

21. The 1956–1965 figure is from Joseph D. Kearney and Thomas W. Merrill, "The Influence of Amicus Curiae Briefs on the Supreme Court," *University of Pennsylvania Law Review* 148 (January 2000): 754 n26.

22. T. R. Goldman, "Inside the Chamber," *California Lawyer*, July 2014, https:// www.callawyer.com/Clstory.cfm?eid=935765&wteid=935765_Inside_the_ Chamber; "Robin Conrad," *National Law Journal*, June 27, 2011, 24; Adam Chandler, *Cert.-Stage Amicus "All Stars": Where Are They Now?*, SCOTUSblog, April 4, 2013, http://www.scotusblog.com/2013/04/cert-stage-amicus-all-stars-where-are-they-now.

23. The case was *Utility Air Regulatory Group v. Environmental Protection Agency* (2014). The Chamber was one of several litigants in opposition to the Environmental Protection Agency (EPA).

24. Tom Turner, "Civil Rights and the Environment," *Earthjustice*, Fall 2014, 10.

25. See Samuel Walker, *In Defense of American Liberties: A History of the ACLU*, 2nd ed. (Carbondale: Southern Illinois University Press, 1999).

26. Alan Johnson, "DeWine Has Intervened in Dozens of U.S. Cases," *Columbus Dispatch*, October 26, 2014, A1.

27. On the use of amicus briefs, see Paul M. Collins Jr., *Friends of the Supreme Court: Interest Groups and Judicial Decision Making* (New York: Oxford University Press, 2008), 28–74.

28. Consolidated cases were counted as a single case. The figures were compiled from listings at the SCOTUSblog website: http://www.scotusblog.com.

29. The cases were, respectively, *National Federation of Independent Business v. Sebelius* (2012) and *Obergefell v. Hodges* (2015).

30. See Josh Blackman, *Unprecedented: The Constitutional Challenge to Obamacare* (New York: Public Affairs, 2013).

31. Charles R. Epp, *The Rights Revolution: Lawyers, Activists, and Supreme Courts in Comparative Perspective* (Chicago: University of Chicago Press, 1998), 44–70.

32. Richard L. Pacelle Jr., *Between Law and Politics: The Solicitor General and the Structuring of Civil Rights, Gender, and Reproductive Rights Litigation* (College Station: Texas A&M Press, 2003).

33. Adam Chandler, "The Solicitor General of the United States: Tenth Justice or Zealous Advocate?" *Yale Law Journal* 121 (December 2011): 733.

34. *Millbrook v. United States* (2013). See Lyle Denniston, "The Government Switches Position," SCOTUSblog, December 3, 2012, http://www.scotus blog.com/2012/12/the-government-switches-position.

35. Charlie Savage, "Justice Dept. Criticized on Spying Statements," *New York Times*, May 14, 2014, A18; Nancy Morawetz, "Convenient Facts: *Nken v. Holder*, the Solicitor General, and the Presentation of Internal Government Facts," *New York University Law Review* 88 (November 2013): 1600–1664.

36. Oral argument, *Kiobel v. Royal Dutch Petroleum Co.*, 10-1491, October 1, 2012, 44.

37. Brief for the United States on the Merits Question, *United States v. Windsor*, 12-307 (2013).

38. See David C. Thompson and Melanie F. Wachtell, "An Empirical Analysis of Supreme Court Certiorari Petition Procedures: The Call for Response and the Call for the Views of the Solicitor General," *George Mason Law Review* 16 (2009): 270–296.

39. Richard L. Pacelle Jr., "Amicus Curiae or Amicus Praesidentis? Reexamining the Role of the Solicitor General in Filing Amici," *Judicature* 89 (May–June 2006): 317–325.

40. These figures and other figures in this section on the Court's receipt and disposition of petitions are based on statistics in the Court's *Journal*: http://www .supremecourt.gov/orders/journal.aspx.

41. Ryan Krog and Kevin T. McGuire, "Issue Fluidity, Judicial Activism, and the Transformation of the Supreme Court's Agenda" (unpublished paper, 2014), 13.

42. Jeffrey Toobin, *The Oath: The Obama White House and the Supreme Court* (New York: Doubleday, 2012), 167–169.

43. *Volkman v. United States* (2014).

44. *Cline v. Oklahoma Coalition for Reproductive Justice* (2013).

45. Ryan C. Black and Christina L. Boyd, "U.S. Supreme Court Agenda Setting and the Role of Litigant Status," *Journal of Law, Economics, & Organization* 28 (June 2012): 286–312.

46. Jessica Gresko, "US Supreme Court Takes Case, but Plaintiff Missing," Associated Press, December 30, 2014. The case was *Chen v. Mayor and City Council of Baltimore* (2015).

47. Jess Bravin, "Justice Kennedy on Choosing Cases, 'Empathy,' and Diversity," *Wall Street Journal Law Blog*, October 10, 2013, http://blogs.wsj.com/law/2013/10/10/justice-kennedy-on-choosing-cases-empathy-and-diversity.

48. John Elwood, "Relist Watch: What Does the Court's Relist Streak Mean?," SCOTUSblog, April 23, 2014, http://www.scotusblog.com/2014/04/relist-watch-what-does-the-courts-relist-streak-mean.

49. *Woodward v. Alabama* (2013).

50. Ryan C. Black and Christina L. Boyd, "The Role of Law Clerks in the U.S. Supreme Court's Agenda-Setting Process," *American Politics Research* 40 (January 2012): 147–173.

51. David R. Stras, "The Supreme Court's Gatekeepers: The Role of Law Clerks in the Certiorari Process," *Texas Law Review* 85 (2007): 972–976; Elizabeth Francis Ward, "Clerks Avoid Getting Their DIGs In," *American Bar Association Journal* 93 (March 2007): 12–13.

52. Bryan A. Garner, "Justice Stephen G. Breyer," *Scribes Journal of Legal Writing* 13 (2010): 152.

53. Barbara Palmer, "The 'Bermuda Triangle?' The Cert Pool and Its Influence Over the Supreme Court's Agenda," *Constitutional Commentary* 18 (2001): 111; Stras, "Supreme Court's Gatekeepers," 976–980.

54. *Texas Department of Housing and Community Affairs v. The Inclusive Communities Project, Inc.* (2015). The earlier cases were *Magner v. Gallagher* (2012) and *Township of Mount Holly v. Mt. Holly Garden Citizens in Action* (2013).

55. Lyle Denniston, "Mixed Signals on Same-Sex Marriage," SCOTUSblog, September 18, 2014, http://www.scotusblog.com/2014/09/mixed-signals-on-same-sex-marriage. The new set of four cases was decided under the title of one of the cases: *Obergefell v. Hodges* (2015).

56. Ryan C. Black and Christina L. Boyd, "Selecting the Select Few: The Discuss List and the U.S. Supreme Court's Agenda-Setting Process," *Social Science Quarterly* 93 (March 2012): 17.

57. Tony Mauro, "Court Aces," *Legal Times*, July 14, 2003, 11.

58. The proportion for the Supreme Court is based on data in the "Statistics" articles in the November issues of the *Harvard Law Review*. The proportion for the courts of appeals is based on data in the Administrative Office of the United States Courts, *Judicial Business of the United States Courts: Annual Report of the Director, 2014*, Table B-5, http://www.uscourts.gov/statistics-reports/judicial-business-2014-tables, and the same report for earlier years.

59. "Confirmation Hearings on the Nominations of Thomas Perrelli Nominee to be Associate Attorney General of the United States and Elena Kagan Nominee to be Solicitor General of the United States," Hearing before the Senate Judiciary Committee, 111th Congress, 1st Session, February 10, 2009 (Washington, D.C.: Government Printing Office, 2009), 99. The transcript used the word *case* rather than *cases*.

60. *American Tradition Partnership v. Bullock*, 183 L. Ed. 2d 448, 449 (2012).

61. This figure does not include two cases in which the Court granted certiorari and immediately remanded the case to the lower court.

62. Ryan C. Black and Ryan J. Owens, *The Solicitor General and the United States Supreme Court: Executive Branch Influence and Judicial Decisions* (New York: Cambridge University Press, 2012), chap. 4.

63. Biskupic, Roberts, and Shiffman, "Special Report: The Echo Chamber."

64. "Notes on Justice Kennedy," *Southern California Appellate News*, February 4, 2010, http://www.socal-appellate.blogspot.com/2010/02/notes-on-justice-kennedy.html.

65. Biskupic, Roberts, and Shiffman, "Special Report: The Echo Chamber."

66. John J. Bursch, "Petitions for Certiorari: Understanding the Hidden Process," *Appellate Issues* 7 (February 2008), http://www.americanbar.org/groups/judicial/conferences/appellate_judges/appellate_lawyers/resources/publications/appellate_issues.html.

67. Gregory A. Caldeira, John R. Wright, and Christopher Zorn, "Organized Interests and Agenda Setting in the U.S. Supreme Court Revisited" (2012), http://papers.ssrn.com/sol3/papers.cfm?abstract_id=2109497.

68. Emily Bazelon, "The Case of the Moldy Washing Machines, Again," *Slate*, February 24, 2014, http://www.slate.com/articles/news_and_politics/jurisprudence/2014/02/moldy_washing_machines_lawsuit_the_supreme_court_won_t_hear_the_class_action.html. The cases were *Sears, Roebuck & Co. v. Butler* (2014); *Whirlpool Corp. v. Glazer* (2014); and *BSH Home Appliances Corp. v. Cobb* (2014).

69. Dahleen Glanton, "O'Connor Questions Court's Decision to Take *Bush v. Gore*," *Chicago Tribune*, April 27, 2013, http://articles.chicagotribune.com/ 2013-04-27/news/ct-met-sandra-day-oconnor-edit-board-20130427_1_ o-connor-bush-v-high-court.

70. The landmark decisions were, respectively, *District of Columbia v. Heller* (2008); *McDonald v. Chicago* (2010); and *Planned Parenthood v. Casey* (1992).

71. Data on the number of petitions accepted are from "Statistical Recap of Supreme Court's Workload during Last Three Terms," in *United States Law Week* (for the 1980–1984 terms) and from the Supreme Court's *Journal* (for the 2010–2013 terms). Those sources were also used for the ratios of petitions to cases accepted that are described later in this section. Data on the number of full decisions are from the "Statistics" articles in the November issues of the *Harvard Law Review*.

72. U.S. Census Bureau, *Statistical Abstract of the United States: 2014* (Washington, D.C.: Government Printing Office, 2013), 233.

73. Linda Greenhouse, "Case of the Dwindling Docket Mystifies the Supreme Court," *New York Times*, December 7, 2006, A1, A30; Robert Barnes, "Justices Continue Trend of Hearing Fewer Cases," *Washington Post*, January 7, 2007, A4; Adam Liptak, "Justices Opt for Fewer Cases, and Professors and Lawyers Ponder Why," *New York Times*, September 29, 2009, A20; John Paul Stevens, *Five Chiefs: A Supreme Court Memoir* (New York: Little, Brown, 2011), 209.

74. David R. Stras, "The Supreme Court's Declining Plenary Docket: A Membership-Based Explanation," *Constitutional Commentary* 27 (Fall 2010): 151–161.

75. Kevin M. Scott, "Shaping the Supreme Court's Federal Certiorari Docket," *Justice System Journal* 27 (2006): 191–207.

Chapter 4

Decision Making

O nce the Supreme Court determines which cases to hear, the justices get to the heart of their work—reaching decisions in those cases. This chapter examines how and why the Court makes its decisions.

Components of the Court's Decision

A Supreme Court decision on the merits, one in which it decides the legal issues in a case, has two components: the immediate outcome for the parties to the case and a statement of general legal rules. In cases that the Court fully considers, it nearly always presents the two components in an opinion. In the great majority of cases, at least five justices subscribe to this opinion. As a result, it constitutes an authoritative statement by the Court.

Except in the few cases the Court hears under its original jurisdiction, the Court describes the outcome in relation to the lower-court decision it is reviewing. The Court can affirm the lower-court decision, leaving that court's treatment of the parties undisturbed. Alternatively, it can modify or reverse the lower-court decision. In general, a reversal overturns the lower-court decision altogether or nearly so, and modification is a more limited, partial overturning. Frequently, the Court "vacates" (makes void) the lower-court decision, an action whose effect is similar to that of reversal.

When the Court does disturb a lower-court decision, it sometimes makes a final judgment in the case. More often, it remands the case to the lower court, sending it back for reconsideration. The Court's opinion provides guidance on how the case should be reconsidered. For example, the opinion in a tax case may say that a court of appeals adopted the wrong interpretation of the federal tax laws and that this court should reexamine the case on the basis of a different interpretation. The Court's opinion in a 2014 case used typical language: "We vacate the judgment of the

Court of Appeals and remand the case for further proceedings consistent with this opinion."[1]

In most cases, the outcome has little impact beyond the parties themselves. Rather, what makes most decisions consequential is the statement in the Court's opinion of legal rules that apply to the nation as a whole. Any court must follow those rules in a case to which they apply, and the rules often shape the behavior of people outside of court. As a result, a decision may affect thousands or even millions of people who were not parties in the case.

The Court chooses which legal rules it establishes in a case, just as it chooses the outcome for the parties. A ruling for one of the parties often could be based on any of several different rules or sets of rules. That reality is underlined when the Court affirms a lower-court decision on a legal ground that differs from the one that the lower court used. The rules chosen by the Court largely determine the long-term impact of its decision. If the Court overturns the death sentence for a particular defendant, it might base that decision on an unusual error in the defendant's trial, and the decision would affect few other defendants. Alternatively, the Court could declare that the death penalty is unconstitutional under all circumstances and thereby make a fundamental policy change.

The Decision-Making Process

When the Court accepts a case for a decision on the merits, it initiates the decision-making process for that case. This process varies from case to case, but it typically involves several stages.

Presentation of Cases to the Court

The written briefs that the Court receives when it considers whether to hear a case usually give some attention to the merits of the case. Once a case has been accepted for oral argument and decision, attorneys for the parties submit new briefs that address only the merits. In the preponderance of cases that reach this stage, interest groups submit amicus curiae briefs stating their own arguments on the merits.

Most of the material in these briefs concern legal issues. The parties muster evidence to support their interpretations of relevant constitutional provisions and statutes. In their briefs they frequently offer arguments about policy as well, seeking to persuade the justices that support for their position constitutes not only good law but good public policy.

Material in the briefs is supplemented by attorneys' presentations in oral argument before the Court. Attorneys for the parties sometimes share their time with the lawyer for an amicus—usually the federal government.

In most cases each side is provided a half hour for its argument. One exception was the set of three cases involving constitutional challenges to the 2010 federal health care law, for which the Court allocated a total of six hours over three days in 2012.[2] When a lawyer's time expires, a red light goes on at the lectern. Chief Justice William Rehnquist enforced the time limit strictly. As Justice Ginsburg explained, Rehnquist's successor, John Roberts, "is a bit more flexible at oral argument: He won't stop a lawyer or a justice in mid-sentence when the red light goes on."[3]

The justices are quite vocal during the arguments, usually leaving lawyers with little time to speak in between questions and comments from the bench. In a 2011 argument, one of the lawyers got only partway through the ritual opening, "Mr. Chief Justice, and may it please the Court," before Elena Kagan asked the first question.[4] In the current Court most of the justices are active questioners, so much so that they frequently interrupt each other. Justice Alito has reported that it can be difficult to get a question in without interrupting a lawyer in midsentence.[5] Speaking about the frequent interventions by the justices, Chief Justice Roberts has said that "it is too much, and I do think we need to address it a little bit."[6]

The most vocal justices on the current Court, measured by numbers of questions and comments, are Antonin Scalia, Sonia Sotomayor, Stephen Breyer, and John Roberts.[7] The least vocal justice by far is Clarence Thomas, who has asked no questions during oral arguments since 2006. His silence is so noteworthy that a brief joke he interjected in a case in 2013 attracted considerable attention.[8] Thomas has said, "I just think there are too many questions. I think that we have capable advocates and we should let the capable advocates talk."[9]

For the justices, oral argument has two broad functions. First, it allows them to gather information about the strengths and weaknesses of the parties' positions and about other aspects of the case that interest them. Second, and probably more important, the argument gives them an opportunity to shape their colleagues' perceptions of a case—the only opportunity they have before the Court reaches its tentative decision at conference. Thus, many of their questions and comments to lawyers are implicitly directed at other justices. In particular, justices try to expose weaknesses in the arguments of the side whose position they oppose. This is one reason for a pattern that observers of the Court have noticed: On the whole, justices ask more questions of the side they ultimately vote against, and their questions to that side tend to be more negative in tone.[10] When justices ask questions of the lawyer whose position they favor, the questions are often designed to shore up the lawyer's case. In one argument, for instance, Justice Sotomayor asked several questions to help one of the lawyers make his case.[11]

At least some justices clearly enjoy the opportunity for self-expression that oral argument provides. Some make humorous comments, a practice that is encouraged by commentators' counts of the number of times that each justice draws laughter in arguments. In one case involving capital punishment, quips by two colleagues drew the testy comment from Justice Anthony Kennedy, "This is very amusing in a capital case."[12]

Justices have indicated that oral argument often shapes their perception of cases and occasionally shifts their judgment about which side to support.[13] Once in a while, the argument seems to have a decisive effect. In *United States v. Jones* (2012), federal agents had installed a GPS device on a car and tracked the car's location for a month without a valid search warrant. The federal government's lawyer responded to questions by saying that if the government tracked all nine Supreme Court justices for a month with GPS devices it had installed on their cars, its actions would not constitute a search and thus would be subject to no legal restrictions. "After that," a commentator said when the Court announced its decision, "it seemed to be mainly a question of how the government would lose, not whether. And this week, sure enough, the tally was Jones 9, Big Brother 0."[14]

Tentative Decisions

After oral argument the Court discusses each case in one of its conferences later the same week. The chief justice begins the discussion of a case, which continues with the other justices from most senior to most junior. As Chief Justice Roberts explained, after Roberts presents his own view, "That means Justice Scalia goes next. On a good day, he'll say, 'Me too, Chief." The justices continue, each indicating their vote in the case and the reasons for their position. By the time the discussion gets to the most junior justice, currently Elena Kagan, the Court's collective decision may be so clear that the other justices pay little attention. "But when it's four to four," Roberts said, "we listen closely to what she has to say."[15]

Once each justice has spoken, there may be little or no further discussion. This reflects the fact that, as Justice Scalia put it, the discussion of a case in conference "is not really an exercise in persuading each other, it's an exercise in stating your views while the rest of us take notes."[16] Justice Kagan recalls that at her first conference to decide cases, the justices spent only ten minutes or so discussing a high-profile case because the justices' positions were firmly set and "the only thing that we would have accomplished is to get a little bit annoyed at each other." But the other case considered at that conference, which involved a procedural issue on which the justices did not feel as strongly, received about forty minutes of discussion.[17]

After each two-week sitting, the writing of the Court's opinion in each case is assigned to a justice. If the chief justice voted with the majority, the chief assigns the opinion. In other cases, the most senior associate justice in the majority makes the assignment.

Steve Petteway, Supreme Court Collection of the United States

The Court's conference room, where the justices meet to reach tentative decisions in cases after oral argument.

Reaching Final Decisions

The justice who was assigned the Court's opinion writes an initial draft, guided by the views expressed in conference. The justice's clerks usually do most of the drafting. Once this opinion is completed and circulated, a justice who was in the majority at conference signs on to it most of the time.[18] But justices sometimes hold back rather than sign on, either because they have developed doubts about their original vote or because they disagree with some of the language in the draft opinion. The language is important because justices are reluctant to join an opinion when they disagree with its reasoning. Members of the original minority also read the draft opinion for the Court, and they sometimes sign on to the opinion because their view of the case has changed.

Justices who do not immediately sign on may indicate fundamental disagreement with the opinion. Exaggerating somewhat, Justice Thomas has described such responses: "Dear Clarence, I disagree with everything in your opinion except your name. Cheers."[19] But justices often indicate that they would be willing to join an opinion if certain changes are made. Justices who had voted with the majority are especially likely to ask for changes. Their memos initiate a process of explicit or implicit negotiation in which the assigned justice tries to gain the support of as many colleagues as possible. At the least, the assigned justice wants to maintain the original majority for the outcome supported by the opinion and to win a majority for the language of the opinion so that it becomes the official statement of the Court. This negotiation process operates primarily through written memos, sent on paper rather than by e-mail. But the justices sometimes interact directly, and law clerks often gather information from clerks for other justices to help identify what revisions are needed to gain a colleague's support for an opinion.[20]

In this effort the justice who was assigned the Court's opinion often competes with other justices, who write alternative opinions supporting the opposite outcome or arguing for the same outcome with a different rationale. Most of the time assigned justices succeed in winning a majority for their opinions, though sometimes with substantial alterations. More often than not, however, they fail to win unanimous support for their opinion. As shown in Table 4-1, which summarizes attributes of the Court's decisions in the 2012 and 2013 terms, unanimity for a single opinion was achieved only about 40 percent of the time.

Occasionally, no opinion gains the support of a majority. This occurred four times in those two terms, and in six other cases there was a majority for only part of one opinion. Without a majority opinion, there is no authoritative statement of the Court's position on the legal issues in the

TABLE 4-1
Selected Characteristics of Supreme Court Decisions, 2012–2013 Terms

Characteristic	Percentage
Vote for Court's decision[a]	
Unanimous	56.0
Nonunanimous	44.0
Support for Court's opinion	
Unanimous for whole opinion	40.7
Unanimous for part of opinion	4.0
Majority but not unanimous	48.7
Majority for only part of opinion	4.0
No majority for opinion	2.7
One or more concurring opinions[b]	39.3
One or more dissenting opinions[c]	44.0
Two or more concurring opinions	11.3
Two or more dissenting opinions	10.7

Source: The decisions included are those decided with opinions and listed in the front section of *United States Supreme Court Reports, Lawyers' Edition,* Vols. 184–189.

a. "Decision" refers to the outcome for the parties. Partial dissents are not counted as votes for the decision.

b. Some concurring opinions are in full agreement with the Court's opinion.

c. Opinions labeled "concurring and dissenting" are treated as dissenting opinions.

case. But the opinion on the winning side with the greatest support—the "plurality opinion"—may specify the points for which majority support exists.

On rare occasions the justices find themselves unable to reach a final decision in a case before the term ends. They then schedule the case for a second set of oral arguments, usually in the following term. The Court took this route in two landmark cases, *Brown v. Board of Education* (1954) and *Roe v. Wade* (1973).

Concurring and Dissenting Opinions

In most cases an opinion gains a majority but lacks unanimous support. Disagreement with the majority opinion can take two forms. First, a justice may cast a dissenting vote, which disagrees with the result reached by the Court as it affects the parties to a case. If a criminal conviction is reversed, for example, a justice who believes it should have been affirmed will dissent. Second, a justice may concur with the Court's decision, agreeing with the result in the specific case but differing with the rationale expressed in the Court's opinion. Table 4-1 shows that both kinds of disagreement are common.

Ordinarily, a justice who disagrees with the majority opinion writes or joins in a dissenting or concurring opinion. The main exception is justices who simply indicate that they join the majority opinion except for one portion, sometimes a single footnote. When the conference vote is not unanimous, the senior dissenting justice assigns the dissenting opinion. This opinion is written at the same time as the assigned opinion for the majority, and often one goal is to persuade enough colleagues to change their positions that a minority becomes a majority.

That goal is no longer relevant after the Court reaches its final decision, but issuing a dissenting opinion can serve several other purposes. For one thing, dissenting opinions give justices the satisfaction of expressing unhappiness with the result in a case and justifying their disagreement. Dissenting opinions sometimes have more concrete purposes as well. Through their arguments, dissenters may try to set the stage for a later Court to adopt their view. In the short term, a dissenting opinion may be intended to subvert the Court's decision by pointing out how lower courts can interpret it narrowly or by urging Congress to overturn the Court's reading of a statute. In *T-Mobile South v. City of Roswell* (2015), the Court held that a city had not followed proper procedures in denying an application to build a cell phone tower. Chief Justice Roberts's dissent described how the lower court could rule in favor of the city on remand and how other cities could avoid any adverse effects from the Court's decision.

When more than one justice dissents, the dissenters usually join in a single opinion—most likely the one originally assigned. But often there are multiple dissenting opinions, each expressing the particular view of the justice who wrote it but sometimes indicating agreement with another opinion.

A concurring opinion that disagrees with the majority opinion on the legal rationale for a decision is labeled a special concurrence. In some cases the disagreement is limited. In some other cases the majority and concurring opinions offer fundamentally different rationales for the outcome they favor. *National Labor Relations Board v. Noel Canning* (2014) concerned the president's power to make "recess appointments" of officials when the Senate is out of session. The Court ruled that President Obama had lacked the power to make such appointments at a time when the Senate was technically in session. But in other respects, the Court gave a broad interpretation to the recess appointment power. Justice Scalia's concurring opinion on behalf of three colleagues disagreed vehemently with that broad interpretation.

Another type of concurring opinion, a regular concurrence, is written by justices who join the majority opinion. Authors of regular concurrences agree with both the outcome for the litigants and the legal rules that the Court establishes. Under those circumstances, why would justices write separate opinions? Most often, they offer their own interpretation of the majority opinion as a means to influence lower courts and other audiences, as well as the Court itself in future cases. For instance, Samuel Alito wrote a concurrence in *Lozano v. Alvarez* (2014) to tell lower courts how they could avoid what he saw as a potential, and undesirable, consequence of the Court's decision. Regular concurrences can have other purposes, such as refuting the arguments in a dissenting opinion.

Content and Style of Opinions

Majority opinions vary in form, but they usually begin with a description of the background of the case before it reached the Court. The opinion then turns to the legal issues, discussing the opposing views on those issues and describing the Court's conclusions about them. A summary of the outcome for the parties ends the opinion. Concurring and dissenting opinions do not need to be comprehensive, so they often focus on specific aspects of the case, and some are brief.

There is also a difference in style, as Justice Alito has explained. "If you're writing a majority opinion, where you have to have at least four people agree with you, you're limited in what you can say. In my dissents I'm writing for myself, so they're more freewheeling." Alito noted that among the opinions he has written, all of his favorites are concurring and dissenting opinions.[21]

Even majority opinions reflect the writing styles of individual justices, despite the substantial role that clerks play in drafting opinions. But distinctive styles come across more clearly in concurring and dissenting opinions.

Justice Scalia sometimes criticizes colleagues' opinions in strong terms, treating them as utterly wrong. In a 2013 dissent, for instance, he referred to "the Court's feeble rejoinder" on one point and then said that another aspect of the majority opinion was "even more bizarre."[22] One study concluded that Scalia is, by a wide margin, "the most sarcastic justice."[23] Justice Kagan also makes strong criticisms in her dissenting opinions, often in colloquial language and short sentences. In a 2013 case, she summarized her disagreement with one point in the majority opinion simply: "Do not be fooled."[24] Her opinions are often tinged with humor. Chief Justice Roberts writes in a lively style, a style that often comes through even in his opinions for the Court.[25]

Legal scholars and other readers of majority opinions sometimes complain that they are not as clear as they might be. A lack of clarity sometimes results from the author's effort to gain support from colleagues. One study found that the larger the number of justices who sign on to a majority opinion, the less clear the opinion is; building a large coalition may require some vagueness in order to patch over disagreements. The study also found considerable variation in clarity across justices.[26]

Both majority opinions and dissents are usually written as arguments for the conclusion they reach rather than presenting the considerations on both sides in an evenhanded way. As part of that style, they emphasize evidence about the law and other aspects of cases that is favorable to their conclusions. They draw that evidence primarily from the briefs and other materials in the case. But in the Internet era justices' opinions frequently cite facts related to cases that they have drawn from their own research or that of Court staff members. The factual material that justices independently gather is not always well founded.[27]

The Decision Announcement and Later Events

The decision-making process for a case ends when all the opinions have been put in final form and all justices have determined which opinions they will join. The Supreme Court is unusual in that it announces its decisions in a court session. Typically, the justice who wrote the majority opinion reads a portion of the opinion. Occasionally—on average, about six times a term in the 2010–2012 terms—the authors of dissenting opinions also read portions of their opinions.[28] As Justice Ginsburg has said in describing her own practice, justices do so when they think the Court's decision is "egregiously" wrong.[29] In *National Labor Relations Board v. Noel Canning* (2014), Justice Scalia took a very unusual step by summarizing his concurring opinion that sharply disagreed with the majority opinion.

The length of time required for a case to go through all the stages from filing in the Court to the announcement of a decision varies a good deal. Of the cases that the Court decided in its 2013 term, the time from the grant of certiorari to oral argument varied from three to more than nine months, and the time from oral argument to decision varied from one to seven months.[30] The Court's decision often comes many years after the incident that triggered the case.

After the Court decides a case—or declines to hear it—the losing party may petition for a rehearing. Such petitions are rarely granted. In *Martinez v. Illinois* (2014), a criminal case, the Court considered the state's argument for a rehearing sufficiently strong that it took the unusual step of asking for a response to that argument from the defendant whose conviction it had overturned. But the result was the usual one: the Court denied a rehearing.[31]

The language of the "slip opinions" that the Court issues when it hands down a decision is sometimes revised in the period of several years before the Court's opinions are published in final form. Some revisions correct typographical errors, but others make more substantive changes. In 2014, a law professor quickly discovered that Justice Scalia's dissent from a decision had made an error in his description of a litigant's argument in an earlier case. He notified the Court, and the error was corrected by the next morning.[32]

Influences on Decisions: Introduction

Of all the questions that might be asked about the Supreme Court, the one that has intrigued people most is how the Court's decisions are best explained. Cases present the justices with choices: which litigant to support, what rules of law to establish. On what bases do they make their choices?

This question is difficult to answer. Like policymakers elsewhere in government, Supreme Court justices act on multiple considerations, those considerations are intermixed, and their relative importance varies among justices and cases.[33] Because of this complexity, people who study the Court disagree sharply about how best to explain the Court's decisions.

The rest of this chapter is devoted to this question. No conclusive answer to the question is possible. But some insight can be gained by examining four broad forces that shape the Court's decisions: the state of the legal rules the Court interprets, the justices' personal values, interaction among the justices, and the Court's political and social environment. The sections that follow consider each of these forces.

The State of the Law

Every case requires the Supreme Court to interpret the law, usually in the form of constitutional provisions or federal statutes. In this sense a justice's job differs from that of a legislator; justices interpret existing law rather than write new law. For this reason, the existing state of the law is a good starting point for explanation of the Court's decisions.

The Law's Significance in Decisions

As a nominee for chief justice in 2005, John Roberts told the Senate Judiciary Committee that "judges and justices are servants of the law, not the other way around. Judges are like umpires. Umpires don't make the rules; they apply them."[34] His statement received considerable attention because it was vivid, but other nominees to the Court and sitting justices have described their work in similar ways. In doing so, they have offered a simple explanation of the justices' work as decision makers: they apply the relevant body of law to the cases they address.

This depiction of the justices' work may be attractive, but it conflicts with two realities. One reality is what might be called the legal ambiguity of the cases the Court decides. In at least the great majority of cases that the Court agrees to hear, the applicable legal rules do not lead clearly to a decision favoring one side or the other. As a result, a good case can be made for either side on the basis of the constitutional or statutory provision that the Court is interpreting. Thus, Justice Sotomayor in 2011 offered her own interpretation of the analogy between justices and umpires:

The baseball rules tell you what the strike zone is, but the umpire has to use judgment about where the ball hit in that strike zone. And for those of you who have ever played umpire, you know a lot of those balls are right on the line, so did it tilt that way or this way?[35]

The second reality is that justices care about more than the law. Most important, like other people in law and politics, they have developed views about what is desirable public policy. When they decide cases involving issues such as affirmative action, abortion, or the role of government in health care, they will be happier if their position in a case and the Court's decision are consistent with their conception of good policy on those issues. In other words, Supreme Court justices have rooting interests in the cases they decide.

Facing cases that are legally ambiguous and caring about the policy issues in those cases, justices may act consciously to reach decisions that accord with their policy preferences. But even if justices try only to interpret the law properly, they will tend toward the interpretation that is most consistent with their preferences. One of Justice Felix Frankfurter's law clerks described that process well in talking about Frankfurter:

He felt very intensely about lots of things, and sometimes he didn't realize that his feelings and his deeply felt values were pushing him as a judge relentlessly in one direction rather than another. I'm sure that you can put these things aside consciously, but what's underneath the consciousness you can't control.[36]

Thus, it is understandable that in most cases the justices disagree with each other about the outcome for the litigants, the legal rules to adopt, or both. The primary reason for those disagreements is the ambiguity of the law. In turn, the most common effect of this ambiguity is that justices with different policy preferences reach different conclusions.

Because of this reality, some observers of the Court take a position directly opposite to the one that justices usually express, arguing that the state of the law has essentially no impact on justices' choices.[37] This argument can be defended, but there is good reason to conclude that legal considerations do have an impact on justices' choices. Even when decisions on either side of a case could be justified under the law, the law may weigh more heavily on one side than on the other. If justices care about making good law, they will be drawn toward the side that seems to have a stronger legal argument.

Surely, most if not all justices do care about making good law. They have been trained in a tradition that emphasizes the law as a basis for judicial decisions. They are evaluated informally by a peer group of judges and legal scholars who assess their ability to reach well-founded interpretations of the law. Perhaps most important, they work in the language of the law. The arguments they receive in written briefs and oral arguments are primarily about the law, and so are the arguments they make to each other in draft opinions and memoranda.[38]

Indeed, some aspects of justices' behavior indicate that the state of the law does affect their choices.[39] Sometimes they take positions that conflict with their conceptions of good policy. And sometimes the justices in the majority are sufficiently unhappy with the effects of their interpretation of a statute that the Court's opinion asks Congress to consider rewriting the statute to override their decision—that is, to establish a policy that the justices feel powerless to adopt themselves because of their reading of the law. While the law is hardly the dominant force in decision making, it exerts a real impact on the Court's decisions.

Means of Interpretation

The role of the law in the Court's decisions can be probed further by considering the techniques that justices use to interpret provisions of the law—techniques that are important in themselves. The justices and legal commentators have developed approaches to legal interpretation based on their views about the value of different techniques.

Plain Meaning. Nearly everyone agrees that interpretation of a legal provision should begin with a search for what is called the "plain meaning" of constitutional and statutory provisions—what the words and sets of words in those provisions mean. This is not always an easy task. The plain meaning of a legal provision is sometimes uncertain, and this is especially true in the cases that the Supreme Court hears. Many of the Court's decisions involve interpretation of the Constitution, and the Constitution is written in broad language whose meaning is difficult to determine. This is true, for instance, of the Fourteenth Amendment provision that prohibits the states from depriving people "of life, liberty, or property, without due process of law." Understandably, the justices have had great difficulty in determining what "due process of law" requires.

Federal statutes are typically less vague than the Constitution, but often their provisions have uncertain meanings. The statutory cases that the Court decides tend to involve issues on which Congress has not spoken clearly. In these cases justices can do their best to ascertain the most reasonable interpretation of the words in a statute, but there may be considerable room for disagreement. In a 2014 decision, for instance, Justice Breyer's majority opinion and Justice Scalia's dissent reached conflicting conclusions about the meaning of the term *perform* in the federal Copyright Act of 1976.[40]

One way to ascertain the meaning of language is to consult dictionaries, and justices have increasingly cited dictionaries in opinions interpreting federal statutes since the 1980s. But dictionaries generally cannot resolve ambiguities. One reason is that dictionaries frequently offer several definitions of a word. Another is that the meaning of a legal provision often depends on combinations of words rather than single words.

In interpreting the Constitution, justices might seek to ascertain the meaning of its language at the time it was written or what that language means to people today. The school of interpretation called originalism, strongly supported by Antonin Scalia and Clarence Thomas, holds that it is the original meaning that counts. Some other justices believe that the current meaning should be taken into account. Thus, while Justice Scalia criticized judges and justices who "have invented this notion of a living Constitution, where the interpretation of the Constitution could change," Justice Ginsburg argued that "no one would say that the Constitution means today what it meant when it was written."[41]

Even when a legal provision seems to have a clear meaning, the justices do not always adhere to it. That is especially true in constitutional law. Over time the Court has accepted several interpretations of the Constitution that seem to depart from the language of its provisions. Although the language of the Fourteenth Amendment's due process clause requires only that government follow proper procedures in taking "life, liberty, or property," the Court interprets the clause as a protection of freedom of expression and freedom of religion.[42] It interprets the same language in the Fifth Amendment to prohibit the federal government from some forms of discrimination.[43] And for more than a century the Court has read the Eleventh Amendment's prohibition of lawsuits against states "by citizens of another state" to prohibit most lawsuits against a state by the state's own residents as well.[44]

Why have justices adopted and adhered to these seemingly inaccurate interpretations? The primary reason is that doing so advances values that are important to them, values such as protecting freedom of speech. The general acceptance of what can be called constitutional fictions shows that no justice always adheres to the plain meaning of the law.

Intent of Framers or Legislators. When the plain meaning of a legal provision is unclear, justices can seek to ascertain the intentions of the people who wrote the provision. Evidence concerning legislative intent can be found in congressional committee reports and floor debates, which constitute what is called the legislative history of a statute or a constitutional amendment. For provisions of the original Constitution, evidence is found in reports of deliberations at the Constitutional Convention of 1787 and other sources.

Sometimes the intent of Congress or the framers of the Constitution is clear. Frequently, however, it is not. The body that adopted a provision may not have spoken on an issue; the members of Congress who wrote the broad language of the Fourteenth Amendment could hardly indicate their intent about all the issues that have arisen under that amendment. And evidence about intent may be contradictory, in part because of competing efforts to influence the courts by members of Congress and congressional staff.

Justices disagree about the use of legislative intent in interpreting statutes. Textualists argue that judges should focus on the plain meaning of legal provisions and that they should ignore evidence of legislative intent. Justice Scalia is the most prominent textualist. In his view, it is illegitimate to consult legislative history: we "are governed by what Congress enacted rather than by what it intended."[45] Further, he sees legislative history as an uncertain and easily distorted guide to congressional intent. Accordingly, Scalia does not refer to legislative history himself and sometimes refuses to join portions of colleagues' opinions that refer to it. Scalia has gained some support for his view from other justices, and the Court's use of legislative history declined after he joined the Court.[46]

In contrast with textualists, some judges and commentators argue that it is both legitimate and desirable to take evidence of legislative intent into account.[47] One school of thought that takes this view is called purposivism, because it emphasizes the goal of ascertaining the purposes that underlie provisions of law. Justice Breyer is the most visible supporter of purposivism on the Supreme Court.

To a considerable extent, disagreements between schools of legal interpretation fall along ideological lines: textualism and originalism, which
Justice Scalia describes as a "sort of subspecies of textualism,"[48] receive
their strongest support from conservatives. In large part, this is because
those two philosophies are perceived as favorable to policies that conservatives support. For instance, liberal justices sometimes support departures from the original meaning of constitutional provisions as a means to
expand civil liberties. The Court's decisions prohibiting the death penalty
for people who are intellectually disabled (in 2002), for murders committed when the defendant was not yet eighteen years old (in 2005), and for
sexual assaults of children (in 2008) were based on the majority's view that
the prohibition of "cruel and unusual punishments" in the Eighth
Amendment should be interpreted on the basis of current values. The
conservative dissenters in each case focused on the meaning of "cruel and
unusual" when the Eighth Amendment was written and strongly criticized
the majority for its approach to interpretation of the Constitution.[49]

Precedent. The Supreme Court's past decisions, its precedents, provide
another guide to decision making. A basic doctrine of the law is stare
decisis (let the decision stand). Under this doctrine a court is bound to
adhere to the rules of law established by courts that stand above it. No
court stands above the Supreme Court, but stare decisis includes an
expectation that courts will generally adhere to their own precedents.

Technically, a court is expected to follow not everything stated in a
relevant precedent but only the rule of law that is necessary for decision
in that case—what is called the holding. In *District of Columbia v. Heller*
(2008), the Court ruled that the Second Amendment protects the right of
individuals to possess guns, and it struck down a Washington, D.C., law on
the ground that the law infringed that right. That was the holding of the
case. The Court's opinion also described some types of gun regulations
that were "presumptively lawful." Because those regulations were not
involved in this case, that part of the Court's opinion was "dictum," which
has no legal force. The distinction between holding and dictum is not
always so clear, however. After the Court upheld the mandate that some
individuals purchase health insurance in 2012 on the basis of congressional power to levy taxes, commentators disagreed about whether the view
of five justices that the power to regulate interstate commerce did not
extend to regulations like the insurance mandate was holding or dictum.[50]

The practice of adhering to precedent would not eliminate ambiguity
in legal interpretation even if the justices always followed that practice.
Most cases before the Supreme Court concern issues that are at least mar-
ginally different from those decided in past cases, so precedents do not
lead directly to a particular outcome. Indeed, justices often "distinguish"

a precedent, holding that it does not govern the current case. Still, the set of precedents that exists in any area of law helps to channel the justices' judgments about cases in that area. This is especially true of analytic frameworks in areas such as freedom of expression that were established by past decisions.[51]

The Court can maintain a precedent but narrow its reach. This is how subsequent Courts have treated some decisions of the Warren Court that expanded the rights of criminal defendants. In some instances this narrowing effectively undercuts the precedent in question. Indeed, dissenting justices sometimes complain that the Court has implicitly overturned a precedent.

The Court explicitly abandons some precedents, and it has done so at an unusually high rate since 1960. By one count, the Court overruled precedents only ninety-four times between 1790 and 1959 but did so seventy-six times in the twenty years from 1960 through 1979. The pace has slowed since then, but the sixty-four decisions overruling precedents between 1980 and 2014, about two per year, is still a much higher rate than in the period prior to 1960.[52] These counts are approximate, because the Court is not always clear about whether it has overruled a precedent. Most overrulings are on constitutional questions. One reason is the view of at least some justices that Congress can easily override statutory precedents with which its members disagree, so the Court should adhere to statutory precedents that Congress has left standing.

The number of times the Court overrules precedents is a small fraction of the times when it follows them. The same is true of individual justices. But most of the time when justices follow a precedent, its validity is not in question, or they simply agree with it. What do justices do when they confront a precedent with which they strongly disagree?

One way to identify such disagreement is when a justice dissents from a legal rule at the time the Court first establishes it. Most of the time, justices continue to reject that precedent in later cases, engaging in what one legal scholar called "perpetual dissents."[53] Yet justices sometimes vote to uphold precedents that they originally opposed. More broadly, the Court as a whole adheres to a good many precedents that no longer accord with the views of most justices. Thus, few of the Warren Court's liberal precedents from the 1960s have been overruled by the more conservative Courts of the post-Warren era.[54]

Justices differ in their willingness to overrule precedents. On the current Court, Justice Thomas stands out for his belief that there is little reason to maintain a specific precedent or a line of Court doctrine if it is faulty. When a questioner asked, "Stare decisis doesn't hold much force for you?" Thomas responded, "Oh, it sure does. But not enough to keep me from going to the Constitution."[55] In contrast, Chief Justice Roberts shows a reluctance to overrule precedents directly even in decisions that undercut them. In 2014 Roberts wrote three majority or plurality opinions in which concurring opinions by other conservative justices argued that certain precedents that Roberts's opinions maintained should be overruled. Thomas wrote two of those concurring opinions and joined the third.[56]

The extent to which precedents actually influence justices is a matter of dispute among commentators. However, they clearly have some effect. The rule of stare decisis does not control the Court's decisions, but it does structure and shape them. The same is true of the law in general: it channels justices' choices, often in subtle ways, but it also leaves them considerable freedom in making those choices.

Justices' Values

If the law leaves justices free to make choices largely on other bases, the most likely basis is their own values. And of those values, justices' policy preferences have the greatest impact. Perceptions of that impact are reflected in the attention that participants in the selection of justices give to the policy views of potential and actual nominees to the Court. They are also reflected in commentaries on the Court, which often emphasize the justices' policy preferences as a basis for their votes and opinions.

The Influence of Policy Preferences

It is difficult to ascertain the actual effect of justices' policy preferences on their behavior as decision makers, simply because their preferences cannot be observed directly. But some evidence strongly suggests that preferences exert a powerful influence on justices' choices. When future justices take strong positions on policy issues, as Ruth Bader Ginsburg did as an advocate for women's rights, those positions are usually reflected in their work as justices. Similarly, justices who speak about their personal views outside the Court, such as Antonin Scalia, generally take positions consistent with those views in the cases they decide.

As with legal considerations, the impact of justices' preferences on their votes and opinions has been a matter of debate. But those preferences are clearly one of the most powerful influences on the justices' choices. And they are the best single explanation for differences in the positions that the nine justices take in the same cases, because no other factor varies so much from one justice to another.

Justices' attitudes on policy issues result from the same array of influences that shape political attitudes generally, including family socialization, religious training, and career experience. Justice John Paul Stevens described the impact of his military experience in World War II and the criminal conviction of his father for embezzlement (later overturned by the Illinois Supreme Court) on his attitudes toward certain issues in the Court.[57] One legal scholar has suggested another way that the justices' life experiences may shape their views: "the best predictor" of whether the Court finds that a search is unreasonable under the Fourth Amendment "is whether the justices could imagine it happening to them."[58]

Justices' policy preferences could shape their decision making in two different ways. Justices might simply take positions in cases that accord with their views of good policy. Alternatively, they might act strategically, departing from the positions they most prefer when doing so could advance the policies they favor. In Chapter 3 I discussed strategy in the selection of cases: Justices might vote whether to hear cases on the basis of their predictions about how the Court would rule on those cases. In decisions on the merits, strategic justices might write opinions that do not fully reflect their own views in order to win the support of other justices. To take another example, the Court collectively could modify the legal rules it establishes in a case in order to reduce the chances that Congress will override the Court's decision and substitute a policy that most justices see as undesirable.

It is not clear to what extent justices behave strategically and what forms their strategies take.[59] But it appears that strategic considerations seldom move justices very far from the positions they most prefer. For this reason, the impact of justices' policy preferences can be considered initially without taking strategy into account. In the two sections that follow I will consider strategy aimed at other justices and at the Court's political environment.

The Ideological Dimension

To a considerable degree, the policy preferences of people in politics and government are structured by ideology: those who take a conservative position on one issue are likely to take conservative positions on other issues as well. This is generally true of Supreme Court justices, so the impact of their preferences can be examined largely in ideological terms.

Defining Liberal and Conservative Positions. On most issues that come to the Court, the opposing positions are labeled as liberal and conservative. In civil liberties, with some exceptions such as gun rights, the position more favorable to legal protection for liberties is considered liberal. Thus, the liberal position gives relatively heavy weight to people's right to equal treatment by government and private institutions, to procedural rights of criminal defendants and others who deal with government, and to substantive rights such as freedom of expression and privacy. In contrast, the conservative position gives relatively great weight to values that compete with these rights, such as national security and effective law enforcement.

Liberal and conservative positions on economic issues are less clearly defined. But the liberal position is basically more favorable to economic "underdogs" and to government policies that are intended to benefit underdogs. In contrast, the conservative position is more favorable to businesses in conflicts with labor unions and consumers and less favorable to government regulation of business practices.

Some cases that come before the Supreme Court, such as boundary disputes between states, have little or no relationship with ideology. On some other issues, including aspects of free expression, ideological lines in American society and thus in the Court have become more complicated. With these cautions, the justices' policy preferences can be understood in ideological terms.

Ideology and the Justices' Positions. If opposing positions in most cases can be identified as liberal or conservative, the justices' voting patterns may be described in terms of the frequency with which they support the conservative side and the liberal side. Table 4-2 shows the ideological patterns of votes on case outcomes for the justices in the 2012 and 2013 terms, based on the definitions of conservative and liberal positions in one source. The table shows that every justice cast a good many votes on both sides, and the difference in voting between the justice with the most liberal record (Sonia Sotomayor) and the justice who voted in a conservative direction most often (Samuel Alito) was not enormous. But that 27 percentage point difference is still substantial. And in the cases that seem most important to observers of the Court, the voting patterns of conservative and liberal justices differ from each other much more.[60]

The relative positions of the justices on a conservative-to-liberal scale tend to remain fairly stable over time. It would be difficult to explain those stable differences except as a result of differences in the justices' policy preferences. Thus, to take one example, it seems clear that Justice Alito is distinctly more conservative than Justice Sotomayor.

Justices' relative ideological positions are reflected in the frequency with which they join the same opinions in a case. In the Court's 2012 and 2013 terms the mean rate of agreement on opinions between pairs of justices was 72 percent. The mean rate of agreement among the four most liberal justices was 88 percent; for the four most conservative justices, the mean rate was 78 percent. In contrast, the mean rate of agreement between the four most liberal justices and the four most conservative justices was 62 percent.[61] To a small degree, rates of agreement on opinions may reflect self-conscious alliances or personal relationships, but they are primarily the result of similar or differing policy preferences.

The general patterns of agreement and disagreement between the justices are often reflected in the lineups of justices in individual cases. In the 2012 and 2013 terms, for instance, about two-thirds of the Court's 5–4 decisions found either the four most liberal justices or the four most conservative justices dissenting, with Justice Kennedy joining one side or the other to create the majority in each case.[62] But divisions on the Court often diverge from ideological lines. One reason is that some justices take more liberal or more conservative positions in certain areas of policy than they do in most others. Justice Scalia, for instance, is relatively favorable to some types of legal claims by criminal defendants. Moreover, the issues

TABLE 4-2
Percentages of Liberal Votes Cast by Justices, 2012–2013 Terms

Justice	Liberal votes
Sotomayor	67.9
Kagan	65.0
Ginsburg	63.4
Breyer	58.6
Kennedy	50.0
Roberts	48.6
Scalia	47.2
Thomas	43.7
Alito	42.1

Source: Analysis of data in The Supreme Court Database (http://scdb.wustl.edu).

Note: Cases are included if they were decided after oral argument and if votes could be classified as liberal or conservative. The database classifies votes on the basis of a set of criteria described at its website.

in individual cases sometimes cut across ideological lines. In *Florida v. Jardines* (2013), a case involving the use of a drug-sniffing dog at a suspect's home, the five-member majority included the three most liberal justices and two of the most conservative. Such divisions, like the frequency of unanimous decisions, make it clear that justices do not respond to cases simply on the basis of their ideological tendencies.[63]

Observers of the Court regularly label justices not just relative to each other but in absolute terms as well: Justice Thomas is called a conservative, Justice Ginsburg a liberal. This conclusion does not follow directly from the justices' votes and opinions. For one thing, their positions in cases are not solely the product of their policy preferences. In addition, the proportions of liberal and conservative votes that a justice casts in a particular period reflect the mix of cases that the Court decides in that period. A justice with a strongly liberal voting record in one era might not have as liberal a record in a different era.

Still, the role of justices' policy preferences in their votes and opinions is sufficiently strong enough that those ideological labels seem appropriate. A justice who casts a preponderance of votes that can be characterized as conservative almost surely holds conservative views on most issues. Indeed, most justices who were perceived as strongly liberal or strongly conservative at the time of their appointment establish records on the Court that are consistent with those perceptions.[64]

Justices' Preferences and Policy Change

If the positions of individual justices reflect their policy preferences, the collective decisions of the Court must also reflect the mix of preferences among the justices. When most of the justices are conservative, the Court will tend to make conservative decisions and move legal doctrine in a conservative direction.

The proportions of liberal and conservative decisions fluctuate from term to term, and that is even more true of the Court's most visible decisions. Observers of the Court often play up this fluctuation, but it generally reflects the particular mix of cases that the Court decides each term rather than a shift in the Court's collective ideological position. But sometimes, the Court's position on a particular issue or its overall ideological position does change, in the sense that the Court would decide the same cases differently from the way it would have decided them in an earlier term.

If the Court's collective positions reflect the policy preferences of individual justices more than anything else, the primary source of changes in Court policies must be a shift in the preferences of the justices as a group. These shifts could come from change in the preferences of people already serving on the Court or from change in the Court's membership. In practice, both are significant but the second is more important.

Changes in Justices' Preferences. Close observers of the Supreme Court often try to predict how the Court will decide a pending case. Typically, they do rather well in their predictions. The primary reason is that individual justices tend to take stable positions on the issues that arise in various policy areas. The views that a justice expressed in past cases about when cars can be searched or when mergers of companies violate the antitrust laws are a good guide to the justice's stance in a future case. On specific legal questions, one legal scholar has suggested, justices tend to adhere to "personal precedent."[65] In turn, the Court's collective position on issues generally remains stable as long as its membership remains unchanged.

But over time, justices are exposed to new influences and confront issues in new forms. The result may be a change in their thinking about specific legal questions or broader issues. Occasionally their position on a specific question differs from the position they took in an earlier case, and sometimes justices acknowledge and explain that change.[66] Justice Ginsburg identified what she saw as a somewhat broader change in William Rehnquist's views. For most of his career as a justice, Rehnquist was relatively unfavorable to legal claims of sex discrimination. But in 2003 he wrote the Court's opinion strengthening the federal Family and Medical Leave Act, with several passages criticizing "stereotypes" about women's roles. Ginsburg thought that this opinion reflected Rehnquist's experience helping to care for his grandchildren after his daughter's divorce.[67]

It is difficult to ascertain whether justices have shifted in their overall ideological positions over time, but it is clear that most justices retain the same basic positions throughout their career. When a justice's position shifts relative to that of the Court as a whole, it is usually because new appointments have altered the Court's ideological composition while the justice has retained the same general views. This seemed to be true of John Paul Stevens, who was initially near the center of the Court but who had the most liberal record of any justice in the second half of his Court career.

Justice Harry Blackmun was one of the few justices whose basic views seemed to change fundamentally. Blackmun came to the Court in 1970 as a Nixon appointee, and early in his tenure he aligned himself chiefly with the other conservative justices. He and Chief Justice Warren Burger, boyhood friends from Minnesota, were dubbed the "Minnesota Twins." In the 1973 term, Blackmun agreed with Burger on opinions in 84 percent of the Court's decisions and with the liberal William Brennan in only 49 percent.[68] Blackmun gradually moved toward the center of the Court, and from the 1980 term onward he usually had higher agreement rates with Brennan than with Burger. In 1985, Burger's last term, it was 30 percentage points higher. In the last few terms before his 1994 retirement, Blackmun was one of the two most liberal justices on the Court. Although the reasons for this change are uncertain, it appears that his experiences in dealing with cases that came to the Court—especially *Roe v. Wade*, in which he wrote the Court's opinion—were important.[69]

Perhaps more common than individual shifts are changes in the collective views of the justices in a particular issue area. These changes typically result from developments in American society that affect the views of the population as a whole. The liberal Warren Court gave unprecedented support to the goal of equality under the law, but it did not strike down legal rules that treated women and men differently. In contrast, the more conservative Burger Court handed down a series of decisions promoting legal equality for men and women. The most fundamental cause of this change was the direct and indirect effect of the feminist movement on justices' views about women's social roles. Similarly, in 1972 the Burger Court summarily dismissed a challenge to the Minnesota prohibition of same-sex marriage. But in 2013 the more conservative Roberts Court struck down a statutory provision that prohibited recognition of same-sex marriages by the federal government, and two years later it directly overturned the 1972 decision by striking down state prohibitions of same-sex marriage.[70] That difference can be explained by the impact of the gay rights movement and associated changes in society on justices' attitudes.

Membership Change. In *Citizens United v. Federal Election Commission* (2010), the Supreme Court overruled two of its precedents that had allowed certain regulations of funding for political campaigns. In his dissenting opinion, Justice Stevens argued that "in the end, the Court's rejection of *Austin* and *McConnell* comes down to nothing more than its disagreement with their results. Virtually every one of its arguments was made and rejected in those cases, and the majority opinion is essentially an amalgamation of resuscitated dissents. The only relevant thing that has changed since *Austin* and *McConnell* is the composition of this Court."[71]

Whether or not Justice Stevens's criticism of the decision in *Citizens United* was justified, he was surely right about the reason why the Court rejected the two precedents. In doing so, he underlined the importance of membership change. If the Court's policies are largely a product of the justices' preferences, and if those preferences tend to be stable, then the most common source of significant policy change is the arrival of new justices on the Court.

As the *Citizens United* decision illustrates, a change in the Court's membership sometimes alters its positions on specific issues. The overturning of a recent precedent usually results from the replacement of justices who helped create that precedent with others who disagree with it. Even when the Court maintains a precedent, a shift in membership may result in a narrower interpretation of the precedent. Retired justice Sandra Day O'Connor has said that the law "shouldn't change just because the faces on the court have changed,"[72] but frequently it does. Indeed, as Justice Ginsburg pointed out, O'Connor's retirement and the resulting appointment of Samuel Alito in 2006 has shifted the Court's position on some issues.[73]

More broadly, shifts in the Court's overall ideological position through new appointments typically lead to change in the general content of its policies. The Court's civil liberties policies since the 1950s demonstrate this effect of membership change.

The early Warren Court was closely divided between liberals and conservatives on civil liberties issues. From 1958 until 1961 there was a relatively stable division between a four-member liberal bloc and a moderate-to-conservative bloc of five. By the standards of the 1920s and 1930s, the Court's decisions were quite liberal, but parties with civil liberties claims won only a little more than half their cases between 1958 and 1961.

President Kennedy's two 1962 appointments created a liberal majority, and the two Johnson appointments later in the decade maintained that majority. The 1962 through 1968 terms were probably the most liberal period in the Court's history. The Court established strikingly liberal positions in a variety of policy areas, and the proportion of pro–civil liberties decisions increased to the extraordinary level of 79 percent.[74]

Between 1969 and 1992 every appointment to the Court was made by a Republican president, and all but Ford sought to use their appointments to make the Court more conservative. Thus, the Court gained a distinctly more conservative set of justices. The proportion of pro–civil

Newly appointed Justice Samuel Alito shaking hands with President George W. Bush before Bush's State of the Union address in 2006. Bush's selection of Alito to succeed Justice Sandra Day O'Connor shifted the Court's ideological balance in a conservative direction.

liberties decisions fell below 45 percent in the 1970s, and it has remained at around that level ever since. If change in the content of cases over time is taken into account, it appears that the Court became increasingly conservative even after the 1970s.[75]

The appointments by Democratic and Republican presidents since 1993 have left the Court's ideological balance largely unchanged, except for the rightward movement resulting from the Alito appointment. As a result, the Court's civil liberties decisions have continued to tend in a conservative direction. That tendency underlines the ability of presidents to shape the Supreme Court through the selection of justices. The many decisions in which the Court has favored civil liberties claims since the 1970s result in part from the close balance between conservative and liberal justices that the Court has had throughout that period.

Role Values

Policy preferences are not the only values that can affect the Court's decisions. Justices may also act on their role values, their views about what constitutes appropriate behavior for the Supreme Court and its members. In any government body, whether it is a court or a legislature, members' conceptions of how they should carry out their jobs structure what they do.

A variety of role values can shape justices' behavior, including their views about the importance of consensus and about the legitimacy of "lobbying" colleagues on decisions. But the role values with the greatest potential impact are justices' beliefs about the considerations they should take into account in reaching their decisions and about the desirability of intervening in the making of public policy.

It is clear that multiple considerations affect justices' votes and opinions. The relative weight of these considerations depends in part on what justices think they ought to do. In particular, justices have to balance their strong policy preferences on many issues with the expectation of others (and themselves) that they will seek to interpret the law accurately.

Some evidence suggests that justices differ in the relative weights they give to these legal and policy considerations.[76] However, these differences are not as sharp as they sometimes appear. For example, at any given time, some justices vote more often than others to uproot some of the Court's precedents. To a degree, this difference reflects differing attitudes toward precedent. But more important are justices' attitudes toward the policies embodied in particular precedents, attitudes that tend to fall along ideological lines.

Intervention in policymaking, beyond what is inevitable for the Court, is often viewed negatively. Justices who seem eager to engage in that intervention are criticized as "activists," and those who seem less prone to do so are praised as "restrained." But activism, like the treatment of precedent, does not seem to differ much among justices.

The most visible form of active intervention in policymaking is striking down federal statutes. The historical patterns are illuminating. During the 1920s and early 1930s, the laws that the Court struck down were primarily government regulations of business practices. Conservative justices were the most willing to strike down such laws, and liberals on the Court and elsewhere argued for judicial restraint. In contrast, in the 1960s and 1970s, the Court struck down primarily laws that conflicted with civil liberties. Liberals were most likely to act against these laws and conservatives to call for judicial restraint.

Since the 1980s the Court has overturned a wide variety of federal laws. No justice has stood out for a willingness or unwillingness to strike down laws. Rather, as in past eras, justices have responded to the ideological content of the statutes in question. The same is true of the decisions in which the Court strikes down state laws on constitutional grounds.[77] In this respect the justices' decisions on whether to declare laws unconstitutional are similar to their decisions on whether to overrule precedents.

All this is not to say that justices' role values have no impact on their behavior. Undoubtedly, such values help to structure the ways in which justices perceive their jobs. But justices' conceptions of good public policy have a more fundamental impact on their choices.

Group Interaction

In discussing legal and policy considerations in decision making, I have focused primarily on justices as individuals. But when justices make choices, they do so as part of a Court that makes collective decisions and as part of American government and society. Justices who seek to make good policy might act strategically by taking their colleagues and other institutions into account when they cast votes and write or join opinions. Whether or not justices act strategically, they can be influenced in a variety of ways by other justices and by their political and social environment. This section examines the justices as a group, and the next section considers the Court's environment.

A Somewhat Collegial Body

Descriptions of the Supreme Court as a collective body offer two competing depictions of the Court. In one depiction, the justices work together closely to reach decisions, and their positions in cases frequently shift as arguments made by some justices change colleagues' minds and as they negotiate over the language of opinions. This depiction is fostered by historical accounts of major decisions such as *Brown v. Board of Education* (1954).[78] In the other depiction, the justices mostly act alone, reaching judgments about cases and adhering to those judgments regardless of what their colleagues think and say. The reality lies somewhere between these two depictions. There are significant limitations on the influence of justices over each other, but there are also strong bases for influence.

The most fundamental limitation on influence among the justices is their strongly held views on many issues of law and policy. When they apply their general positions on an issue to a specific case, the resulting judgment about that case is often too firm for colleagues to sway. As William Rehnquist wrote, when justices who have prepared themselves "assemble around the conference table on Friday morning to decide an important case presenting constitutional questions that they have all debated and written about before, the outcome may be a foregone conclusion."[79]

Balanced against that powerful limitation are two powerful incentives for justices to try to influence their colleagues and to accept influence from them. Both of these incentives have important strategic elements.

One incentive is institutional: Justices want to achieve opinions that at least five members endorse so that the Court can lay down authoritative legal rules. And to give more weight to the Court's decisions, they generally would like to reach greater consensus. Justices may operate on this incentive simply because they think that legal clarity is good in itself, but the desire to maximize the impact of the legal policies they favor also plays a part.

A second incentive is more personal: justices' interest in winning majority support for their positions. Justices want the Court to adopt the legal rules they prefer, and most justices get satisfaction from being on the winning side. Thus, they have good reason to engage in efforts at persuasion. They also have reason to be flexible in the positions they take in cases, because flexibility can help them win colleagues' support for rules that are close to the ones they prefer.

The extent to which justices seek and accept influence varies among cases. Justice Kagan has contrasted cases in which justices "just see the law differently" with those "where you can persuade each other."[80] On the whole, justices are more open to influence in cases that involve issues on which they lack strong feelings. On the other hand, they may make greater efforts at persuasion in cases they care most about, and more negotiation and compromise may be necessary in those cases to achieve a majority opinion.

The tentative votes that the justices cast on case outcomes usually become their final votes. In the Burger Court, only 7.5 percent of the justices' individual votes to reverse or affirm switched from one side to the other. On the other hand, at least one switch occurred in 37 percent of the cases. Most vote switches increase the size of the majority, as the Court works toward consensus. During the Burger Court, the justices who initially voted with the majority switched their votes 5 percent of the time, but those who initially voted with the minority switched 18 percent of the time.[81] Occasionally, however, shifts of position turn an initial minority into a majority. This occurred in about 7 percent of the cases decided by the Burger Court.[82]

Even if the justices adhere to their original votes, the content of the Court's opinion may change.[83] The most common course of events in a case is for a justice to write a draft opinion for the Court and then gain the support of a majority for that opinion with no difficulty. But other justices who voted on the majority side in conference frequently ask for changes in the draft opinion, and most of the time justices who make these requests indicate that they cannot join the opinion unless the changes are made. A study of Justice Harry Blackmun's draft opinions showed that he almost always made the requested changes. Because of this responsiveness, the colleagues who requested changes in the original draft usually joined Blackmun's final opinion; they wrote concurring opinions in only about 20 percent of those cases. Not surprisingly, however, Blackmun became much less willing to accommodate colleagues when he had already secured majority support for his opinion.[84]

Whether or not colleagues request changes in opinions for the Court, those opinions frequently are revised during the decision process. In the Burger Court, in slightly more than half of all cases the author of the

Court's opinion circulated at least three drafts of the opinion.[85] Although successive drafts usually differ only on minor matters, they sometimes proclaim quite different legal rules. Moreover, the first draft of a majority opinion often reflects the writer's efforts to take into account the views that colleagues expressed in conference, so those colleagues influence the opinion even if they fully accept that first draft.

Patterns of Influence

To the extent that justices actually influence their colleagues' choices, inevitably some are more influential than others. In general, the primary requisites for influence are the same as in any other group: an interest in exerting influence and skill in doing so.

What we know now about justices who served in past eras underlines the importance of both these considerations. For instance, Justice William O. Douglas, who served for a record thirty-six years between 1939 and 1975, had relatively little influence with other justices because he made only limited efforts to achieve it. Douglas's longtime colleague Felix Frankfurter actively sought influence over his colleagues, and his eminence as a legal scholar should have put him in a good position to persuade his colleagues to support his positions. But Frankfurter's weak interpersonal skills—especially his inability to hide his lack of respect for colleagues—worked against him. William Brennan, who served from 1956 to 1990, shared Frankfurter's strong interest in exerting influence, but he was far more skilled in working with colleagues. This skill helped Brennan in his efforts to forge a liberal majority for the expansion of civil liberties in the Warren Court and to limit the Court's conservative shift in the Burger Court.

It is more difficult to assess the influence of justices who are currently sitting on the Court, but some assessments have been offered. In a 2014 biography of Sonia Sotomayor, Joan Biskupic contrasted her with Elena Kagan: "Kagan's pattern on the bench and in opinions indicates that she sees herself operating strategically as one of nine justices. Sotomayor, in contrast, is more of a solo operator, engrossed in her own determinations on a case, less interested and adept at getting others to adopt them."[86] But Biskupic also reported that Sotomayor's strong draft dissent in a 2013 affirmative action case triggered a partial retreat by the majority and a final opinion for the Court that Sotomayor was able to join.[87]

Antonin Scalia's influence has been a matter of interest. Some observers of the Court think that Scalia's frequent strong criticism of colleagues in his opinions has alienated some of them and thus weakened his capacity for persuasion. According to one account, Chief Justice Rehnquist responded to a Scalia opinion attacking Sandra Day O'Connor by calling him to say that he was annoying O'Connor "again. Stop it!"[88] But Scalia himself dismissed the possibility that the tone of his opinions ever "cost me a majority,"[89] and it is clear that he has shaped other justices' approach to matters such as methods for interpretation of statutes.

Another source of influence is a justice's position on the ideological spectrum. The vote of a "swing" justice at the ideological center of the Court often will determine which side wins in cases that closely divide the Court along ideological lines. In itself, this does not mean that the swing justice is influential, because every justice in a 5–4 majority contributes to that result with one vote. Swing justices do have a degree of extra influence, however, because their positions are seen as relatively unpredictable and their support as crucial to the outcome of some cases. Lawyers work to devise arguments that appeal to the swing justice, and colleagues also work hard to win the support of that justice.

Since 2006 Anthony Kennedy has clearly been the swing justice, because four justices are well to his ideological left and the other four are to his right. On a series of major decisions on issues such as abortion and the death penalty, he has created liberal or conservative majorities with his vote. Justice Kagan joked in 2014 that "there are four of us who think one thing. There are four of us who think another thing, and then we wait and see what Justice Kennedy does."[90] As a result, lawyers and colleagues show considerable deference to him. One observer of the Court suggested in 2009 that "two blocs of four justices seem to spend much of their energy competing for the affections of the one in the middle"—Justice Kennedy.[91]

Even so, it exaggerates the influence of Kennedy or any other swing justice to say, as one headline did, that "This Is Kennedy's Court—the Rest of the Justices Just Sit on It."[92] Nor can any other justice dominate the Court. To the extent that the justices do influence each other, every justice has considerable influence as one out of only nine members of the Court.

The Chief Justice

Compared with other justices, the chief justice has both advantages and disadvantages in achieving influence over colleagues. The disadvantage is the chief's administrative duties, which reduce the time that the chief can spend on cases. The primary advantage is a set of formal powers. The chief presides over the Court in oral argument and in conference. In conference the chief speaks first on cases, and by doing so the chief can direct discussion and frame alternatives. Aided by clerks, the chief makes up the initial version of the discuss list from the petitions for certiorari. This task gives the chief the largest role in determining which cases are set aside without group discussion. Another power, over opinion assignment, merits more extensive consideration.

Opinion Assignment. The chief justice is usually in the majority in conference votes on decisions and thus assigns the Court's opinion in the preponderance of cases. In making assignments, chiefs balance different considerations.[93]

Administrative considerations relate to spreading the workload and opportunities among the justices. Chief justices generally try to make sure that each colleague gets about the same number of opinions for the Court. As a result, each justice typically gets at least one case from each of the Court's two-week sittings. And as Chief Justice Roberts put it, "You want to make sure everyone has their fair share of interesting cases and has their fair share of what we call the dogs, the uninteresting cases."[94] Chiefs may also take into account the workload of opinion writing that a justice already faces at a given time.

Other considerations relate to the substance of the Court's decisions. Because opinion writers have to take their colleagues into account, scholars disagree about how much difference it makes which justice is assigned the Court's opinion. But justices perceive that the opinion writer has disproportionate influence over what the Court says, so that opinion assignment is consequential. As a result, chief justices tend to favor themselves and colleagues who are close to them ideologically when assigning opinions in the cases they care most about. Not surprisingly, Chief Justice Roberts assigns the Court's opinion to himself at a high rate in the most important cases.[95]

The chief might also act to help the conference majority remain a majority. When there is a close vote at conference, the chief often assigns the opinion to a relatively moderate member of that majority. One reason is that a moderate may be in a good position to write an opinion that will maintain the majority and perhaps win over justices who were initially on the other side. Justice Ginsburg has pointed out a second, practical reason for assigning an opinion to the justice who is wavering the most in a 5–4 vote: if that justice shifts to the other side, he or she will remain in the majority and can still write the Court's opinion.[96]

Because chief justices favor ideological allies in assigning important opinions, in effect they reward the justices who vote with them the most often. They might also use the assignment power more directly to reward and punish colleagues. Chief Justice Roberts said in 2006 that "you can always give all the tax opinions to a justice, if you want to punish them."[97] Roberts added that he had not yet taken that kind of action. But according to Justice Blackmun, Chief Justice Burger might assign one of the "crud" opinions "that nobody wants to write" to a justice who was "in the doghouse" with Burger.[98]

The associate justice who assigns the Court's opinion when the chief is in the minority is under fewer constraints. Justice Stevens confessed that when assigning cases as senior associate justice, he sometimes gave himself an interesting case to keep the chief justice from assigning him a case from the same sitting that he wanted to avoid.[99] As the most senior justice among the Court's liberals since 2010, Justice Ginsburg assigns many dissenting opinions. She has acknowledged that she probably takes "more than a fair share of the dissenting opinions in the most-watched cases."[100]

Variation in Influence. Chief justices have differed considerably in their influence over the Court. These differences reflect the chief's interest in leading the Court, the chief's skill as a leader, and the willingness of the associate justices to be led.

Warren Burger sought to be a strong leader. He had some success in securing administrative changes in the federal courts and procedural changes in the Court itself. But he was not especially influential in the decision-making process.

Burger's limited impact on the Court's decisions stemmed largely from his own qualities and predilections. Colleagues chafed at what they considered a poor style of leadership in conference, and they disliked Burger's occasional practice of casting "false" votes so that he could assign the Court's opinion.[101] He was also accused of bullying his colleagues. One scholar concluded that Potter Stewart "loathed" Burger,[102] and other colleagues also disliked his leadership style. But Burger also faced obstacles that were beyond his control. Perhaps most important, as a fairly strong conservative he had the disadvantage of standing near one end of the Court's ideological spectrum.

William Rehnquist became chief justice in 1986 after serving on the Court for fifteen years. He brought important strengths to the position, especially his well-respected intellectual abilities and a pleasant manner of interaction with people. Having served in the Burger Court as an associate justice, Rehnquist learned—in one observer's words—"how *not* to be Chief Justice."[103] In any event, Rehnquist was an effective chief justice, and his leadership was widely praised even by justices who did not share his conservative views on most judicial issues.[104] Reflecting his preferences, the Court's discussions of cases at conference were shorter and tighter than they had been in the recent past. Rehnquist's leadership was one source of the sharp decline in the number of cases accepted by the Court. In decision making he enhanced his influence by taking strong positions with an affable style.

Both colleagues and observers of the Court have attested to John Roberts's strengths as leader of the Court. "With regard to all of his special responsibilities" as chief justice, Justice Stevens said, "John Roberts is an excellent chief justice."[105]

As a participant in the Court's decision making, Roberts has proved to be a skillful strategist. He has sought to move the Court's policies to the right through gradual steps; as one legal scholar said, "The chief justice is

Chief Justice John Roberts with four of his colleagues at President Obama's inauguration in 2013. (From front to back, the colleagues are Anthony Kennedy, Clarence Thomas, Sonia Sotomayor, and Antonin Scalia.) Since his appointment in 2005, Roberts has proved to be a skillful leader of the Court.

a patient man playing a long game."[106] For instance, in a 2009 case he wrote a compromise majority opinion that avoided deciding the controversial issue of whether one provision of the federal Voting Rights Act was unconstitutional. Four years later he wrote the Court's opinion in another case, this time holding that provision unconstitutional. His 2013 opinion used language that he had included in the 2009 opinion as a major basis for the Court's new ruling. The 2013 opinion chided the Court's liberal dissenters in the case for not accepting the implications of that language, especially since two of the dissenters had signed onto his 2009 opinion.[107]

Roberts also seems to be sensitive to the Court's standing. In *National Federation of Independent Business v. Sebelius* (2012), the Court seemed likely to strike down a key provision of the federal health care act sponsored by President Obama, the mandate that some individuals purchase health insurance. But Roberts, writing the decisive opinion in the case, unexpectedly held that this provision was within the taxing power of Congress and thus was valid. By joining the Court's four Democratic appointees in upholding the individual mandate, he avoided the charge that the Court was overturning a major law on a party-line vote and thereby protected the Court from becoming a campaign issue in that year's presidential election.[108]

Thus, Roberts appears to be establishing a strong role as justice and chief justice. His long-term success will depend not only on his skills but also on whether the Court retains a conservative majority that facilitates his leadership in the decision-making process.

Harmony and Conflict

A faithful reader of the justices' opinions might well conclude that they are a highly contentious group. A 2014 opinion charged that a justice's colleagues held a view that was "out of touch with reality," and a 2013 opinion dismissed the majority opinion as "legalistic argle-bargle." According to another 2013 opinion, the Court's decision was based on a supposed rule of law "that is nowhere to be found in the annals of Anglo-American jurisprudence." And a 2014 opinion concluded that the majority opinion "takes the tack of throwing everything against the wall in the hope that something might stick. A vain hope, as it turns out."[109]

Beyond sharply written opinions, some observers of the Court have perceived personal frictions among the justices. After Chief Justice Roberts voted to uphold the individual mandate in the health care law of 2010, for instance, one reporter spoke of deep bitterness toward Roberts from the other conservative justices.[110]

According to the justices themselves, however, any perceptions of discord are mistaken. "Sometimes you read these opinions," said Justice Kagan, "and you think 'they must hate each other.' It's just not true."[111] Justice Breyer reported in 2013 that "I have never heard a voice raised in anger" at the Court's conferences, "and I have never heard someone say something mean about somebody else, not even as a joke."[112] Justices sometimes refer to their good working relationships with each other, and Justice Scalia has said that "everybody I've served with on the Court I've regarded as a friend."[113]

It is very difficult to determine the actual state of relations among the justices from outside the Court, but it seems likely that these relations involve a mix of harmony and conflict. Justices have a strong incentive to maintain good relations with each other, because harmony makes the Court a more pleasant place to work and facilitates the process of reaching decisions. Still, all the sources of strife that exist in other groups can operate in the Court as well. The justices care a great deal about many of the issues they address in their decisions—issues on which they often have sharp disagreements—and they sometimes work under considerable pressure. As one justice described it, "The term always starts friendly and relaxed, and gets tense at the end when the most difficult cases pile up. It's still collegial, but there is an overlay of frustration."[114]

One thing seems clear: the current Court is more harmonious than several past Courts, in which some pairs of justices were actually unable to work with each other. The absence of such deep conflicts undoubtedly improves the functioning of the Court.

The Court's Environment

When the Supreme Court hears a case on a controversial issue, people who care about the issue often try to influence the Court's decision.

Beyond submitting amicus briefs, interest groups sometimes hold rallies and demonstrations to show support for their positions. Commentators write articles and op-eds to argue for one side or the other. Members of Congress often weigh in on the issue, and sometimes the president does so as well.

In the view of Justice Thomas, none of this activity makes any difference. Speaking about the challenges to the Obama health care program that the Court heard in 2012, Thomas likened the efforts to influence the Court's decision from outside the legal process to basketball fans who try to distract free throw shooters. "Why do you think they're never distracted? They're focusing on the rim, right? That's the same thing here. You stay focused on what you're supposed to do. All that other stuff is just noise."[115]

There is considerable basis for Justice Thomas's conclusion. In comparison with Congress and the president, the Supreme Court is more isolated from the world around it and more insulated from the influence of that world. The isolation is reflected in the relatively limited contact between the justices and other participants in politics, such as members of Congress and representatives of interest groups. The primary source of insulation is the justices' life terms; no matter whom they displease, they can be removed from office only through impeachment proceedings, a quite unlikely prospect.

But this does not necessarily mean that the Court's environment has no effect on the justices. Certainly they are aware of events and developments in American society and in the political world. They might take their environment into account for strategic reasons, acting to avoid negative responses to their decisions that would endanger the policies they favor or even damage the Court itself. Strategic considerations aside, justices might simply like to be viewed positively by people outside the Court. For both reasons, the Court's environment could affect the justices' choices as decision makers.

Mass Public Opinion

Supreme Court justices would seem to be especially immune from influence by the general public. The public has no direct power over the Court, and the great majority of the Court's decisions are essentially invisible to the public. Yet some observers of the Court have argued that the justices pay attention to public opinion. As these observers see it, the justices listen to the public primarily because public support strengthens the Court's ability to secure acceptance of its decisions from public officials who are responsible for carrying out those decisions and who can limit or overturn them.

It is not clear that justices need to worry about maintaining public support. The Court is viewed more positively by the public than are the other branches of government, and even highly unpopular decisions have little long-term effect on public support for the Court as an institution. Yet justices themselves sometimes refer to the Court's need to act in ways that maintain its legitimacy with the general public, and they may perceive that the Court's public standing is more fragile than it actually is. Surveys that show declining public support for the Court in recent years probably reflect a general unhappiness with government more than disapproval of the Court itself, but those surveys might still make the justices nervous. One observer of the Court reported in 2012 that "the current court is almost fanatically worried about its legitimacy and declining public confidence in the institution."[116] Further, justices might simply feel more comfortable when the Court's decisions and their own positions in cases garner approval from the general public.

If the justices do take public opinion into account when they decide cases, one effect might be to draw them to support the majority view among the public on issues that many people know and care about. Some observers argue that the justices collectively do fall in step with public opinion on major issues. "Time and time again," one legal scholar has said, the Court's decisions "plainly reflect the tug of public views."[117] Yet the Court sometimes makes highly unpopular decisions, even when reactions to earlier decisions have made it clear that a decision will arouse strong disapproval. That has been the case, for instance, with its rulings on flag burning and religious observances in public schools. It is very difficult to determine whether a concern with public opinion has deterred the Court from making such unpopular decisions even more often.

Another possible effect of concern with public opinion is more subtle but also more pervasive. It might be that as the general public moves left or right on an ideological scale, the Court moves along with it to avoid straying too far from public opinion in its decisions as a whole. Indeed, some studies have found a tendency for the Court and the public to move in the same ideological direction over time. But even if that tendency exists, it is uncertain whether the justices are being pulled along by the public or whether the justices and the public are responding in the same way to developments in government and society.[118]

The same is true of the justices' decisions in particular areas of public policy. To a degree, the Court's decisions over the past half century on measures to control illegal drugs, the legal status of women, and government policies related to sexual orientation have tracked public opinion on those issues. It might be that the justices have sought to align themselves with changing public views, and changes in those views might enable the justices to take positions that had seemed untenable in the past. Perhaps, for instance, the five justices who voted to overturn the federal Defense of Marriage Act (DOMA) in 2013 felt freer to take that step because the long streak of election results opposing same-sex marriage in votes on initiatives and referenda had been decisively broken in November 2012.[119] But in such situations the justices might be acting primarily on their own views—views shaped by the same forces that affect public opinion.

Justices' interest in maintaining public support for the Court might manifest itself in other ways. Perhaps they seek to minimize the number of laws they strike down in order to avoid the appearance of judicial activism. In the current era some justices might try to dispel the idea that they respond to certain cases on a partisan basis. Such effects of public opinion are likely to operate only at the margins. On the whole justices seem largely independent of the public, and certainly they have much greater independence than do elected officials.

Elite Opinion: Friends and Acquaintances, the Legal Community, and the News Media

Whether or not justices respond to the general public, they can be influenced by more specific sets of relevant people. One set is the justices' personal friends and acquaintances. We would expect justices, like other people, to pay attention to the views of those who are most important to them. If the people who are close to a justice share a strong point of view about certain issues that come before the Court, they may exert a subtle influence on the justice to take positions consistent with that point of view.

The legal community is important as a professional reference group. Justices draw many of their acquaintances from that community. Most justices interact a good deal with practicing lawyers, law professors, and lower-court judges, and most of the justices' public appearances are before legal groups. Lawyers are also the primary source of expert evaluations of the Court, often presented in the law reviews that law schools publish and in legal blogs that have attracted more attention in recent years. The same publications are sources of ideas and arguments about legal issues that the justices address. At least some of the justices pay attention to them. Justice Kagan, for instance, reported that there are three legal blogs that she reads every day.[120]

Scrutiny by the legal community helps to make legal considerations important to the justices in reaching decisions. And the arguments of legal scholars on issues may influence the justices' thinking. There is some evidence that these arguments helped to shape the positions that justices took in the Court's 2012 decision on the federal health care law of 2010.[121]

The news media may also be important to the justices. The media are the public's primary source of information about the Court, so they can shape public attitudes toward the justices. And whether or not the news media influence public views of the Court, justices understandably prefer to be depicted positively in news reports. For these reasons, many justices pay attention to coverage of the Court.

Most of the people in the justices' personal circles, the legal community, and the news media are from elite groups in American society. To the extent that these elites have a distinctive point of view, they may move justices toward that point of view. Indeed, some conservative commentators have argued that several justices who were appointed to the Court by Republican presidents between 1970 and 1990 adopted more liberal positions over time because of their desire to win praise from elite groups that leaned to the left, including legal scholars and reporters who wrote about the Court.[122]

It is uncertain whether this possible influence on justices to move to the left actually operated, but in any event the elite world has changed. In the past few decades political polarization has created distinct elite groups on the left and right, including legal scholars and news outlets. Even more than in the past, justices can seek approval from groups that share their point of view. It may be, then, that conservative and liberal justices today respond largely to different subsets of the political and social elites in the United States. Whatever their effects may be, these elites almost surely have greater influence on the justices than does the public as a whole.[123]

Litigants and Interest Groups

Simply by bringing cases to the Supreme Court, litigants, interest groups, and the lawyers who represent them influence the Court's policies. Once the Court has accepted a case, litigants and interest groups may influence its decision on the merits through advocacy in briefs, including amicus briefs, and oral arguments.

Certainly, justices and their law clerks pay attention to the material presented by the participants in cases. That attention is reflected in the Court's opinions, which frequently use language in the parties' briefs and cite material in amicus briefs.[124] Indeed, justices sometimes accept and use questionable assertions of fact from amicus briefs.[125] When justices question lawyers closely during oral argument, they are often looking for responses to strong arguments by the other side.

Justices may react to the identities of the litigants in a case, and this possibility is reflected in the efforts by interest groups that sponsor cases to find litigants who might be viewed sympathetically by the justices. The identities of the groups that submit amicus briefs may also influence the justices. In *Young v. United Parcel Service* (2015), the amici supporting an employee's case under the federal Pregnancy Discrimination Act came from both sides of the ideological spectrum, and the brief for several pro-life groups undoubtedly was intended to appeal to conservative justices who were not generally inclined to favor employees' claims against businesses. The employee did win the votes of Chief Justice Roberts and Justice Alito and thereby gained a 6–3 victory, but it is impossible to know whether that amicus brief made a difference.

The federal government is probably in the best position to benefit from justices' favorable perceptions. The government enjoys a high rate of success as a party and amicus in the Court's decisions on the merits. One source of the government's success is the expertise of the advocates in the solicitor general's office. But the justices' sympathies for the government's interests and its respect for the solicitor general's professionalism also play a part.[126]

Thus, the identities of the participants in cases may influence the Court, and the arguments they make certainly have an effect. But neither influence is as strong as justices' preexisting attitudes toward the issues they address. Whatever influence the federal government has over the Court, the government wins the justices' support far more often when its arguments accord with their ideological positions than when the two conflict.[127]

Congress and the President

Other government bodies take actions that affect the Court and the impact of its policies. Because of this effect, justices may take those policymakers into account when they reach decisions. The president and Congress are especially important to the Court, so they have the greatest potential influence on the Court's decisions.

Congress. Congressional powers over the Court range from overriding the Court's interpretations of statutes to controlling salary increases for the justices. Because of this array of powers, justices have some reason to consider congressional reactions to their decisions. Relations with Congress can affect their prestige and their comfort. And justices who think strategically in a broad sense, who care about the impact of the Court's policies, want to avoid congressional actions that undercut those policies.

If justices do act strategically toward Congress, one potential form of strategy involves decisions that interpret federal statutes. These decisions are more vulnerable than the Court's interpretations of the Constitution because Congress and the president can override them simply by enacting a new statute. Indeed, Congress considers such overrides quite frequently, and it enacts them into law fairly often.

For this reason, justices might try to calculate whether their preferred interpretation of a statute would be sufficiently unpopular in Congress to produce an override. If so, justices would modify their interpretation to make it more acceptable to members of Congress and thereby avoid an override. By making this implicit compromise with Congress, the justices could get the best possible result under the circumstances—not the interpretation of a statute that they favor the most but one that is closer to their preferences than the new statute that Congress would enact to override the Court's decision. It may be, however, that most justices are not bothered much when Congress overrides their decisions. And justices might find it so difficult to predict overrides that little can be gained by trying to make those predictions.

It is not yet clear how often justices pursue this strategic approach. One possibility is that they do so selectively, when they perceive that a decision disfavored by Congress is a very good candidate for an override. If so, to take one example, justices might avoid handing down highly conservative statutory decisions on issues such as civil rights when the president is a Democrat and both houses of Congress have solid Democratic majorities. By the same token, when party control of Congress and the presidency is divided, as it has been between 2011 and 2016, justices might feel great freedom to interpret statutes as they wish on issues on which the parties differ.

When Court decisions interpret the Constitution rather than statutes, those decisions are considerably more difficult to overturn directly. But constitutional decisions also have the potential to arouse strong negative reactions from Congress when the Court overturns major government policies. Justices may have reason to avoid arousing such reactions or to reduce conflict with Congress when it arises.

In some historical periods, justices seem to have taken this approach. The first such period was the early nineteenth century, when Chief Justice John Marshall's Court faced congressional attacks because of its policies. As the Court's dominant member, Marshall was careful to limit the frequency of decisions that would further anger the Court's opponents. In the late 1930s the Court's shift from opposition to support of New Deal legislation may have reflected an effort by one or two justices to end a serious confrontation with the other branches. In the late 1950s members of Congress reacted to the Court's expansions of civil liberties by trying to override some of its policies and limit its jurisdiction. A few justices then shifted their positions on some contentious issues. As a result, the Court reversed some of its collective positions and thereby helped to quiet congressional attacks on the Court.

The period from the 1960s to the present has featured strong criticism of the Court by members of Congress in response to decisions on a variety of civil liberties issues, including school desegregation, legislative districting, abortion, school prayer, and flag burning. On each of these issues, members have introduced bills to overturn the Court's decisions, to limit its jurisdiction over the issue, or both. There have also been proposals to attack the Court more broadly, such as constitutional amendments that would limit the justices' tenure to a set number of years.

There have been no clear signs of retreat by the Court in the face of these actions, and the Court has maintained many of the policies that aroused congressional criticism. Yet it may be that such criticism and even the ideological composition of Congress have a more subtle effect on the justices' inclination to strike down statutes.[128] Such an effect might help to explain the relatively small numbers of federal statutes that the Court has declared unconstitutional over its history.

The President. Presidents have multifaceted relationships with the Supreme Court, and these relationships provide several sources of potential influence. Two of these sources, discussed already, are the power to appoint justices and the government's frequent participation in Supreme Court litigation. The appointment power gives presidents considerable ability to determine the Court's direction. The president helps to shape the federal government's litigation policy and thereby influences the Court's decisions through appointment of the solicitor general and occasional intervention in specific cases.

Justices might be inclined to favor the interests of the president who appointed them in cases that the president cares about, though this inclination probably would not be conscious. A justice who is a close acquaintance of the president might have a similar inclination, but such acquaintanceship has become much less common than it once was. Nor is such acquaintanceship likely to have a substantial impact on a justice. President Obama has expressed his strong admiration for Justice Ginsburg. For her part, Ginsburg displays in her chambers both a picture of her with Obama and a gift from him, a framed copy of the statute that Congress enacted in 2009 after her dissent from a 2007 decision advocated such a statute to override the decision.[129] It seems unlikely, however, that this mutual admiration exerts much effect on Ginsburg's choices as a decision maker.

Presidents influence responses to the Court's decisions by Congress and the federal bureaucracy. They can also shape the public's view of the Court and its decisions. For those reasons, justices may have an incentive to keep the peace with the president. On rare occasions, presidents try to take advantage of their influence by speaking about pending cases in an effort to influence their outcome. While the Court was considering the constitutional challenges to his health care law in 2012, President Obama expressed his strong view that the Court should uphold the law, an expression that opponents of the law depicted as pressuring the justices.[130] Whether Obama's statements had any effect on Chief Justice Roberts's unexpected vote to uphold the key provision in the health care law is impossible to ascertain. In this instance and most others, however, it seems clear that direct presidential influence on the Court is no more than marginal.

Conclusion

Of all the considerations that influence the Supreme Court's decisions, the justices' policy preferences appear to be the most important. The application of the law to the Court's cases is usually ambiguous, and constraints from the Court's environment are generally weak. As a result, justices have considerable freedom to take positions that accord with their own conceptions of good policy. For this reason, the Court's membership has the greatest impact on the Court's direction.

If justices' preferences explain a great deal, they do not explain everything. The law and the political environment rule out some possible options for the Court, and they influence the justices' choices among the options that remain. The group life of the Court affects the choices of individual justices and the Court's collective decisions. In particular, justices frequently adjust their positions in cases to win support from colleagues and help build majorities. Factors other than policy preferences are reflected in results that might seem surprising—strikingly liberal decisions from conservative Courts and the maintenance of precedents even when most justices no longer favor the policies they embody.

Thus, what the Court does is a product of multiple and intertwined forces. These forces operate together in complicated ways to shape the Court's decisions. Efforts to understand why the Court does what it does must take into account the complexity of the process by which the justices make their choices.

NOTES

1. *United States v. Clarke*, 189 L. Ed. 2d 330, 338 (2014).
2. The cases were *Florida v. Department of Health and Human Services* (2012); *U.S. Department of Health and Human Services v. Florida* (2012); and *National Federation of Independent Business v. Sebelius* (2012).
3. Jeffrey Rosen, "RBG Presides," *New Republic*, October 13, 2014, 21.
4. *Hosanna-Tabor Evangelical Lutheran Church v. Equal Employment Opportunity Commission*, 10-553, Transcript of oral argument, October 5, 2011, 45.
5. Brian Lamb, Susan Swain, and Mark Farkas, eds., *The Supreme Court: A C-Span Book Featuring the Justices in Their Own Words* (New York: PublicAffairs, 2010), 157.
6. Adam Liptak, "A Most Inquisitive Court? No Argument There," *New York Times*, October 6, 2013, A14.
7. "Oral Argument" (2011–2013 Terms), SCOTUSblog Stat Pack Archive, http://www.scotusblog.com/reference/stat-pack.
8. Adam Liptak, "Breaking the Silence," *New York Times*, January 15, 2013, A14.
9. Kaitlynn Riely, "A Supreme Presence in Pittsburgh," *Pittsburgh Post-Gazette*, April 10, 2013, A-1.
10. Timothy R. Johnson, Ryan C. Black, Jerry Goldman, and Sarah A. Treul, "Inquiring Minds Want to Know: Do Justices Tip Their Hands with Questions at Oral Argument in the U.S. Supreme Court?" *Washington University Journal*

of Law & Policy 29 (2009): 241–261; Ryan C. Black, Sarah A. Treul, Timothy R. Johnson, and Jerry Goldman, "Emotions, Oral Arguments, and Supreme Court Decision Making," *Journal of Politics* 73 (April 2011): 572–581.

11. *Chafin v. Chafin*, 11-347, Transcript of oral argument, December 5, 2012, 6–12.

12. *Trevino v. Thaler*, 11-10189, Transcript of oral argument, February 25, 2013, 43.

13. Lamb, Swain, and Farkas, *The Supreme Court*, 61, 132.

14. Garrett Epps, "Justice Scalia Turns to 18th-Century Wisdom for Guidance on GPS," *Atlantic*, January 24, 2012, http://www.theatlantic.com/technology/archive/2012/01/justice-scalia-turns-to-18th-century-wisdom-for-guidance-on-gps/251883.

15. Joe Duggan, "Chief Justice Says Law, Not Politics, Drives Supreme Court's Rulings," *Omaha World-Herald*, September 19, 2014.

16. Lamb, Swain, and Farkas, *The Supreme Court*, 63.

17. Melissa Harris, "Justice Elena Kagan Gives an Inside Look at the U.S. Supreme Court," *Chicago Tribune*, February 3, 2015, http://www.chicagotribune.com/business/ct-confidential-elena-kagan-0204-biz-20150203-column.html.

18. The process of responding to draft majority opinions is described in Forrest Maltzman, James F. Spriggs II, and Paul J. Wahlbeck, *Crafting Law on the Supreme Court: The Collegial Game* (New York: Cambridge University Press, 2000), 62–72.

19. Kevin Merida and Michael A. Fletcher, "Thomas v. Blackmun: Late Jurist's Papers Puncture Colleague's Portrait of a Genteel Court," *Washington Post*, October 10, 2004, A15.

20. Clare Cushman, *Courtwatchers: Eyewitness Accounts in Supreme Court History* (Lanham, Md.: Rowman & Littlefield, 2011), 198–199.

21. Matthew Walther, "Sam Alito: A Civil Man," *The American Spectator* 47 (May 2014): 30.

22. *McQuiggen v. Perkins*, 185 L. Ed. 2d 1019, 1039-40 (2013).

23. Richard L. Hasen, "The Most Sarcastic Justice," *The Green Bag* 18 (Winter 2015): 215–227.

24. *American Express Company v. Italian Colors Restaurant*, 186 L. Ed. 2d 417, 436 (2013). See Laura Krugman Ray, "Doctrinal Conversation: Justice Kagan's Supreme Court Opinions," *Indiana Law Journal Supplement* 89 (2012): 1–11.

25. Ross Guberman, "The Supreme Writer on the Court: The Case for Roberts," The Volokh Conspiracy blog, July 8, 2013, http://volokh.com/2013/07/08/the-supreme-writer-on-the-court-the-case-for-roberts.

26. Ryan J. Owens and Justin P. Wedeking, "Justices and Legal Clarity: Analyzing the Complexity of U.S. Supreme Court Opinions," *Law & Society Review* 45 (2011): 1027–1061.

27. Allison Orr Larsen, "Confronting Supreme Court Fact Finding," *Virginia Law Review* 98 (October 2012): 1255–1312.

28. Stephen Wermiel, "Dissenting from the Bench," SCOTUSblog, July 2, 2013, http://www.scotusblog.com/2013/07/scotus-for-law-students-sponsored-by-bloomberg-law-dissenting-from-the-bench.

29. Greg Moran, "No Retirement Plans for Justice Ginsburg," *San Diego Union Tribune*, February 8, 2013, http://www.utsandiego.com/news/2013/feb/08/justice-ginsburg-retirement-san-diego.

30. Kedar Bhatia, *Final Stat Pack for October Term 2013 and Key Takeaways*, SCOTUSblog, June 30, 2014, pp. 30–31, http://www.scotusblog.com/2014/06/final-stat-pack-for-october-term-2013-and-key-takeaways-2.

31. Amy Howe, "A Rare Call for a Rehearing Response," SCOTUSblog, July 22, 2014, http://www.scotusblog.com/2014/07/a-rare-call-for-a-rehearing-response.
32. Richard J. Lazarus, "The (Non)Finality of Supreme Court Opinions," *Harvard Law Review* 128 (December 2014): 604–606. The case was *Environmental Protection Agency v. EME Homer City Generation* (2014).
33. See Richard L. Pacelle Jr., Brett W. Curry, and Bryan W. Marshall, *Decision Making by the Modern Supreme Court* (New York: Cambridge University Press, 2011).
34. U.S. Senate, *Confirmation Hearing on the Nomination of John G. Roberts, Jr. to be Chief Justice of the United States,* 109th Cong., 1st sess., 2005, 55.
35. Sonia Sotomayor, "Landon Lecture," Kansas State University, January 27, 2011, http://www.k-state.edu/media/newsreleases/landonlect/sotomay ortext127.html. See William Blake, "Umpires as Legal Realists," *P.S.: Political Science & Politics* 45 (April 2012): 271–276.
36. Norman I. Silber, *With All Deliberate Speed: The Life of Philip Elman* (Ann Arbor: University of Michigan Press, 2004), 51.
37. Jeffrey A. Segal and Harold J. Spaeth, *The Supreme Court and the Attitudinal Model Revisited* (New York: Cambridge University Press, 2002), chap. 2.
38. Walter Murphy, *Elements of Judicial Strategy* (Chicago: University of Chicago Press, 1964), 44n. See Jack Knight and Lee Epstein, "The Norm of Stare Decisis," *American Journal of Political Science* 40 (November 1996): 1018–1035.
39. Evidence of the impact of law is discussed and presented in Stefanie A. Lindquist and David E. Klein, "The Influence of Jurisprudential Considerations on Supreme Court Decision Making: A Study of Conflict Cases," *Law & Society Review* 40 (2006): 135–161; and Michael A. Bailey and Forrest Maltzman, *The Constrained Court: Law, Politics, and the Decisions Justices Make* (Princeton, N.J.: Princeton University Press, 2011), chaps. 4, 5.
40. *American Broadcasting Companies v. Aereo, Inc.* (2014).
41. Carl Smith, "Quizzing Justice," *The Reflector* (Mississippi State University), January 25, 2008; Sally Friedman, "Supreme Court Justice Ginsburg Advocates Women Pursuing Law," *Philadelphia Bulletin*, March 11, 2008. An apparent typographical error in the Scalia quotation was corrected.
42. *Gitlow v. New York* (1925); *Cantwell v. Connecticut* (1940).
43. *Bolling v. Sharpe* (1954).
44. *Hans v. Louisiana* (1890).
45. *Lawson v. FMR LLC,* 188 L. Ed. 2d 158, 187 (2014). See Antonin Scalia and Bryan A. Garner, *Reading Law: The Interpretation of Legal Texts* (St. Paul, Minn.: Thomson/West, 2012).
46. James J. Brudney and Corey Ditslear, "The Decline and Fall of Legislative History? Patterns of Supreme Court Reliance in the Burger and Rehnquist Eras," *Judicature* 89 (January–February 2006): 220–229.
47. Robert A. Katzmann, *Judging Statutes* (New York: Oxford University Press, 2014).
48. Chris Wallace, "Justice Antonin Scalia on Issues Facing SCOTUS and the Country," Fox News Sunday, July 29, 2012, http://www.foxnews.com/on-air/fox-news-sunday-chris-wallace/2012/07/29/justice-antonin-scalia-issues-facing-scotus-and-country#p//v/1760654457001.
49. The decisions were *Atkins v. Virginia* (2002); *Roper v. Simmons* (2005); and *Kennedy v. Louisiana* (2008).
50. *National Federation of Independent Business v. Sebelius* (2012).

51. Mark J. Richards and Herbert M. Kritzer, "Jurisprudential Regimes in Supreme Court Decision Making," *American Political Science Review* 96 (June 2002): 305–320; Brandon L. Bartels, "The Constraining Capacity of Legal Doctrine on the U.S. Supreme Court," *American Political Science Review* 103 (August 2009): 474–495; Mark J. Richards, *The Politics of Freedom of Expression: The Decisions of the Supreme Court of the United States* (New York: Palgrave Macmillan, 2012).

52. Congressional Research Service, *The Constitution of the United States of America: Analysis and Interpretation* (Washington, D.C.: Government Printing Office, 2014), 2583–2595; updated by the author. In many of these decisions, the Court overruled multiple precedents.

53. Harold J. Spaeth and Jeffrey A. Segal, *Majority Rule or Minority Will: Adherence to Precedent on the U.S. Supreme Court* (New York: Cambridge University Press, 1999); Allison Orr Larsen, "Perpetual Dissents," *George Mason Law Review* 15 (Winter 2008): 447–478.

54. Donald R. Songer, "The Dog That Did Not Bark: Debunking the Myths Surrounding the Attitudinal Model of Supreme Court Decision Making," *Justice System Journal* 33 (2012): 340–362.

55. Adam Liptak, "Thomas Is Getting a New Chance to Break Precedent (if Not Silence)," *New York Times*, February 25, 2014, A15.

56. *McCullen v. Coakley* (2014); *Halliburton Co. v. Erica P. John Fund, Inc.* (2014); *McCutcheon v. Federal Election Commission* (2014).

57. Diane Marie Amann, "John Paul Stevens, Human Rights Judge," *Fordham Law Review* 74 (March 2006): 1582–1583; Ken Kobayashi, "Justice Stevens Recalls War Years in Honolulu," *Honolulu Advertiser*, July 20, 2007; Jeffrey Rosen, "The Dissenter," *New York Times Magazine*, September 23, 2007, 54.

58. Erwin Chemerinsky, "The Court and the Fourth Amendment," *National Law Journal*, May 7, 2012, 50.

59. For two differing positions, see Lee Epstein and Jack Knight, *The Choices Justices Make* (Washington, D.C.: CQ Press, 1998); and Saul Brenner and Joseph M. Whitmeyer, *Strategy on the United States Supreme Court* (New York: Cambridge University Press, 2009).

60. Geoffrey R. Stone, "The Behavior of Supreme Court Justices When Their Behavior Counts the Most: An Informal Study," *Judicature* 97 (September/October 2013): 82–89.

61. Data on rates of agreement are from "The Statistics," *Harvard Law Review* 127 (November 2013): 410; and "The Statistics," *Harvard Law Review* 128 (November 2014): 403. The mean rates of agreement between pairs of justices are averages between the two terms.

62. "The Statistics" (November 2013): 414; "The Statistics" (November 2014): 407.

63. Paul H. Edelman, David E. Klein, and Stefanie A. Lindquist, "Consensus, Disorder, and Ideology on the Supreme Court," *Journal of Empirical Legal Studies* 9 (March 2012): 129–148.

64. Jeffrey A. Segal, Lee Epstein, Charles M. Cameron, and Harold J. Spaeth, "Ideological Values and the Votes of Justices Revisited," *Journal of Politics* 57 (August 1995): 812–823.

65. Richard M. Re, "Personal Precedent in Bay Mills," Re's Judicata, June 4, 2014, http://richardresjudicata.wordpress.com/2014/06/04/personal-precedent-in-bay-mills.

66. Adam Liptak, "Supreme Court Justices Admit Inconsistency, and Embrace It," *New York Times*, December 23, 2014, A15.

67. Adam Liptak, "Another Factor Said to Sway Judges to Rule for Women's Rights: A Daughter," *New York Times,* June 17, 2014, A14. The decision was *Nevada Department of Human Resources v. Hibbs* (2003).

68. Figures on agreement between Blackmun and his colleagues are taken from the annual statistics on the Supreme Court term in the November issues of *Harvard Law Review,* vols. 85–100 (1972–1987). See also "The Changing Social Vision of Justice Blackmun," *Harvard Law Review* 96 (1983): 717–736.

69. See Linda Greenhouse, *Becoming Justice Blackmun: Harry Blackmun's Supreme Court Journey* (New York: Times Books, 2005).

70. *Baker v. Nelson* (1972); *United States v. Windsor* (2013); *Obergefell v. Hodges* (2015).

71. *Citizens United v. Federal Election Commission,* 175 L. Ed. 2d 753, 829 (2010).

72. Hope Yen, "O'Connor: Supreme Court Rulings Shouldn't Differ Based on Who Sits on Court," Associated Press, May 20, 2007.

73. Rosen, "RBG Presides," 20.

74. The percentages of pro–civil liberties decisions presented here are based on analysis of data in the Supreme Court Database, http://scdb.wustl.edu. The unit of analysis is the case citation. Civil liberties cases are those in issue areas 1–6.

75. The Court's increased conservatism after the 1970s is suggested by the analysis presented in Michael A. Bailey, "Is Today's Court the Most Conservative in Sixty Years? Challenges and Opportunities in Measuring Judicial Preferences," *Journal of Politics* 75 (July 2013): 821–834.

76. Bailey and Maltzman, *The Constrained Court,* chaps. 4, 5.

77. Lee Epstein and Andrew D. Martin, "Is the Roberts Court Especially Activist? A Study of Invalidating (and Upholding) Federal, State, and Local Laws," *Emory Law Journal* 61 (2012): 737–758.

78. Richard Kluger, *Simple Justice: The History of* Brown v. Board of Education *and Black America's Struggle for Equality* (New York: Knopf, 1976), 582–699.

79. William H. Rehnquist, "Chief Justices I Never Knew," *Hastings Constitutional Law Quarterly* 3 (Summer 1976): 647.

80. Tal Kopan, "Elena Kagan Talks Diversity and (Dis)agreement on the Supreme Court," Under the Radar Blog, *Politico,* December 14, 2012, http://www.politico.com/blogs/under-the-radar/2012/12/elena-kagan-talks-diversity-and-disagreement-on-the-151963.html.

81. Forrest Maltzman and Paul J. Wahlbeck, "Strategic Policy Considerations and Voting Fluidity on the Burger Court," *American Political Science Review* 90 (September 1996): 587.

82. Segal and Spaeth, *The Supreme Court and the Attitudinal Model Revisited,* 286.

83. See Maltzman, Spriggs, and Wahlbeck, *Crafting Law on the Supreme Court.*

84. Pamela C. Corley, "Bargaining and Accommodation on the United States Supreme Court: Insight from Justice Blackmun," *Judicature* 90 (January–February 2007): 157–165.

85. Maltzman, Spriggs, and Wahlbeck, *Crafting Law on the Supreme Court,* 116.

86. Joan Biskupic, *Breaking In: The Rise of Sonia Sotomayor and the Politics of Justice* (New York: Farrar, Straus and Giroux, 2014), 11.

87. Ibid., 205–209. The case was *Fisher v. University of Texas* (2013).

88. Jeffrey Toobin, *The Nine: Inside the Secret World of the Supreme Court* (New York: Doubleday, 2007), 129.

89. Jennifer Senior, "In Conversation: Antonin Scalia," *New York Magazine,* October 2013, 80.

90. Michael Hotchkiss, "Kagan Discusses the Constitution, the Supreme Court and Her Time at Princeton," Princeton University Office of Communications, November 21, 2014, https://www.princeton.edu/main/news/archive/S41/65/85E33/index.xml?section=featured.

91. Linda Greenhouse, "Every Justice Creates a New Court," *New York Times*, May 27, 2009, A25.

92. Andrew Cohen, "This Is Kennedy's Court—the Rest of the Justices Just Sit on It," *Atlantic*, May 29, 2013, http://www.theatlantic.com/national/archive/2013/05/this-is-kennedys-court-the-rest-of-the-justices-just-sit-on-it/276309.

93. This discussion of criteria for opinion assignment is based largely on the findings for the 1953–1990 period in Forrest Maltzman and Paul J. Wahlbeck, "A Conditional Model of Opinion Assignment on the Supreme Court," *Political Research Quarterly* 57 (December 2004): 551–563; Forrest Maltzman and Paul J. Wahlbeck, "May It Please the Chief? Opinion Assignments in the Rehnquist Court," *American Journal of Political Science* 40 (May 1996): 421–443; and Paul J. Wahlbeck, "Strategy and Constraints on Supreme Court Opinion Assignment," *University of Pennsylvania Law Review* 154 (2006): 1729–1755.

94. Jan Crawford Greenburg, "Interview with Chief Justice Roberts," November 28, 2006, http://abcnews.go.com/Nightline/story?id=2661589&page=6.

95. Linda Greenhouse, "Chief Justice Roberts in His Own Voice: The Chief Justice's Self-Assignment of Majority Opinions," *Judicature* 97 (September/October 2013): 90–97.

96. Bill Barnhart and Gene Schlickman, *John Paul Stevens: An Independent Life* (DeKalb: Northern Illinois University Press, 2010), 230.

97. Greenburg, "Interview with Chief Justice Roberts."

98. Ruth Marcus, "Alumni Brennan, Blackmun Greet Harvard Law Freshmen," *Washington Post*, September 6, 1986, 2.

99. Adam Liptak, "As Justices Get Back to Business, Old Pro Reveals Tricks of the Trade," *New York Times*, October 4, 2011, A15.

100. Rosen, "RBG Presides," 21.

101. See Timothy R. Johnson, James F. Spriggs II, and Paul J. Wahlbeck, "Passing and Strategic Voting on the U.S. Supreme Court," *Law & Society Review* 39 (June 2005): 349–377.

102. David J. Garrow, *Liberty and Sexuality: The Right to Privacy and the Making of Roe v. Wade* (New York: Macmillan, 1994), 558.

103. Linda Greenhouse, "How Not to Be Chief Justice: The Apprenticeship of William H. Rehnquist," *University of Pennsylvania Law Review* 154 (2006): 1367, emphasis in original.

104. Jeffrey Rosen, "Rehnquist the Great?" *Atlantic Monthly*, April 2005, 79–80.

105. John Paul Stevens, *Five Chiefs: A Supreme Court Memoir* (New York: Little, Brown, 2011), 210.

106. Richard L. Hasen, "The Chief Justice's Long Game," *New York Times*, June 26, 2013, A23.

107. The decisions were *Northwest Austin Municipal Utility District No. 1 v. Holder* (2009) and *Shelby County v. Holder* (2013).

108. Marcia Coyle and Tony Mauro, "Tough Medicine," *National Law Journal*, July 2, 2012, 1, 4–5.

109. The opinions, in order, were in *Schuette v. Coalition to Defend Affirmative Action*, 188 L. Ed. 2d 613, 670 (2014) (Sotomayor); *United States v. Windsor*, 186 L. Ed. 2d 808, 845 (2013) (Scalia); *Florida v. Jardines*, 185 L. Ed. 2d 495, 507 (2013) (Alito); and *Harris v. Quinn*, 189 L. Ed. 2d 620, 663 (2014) (Kagan).

110. Jan Crawford, "Discord at Supreme Court Is Deep, and Personal," CBS News, July 8, 2012, http://www.cbsnews.com/news/discord-at-supreme-court-is-deep-and-personal.

111. Andrew Cohen, "Justice Elena Kagan, Comedian," *Atlantic*, September 11, 2012, http://www.theatlantic.com/national/archive/2012/09/justice-elena-kagan-comedian/262174.

112. Colleen Walsh, "A Reflective Justice Breyer," *Harvard Gazette*, October 2, 2013, http://news.harvard.edu/gazette/story/2013/10/a-reflective-justice-breyer.

113. Senior, "In Conversation: Antonin Scalia," 27.

114. Marcia Coyle and Tony Mauro, "Justices Say Any Rifts Are Temporary," *National Law Journal*, July 16, 2012, 4.

115. Eric Lichtblau, "Groups Blanket Supreme Court on Health Care," *New York Times*, March 25, 2012, A1.

116. Dahlia Lithwick, "It's Not About the Law, Stupid," *Slate*, March 22, 2012, http://www.slate.com/articles/news_and_politics/jurisprudence/2012/03/the_supreme_court_is_more_concerned_with_the_politics_of_the_health_care_debate_than_the_law_.html.

117. Barry Friedman, *The Will of the People: How Public Opinion Has Influenced the Supreme Court and Shaped the Meaning of the Constitution* (New York: Farrar, Straus, & Giroux, 2009), 371. A contrary view is presented in Richard H. Pildes, "Is the Supreme Court a 'Majoritarian' Institution?" *Supreme Court Review*, 2010, 103–158.

118. See Micheal W. Giles, Bethany Blackstone, and Richard L. Vining Jr., "The Supreme Court in American Democracy: Unraveling the Linkages between Public Opinion and Judicial Decision Making," *Journal of Politics* 70 (April 2008): 293–306; and Christopher J. Casillas, Peter K. Enns, and Patrick C. Wohlfarth, "How Public Opinion Constrains the U.S. Supreme Court," *American Journal of Political Science* 55 (January 2011): 74–88.

119. Adam Liptak, "States' Votes for Gay Marriage Are Timely, with Justices Ready to Weigh Cases," *New York Times*, November 8, 2012, 7. The case was *United States v. Windsor* (2013).

120. Anna Ivey, "Introduction," *Journal of Law* 3 (2013), 277.

121. Neal Kumar Katyal, "Foreword: Academic Influence on the Court," *Virginia Law Review* 98 (October 2012): 1189–1194.

122. Thomas Sowell, "Blackmun Plays to the Crowd," *St. Louis Post-Dispatch*, March 4, 1994, 7B; Michael Barone, "Justices Have Typically Felt Little Compunction about Overturning Laws and Making Public Policy," *Chicago Sun-Times*, July 13, 2005, 55.

123. Neal Devins and Lawrence Baum, "Split Definitive: How Party Polarization Turned the Supreme Court Into a Partisan Court" (2014), http://ssrn.com/abstract=2432111.

124. Pamela C. Corley, "The Supreme Court and Opinion Content: The Influence of Parties' Briefs," *Political Research Quarterly* 61 (September 2008): 468–478; Anthony J. Franze and R. Reeves Anderson, "The Supreme Court's Reliance on Amicus Curiae in the 2012–13 Term," *National Law Journal*, September 18, 2013.

125. Allison Orr Larsen, "The Trouble with Amicus Facts," *Virginia Law Review* 100 (December 2014): 1757–1818.

126. See Ryan C. Black and Ryan J. Owens, *The Solicitor General and the United States Supreme Court: Executive Branch Influence and Judicial Decisions* (New York: Cambridge University Press, 2012), chaps. 5–7.

127. See Rebecca E. Deen, Joseph Ignagni, and James Meernik, "Individual Justices and the Solicitor General: The Amicus Curiae Cases, 1953–2000," *Judicature* 89 (September–October 2005): 68–77.

128. Tom S. Clark, *The Limits of Judicial Independence* (New York: Cambridge University Press, 2011); Anna Harvey, *A Mere Machine: The Supreme Court, Congress, and American Democracy* (New Haven, Conn.: Yale University Press, 2013).

129. Jeffrey Toobin, "Heavyweight: How Ruth Bader Ginsburg Has Moved the Supreme Court," *New Yorker*, March 11, 2013, 45, 47. The decision was *Ledbetter v. Goodyear Tire & Rubber Co.* (2007).

130. Mark Landler, "President Confident Health Law Will Stand," *New York Times*, April 3, 2012, A17; David Lightman, "Senate's Mitch McConnell Tells Obama to 'Back Off' Supreme Court," McClatchy-Tribune News Service, April 5, 2012.

Chapter 5

Policy Outputs

The last two chapters examined the processes that shape the Supreme Court's policies. In this chapter I consider the substance of those policies by discussing several questions. What kinds of issues does the Court address? How active is the Court as a policymaker? Finally, what is the ideological content of its policies? I conclude the chapter by developing an explanation for historical patterns in the Court's outputs.

Areas of Activity: What the Court Addresses

The Supreme Court addresses issues in fields as different as antitrust, criminal law, and freedom of speech. In this sense the Court's agenda is highly diverse. But the Court devotes most of its efforts to a few types of policy. To a considerable degree, then, the Court is a specialist.

The Court's Current Activity

The shape of the Court's agenda can be illustrated with the cases that it heard in the 2013 term. It is useful to begin by describing the issues in a fairly representative sample of cases decided during that term.

1. Under the federal Fair Labor Standards Act (FLSA), does the term *changing clothes* apply to protective gear so that a labor union and a company can agree that workers will not be paid for the time they spend putting protective gear on and taking if off? (*Sandifer v. U.S. Steel Corp.*, 2014)

2. Does a Massachusetts statute that prohibits people from knowingly standing on a "public way or sidewalk" within thirty-five feet of an entrance to an abortion clinic violate the First Amendment' protection of freedom of speech? (*McCullen v. Coakley*, 2014)

3. When a business sells a service that allows people to select and watch television shows over the Internet at around the time they are

broadcast, does it "perform" those shows "publicly" under the federal Copyright Act of 1976? (*American Broadcasting Companies, Inc. v. Aereo, Inc.*, 2014)

4. Under a federal criminal statute, is a defendant guilty of aiding and abetting the use of a gun in connection with a drug trafficking crime if the defendant did not know in advance that another participant in the crime would be armed? (*Rosemond v. United States*, 2014)

5. Under the federal General Railroad Right-of-Way Act of 1875, did a railroad's right of way over federal land transfer to the federal government when the railroad abandoned the right of way, even though the government no longer owned the land? (*Marvin M. Brandt Revocable Trust v. United States*, 2014)

6. Does the protection of whistleblowers under the federal Sarbanes-Oxley Act apply to employees of privately held companies that perform work for publicly held companies? (*Lawson v. FMR LLC*, 2014)

7. Does a state constitutional provision that prohibits state universities from granting "preferential treatment" to applicants for admission on the basis of race violate the equal protection clause of the Fourteenth Amendment because it rules out affirmative action programs? (*Schuette v. Coalition to Defend Affirmative Action*, 2014)

8. Under federal law, does money in an individual retirement account that a person has inherited qualify as "retirement funds" that are exempt from going to the person's creditors in a bankruptcy? (*Clark v. Rameker*, 2014)

9. In a case in which a 911 caller reported that a truck had run her off the road, did a highway patrol officer have the reasonable suspicion of drunk driving that the Fourth Amendment requires in order to stop a truck that matched the caller's description? (*Navarette v. California*, 2014)

10. Does a regulation of the federal Department of Health and Human Services requiring that certain employers provide insurance coverage for contraceptives violate the federal Religious Freedom Restoration Act when it conflicts with the religious views of the owners of "closely held" corporations? (*Burwell v. Hobby Lobby Stores, Inc.*, 2014)

Table 5-1 provides a more systematic picture of the Court's agenda in the 2013 term by summarizing the characteristics of the seventy-two decisions with full opinions in that term. The Court's decisions were closely connected with the other branches of government. The federal government or one of its agencies was a party in one-third of all cases. State governments were parties in nearly as many cases, so that well over half of all cases had at least one government party. Moreover, most of the disputes between private parties were based directly on government policy in fields such as environmental protection and labor-management relations.

The 2013 term was typical of the Court's work in the current era in several respects. First, the majority of cases involved disagreements about the meaning of federal statutes. Observers of the Court tend to focus on its interpretations of the Constitution, but the justices devote most of their work to statutory interpretation.

Second, the Court's single biggest area of activity was civil liberties. As in earlier discussions, the term *civil liberties* refers here to three general types of rights: the right to fair procedure in dealings with government, the right to equal treatment by government and by private institutions, and certain substantive rights protected against government violations such as freedom of expression and freedom of religion. By that definition, about 40 percent of the Court's decisions fell into this area in the 2013 term and an even higher proportion in most other recent terms.

TABLE 5-1
*Characteristics of Decisions by the Supreme
Court with Full Opinions, 2013 Term*

Characteristic	Number	Percentage
Number of decisions	72	NA
Cases from lower federal courts	65	90
Cases from state courts	7	10
Original cases	0	0
Federal government party[a]	24	33
State or local government party[a]	19	26
No government party	29	40
Constitutional issue decided[b]	21	29
No constitutional issue decided	51	71
Civil liberties issue present[c]	27	38
No civil liberties issue	45	62
Criminal cases[d]	19	26
Civil cases	53	74

Source: The cases listed were those decided with opinions and listed in the front section of *United States Supreme Court Reports, Lawyers' Edition,* vols. 187–189.

Note: NA = not applicable. Consolidated cases decided with one set of opinions were counted once.

a. Cases with both a federal government party and another government party were listed as federal government. Government as party includes agencies and individual government officials.
b. In several additional cases the parties raised constitutional issues, or those issues were present in the underlying case. Cases involving federal preemption of state laws are not treated as constitutional.
c. Includes cases in which the Court did not decide the civil liberties issue directly.
d. Includes actions brought by prisoners to challenge the legality of their convictions but excludes cases concerning rights of prisoners.

Third, the Court gave considerable attention to criminal cases, as it has done for more than a century. The great majority of these cases fall into two categories: interpretations of federal statutes that define crimes and set rules for sentencing and interpretations of constitutional protections of defendants' procedural rights.

Federalism—the division of power between federal and state governments—was not a major part of the Court's agenda in the 2013 term. But it has been a concern of the Court throughout its history, and it has been especially prominent in the past two decades. Federalism overlaps with other categories, and most federalism cases involve economic issues. One example was *National Federation of Independent Business v. Sebelius* (2012), the case in which the Court reached a mixed decision about federal power in the health care field.

Taken together, civil liberties, economic policy, and federalism cover a large portion of the issues that arise in American government. Still, the Court's emphasis on those issues constitutes something of a specialized focus. Most striking is its concentration on civil liberties. Although civil liberties is a broad category, the fact that about half the Court's decisions in the current era concern this single kind of issue indicates the Court's specialization.

Change in the Court's Agenda

The Court's agenda is not static. Even over a few terms, the Court's attention to specific categories of cases sometimes increases or decreases considerably. The shape of its agenda as a whole has changed more slowly, but the changes have been fundamental.[1]

Changes in Specific Portions of the Agenda. Sometimes an issue that has occupied a very small place on the Court's agenda, or no place at all, becomes more prominent. More often than not, this change comes from new federal legislation. Before federal law prohibited employment discrimination, for instance, people who felt that they had been subjected to discrimination had little basis for bringing cases to court. The series of statutes that Congress enacted beginning in 1963 provided that basis, and those statutes generated a substantial number of legal questions that the Court chose to resolve. The Court has now heard more than 130 cases on employment discrimination.

Another example concerns employee pension plans. Until 1980 the Court decided few cases involving those issues, but since then these cases have been common. The source of this change is simple: Congress enacted the Employee Retirement Income Security Act of 1974 (ERISA). This regulation of pension plans raised a variety of legal questions that the courts had to address. The justices have seen a need to resolve many of these questions themselves, even though they have limited interest in the complex issues that arise under ERISA. As a result, the Court has heard more than fifty cases interpreting ERISA.

The Court itself can open up new areas on its agenda with decisions that create legal rights or add to existing rights. The Court's decision in *Batson v. Kentucky* (1986) allowed criminal defendants to challenge the use of peremptory challenges to prospective jurors by prosecutors on the ground that the challenges were used in a racially discriminatory way. Since then, the Court has decided a series of cases about who has the right to raise a *Batson* claim and how judges should determine whether challenges were used with discriminatory intent. A similar result followed *Strickland v. Washington* (1984), which set up new standards to determine whether a criminal defendant was effectively denied the right to counsel by a lawyer's poor performance.

Just as issues can rise on the Court's agenda, they can also recede. Often, a new statute or Court decision raises a series of issues that the Court resolves during a particular period, but after that wave of cases the Court can move away from that field. In *Benton v. Maryland* (1969) the Court ruled that the constitutional protection against double jeopardy for criminal offenses applied to the states. This decision opened the way for state cases with double jeopardy issues to reach the Court, and the Court decided more than fifty cases in that field in the 1970s and 1980s. But with so many issues resolved, the Court has heard only occasional double jeopardy cases since then.

Changes in the Agenda as a Whole. Beyond changes in specific areas, the overall pattern of the Court's agenda may change over a period of several decades. The current agenda reflects a fundamental change that occurred between the 1930s and 1960s. In the half century up to the 1930s, the largest part of the Court's agenda was devoted to economic issues. Also important but clearly secondary were cases about federalism. Issues of procedural due process constituted a small proportion of the agenda, and relatively few cases fell in other areas of individual civil liberties.

Over the next three decades, the Court evolved into an institution that gave most of its attention to individual liberties. The proportion of decisions dealing with civil liberties grew from 8 percent of the agenda in the 1933–1937 terms to 59 percent in the 1968–1972 terms.[2] Cases about the rights of criminal defendants became far more numerous, and other civil liberties areas such as racial equality took a large share of the agenda. At the same time, some kinds of economic cases declined precipitously. In the 1933–1937 terms, one of every three cases involved federal taxation or economic disputes between private parties. By the 1968–1972 terms, those two areas accounted for only 6 percent of the Court's agenda. Federalism also took a reduced share of the agenda, falling from 14 percent in 1933–1937 to 5 percent in 1968–1972.

Many forces contributed to this change, from public opinion to federal legislation. Interest groups that supported civil liberties cases played a key role by bringing relevant cases to the Court. But actions by the Court itself had the most direct effect. Perhaps most important, the justices became more interested in protecting civil liberties and thus in hearing claims that government policies infringed on liberties. Partly because they had to make room for civil liberties cases, the justices gave more limited attention to other fields. They continued to hear a good many cases involving economic issues, but economics declined considerably as part of the Court's work.

The Court's agenda has changed in some respects since the 1960s. Within the civil liberties field, cases involving criminal law and procedure have taken a larger share of the agenda, while issues of equality and First Amendment rights have declined. Meanwhile, federalism cases have become somewhat more common. But the broad contours of the agenda have remained fairly stable. In particular, as the agenda for the 2013 term illustrates, the Court continues to hear more cases in civil liberties than in any other field. Thus, the Court's work still reflects the changes in its agenda that occurred between the 1930s and the 1960s.

A Broader View of the Agenda

The Supreme Court's current agenda distinguishes the Court from other policymakers. In some respects the Court's agenda resembles the agendas of other appellate courts, especially state supreme courts and federal courts of appeals. All these courts hear many cases with government parties and additional cases based on policies of the other branches. Nearly all appellate courts hear large numbers of criminal cases, and most give much of their attention to cases with economic issues. Where the Court stands out is in the prominence of civil liberties issues on its agenda. Except for the rights of criminal defendants, most other appellate courts hear few cases about civil liberties.

Like the Court, the president is something of a specialist. But the president's agenda has its own emphases: foreign policy and management of the economy. In contrast, the Court makes few decisions about foreign policy. Although the Court is active in economic policy, its decisions in that field do not often address government policies that have broad effects on the economy; its rulings on the federal health care law sponsored by President Obama are exceptional.[3]

In contrast, Congress is a generalist that spreads its activity across a very broad set of issues. One result is that the congressional agenda covers virtually all the types of policy that the Supreme Court deals with. But Congress gives relatively little attention to some of the issues that are central to the Court, especially in civil liberties. And Congress gives a high priority to several fields that are less important to the Court, ranging from foreign policy to agriculture.

These differences provide some perspective on the Court's role by underlining the limited range of its work. Its jurisdiction is broad, but the bulk of its decisions are made in only a few policy areas. The Court's specialization affects its role as a policymaker. By deciding as many civil liberties cases as it does, the Court can do much to shape law and policy in this area. In contrast, the Court's more limited activity in some major areas severely narrows its potential impact in those fields. That is especially true of foreign policy.

Even in the areas in which it is most active, the Court addresses only certain types of issues. In criminal justice, for instance, the Court does much to define the rights of criminal defendants and the scope of federal criminal statutes. But its cases do not affect the funding of criminal justice agencies, and they have little direct impact on decisions to prosecute.

One effect of the Court's narrow focus is that it does not deal with most of the issues that are high on the agendas of government and the public. U.S. military action in Iraq, Afghanistan, and other countries in the twenty-first century has proceeded with essentially no involvement by the Court. The major decisions on revival of the economy after the Great Recession of 2008–2009 were made in the other branches of government, and the Court continues to play a very limited role in decisions about management of the economy.

A demonstrator at the Supreme Court on the day of oral arguments in King v. Burwell *(2015), in which the Court ruled on a key issue involving the health care law sponsored by President Obama. The Court's decisions on that law are a striking exception to its generally limited role in national economic policy.*

These realities should caution against exaggerating the Supreme Court's power as a policymaker. Although the importance of its role can be debated, the relatively narrow range of its activities inevitably limits its power. The Court could not possibly be dominant as a policymaker except in federalism, civil liberties, and some limited areas of economic policy. For reasons that are discussed later in this chapter and in Chapter 6, even in those areas the Court is far from dominant.

The Court's Activism

The prominence of various areas of policy on the Court's agenda helps determine where it plays a significant role, but its impact also depends on what it actually decides in those policy areas. One important element of those decisions is the extent of the Court's activism.

The term *judicial activism* has multiple meanings, and people most often use the term simply as a negative label for decisions they dislike. What I mean by activism is that a court makes significant changes in public policy— especially in policies established by the other branches. The most important form of activism is the use of judicial review: the power to overturn acts of other policymakers on the ground that they violate the Constitution.

Overturning Acts of Congress

The most familiar use of judicial review comes in Supreme Court decisions holding that federal statutes are unconstitutional. Such a ruling represents a clear assertion of power by the Court, because it directly negates a decision by another branch of the federal government.

According to one count, shown in Table 5-2, by the end of 2014 the Court had overturned 177 federal laws completely or in part.[4] (When different provisions of a statute were struck down in different decisions, each decision is counted once.) This number in itself is noteworthy. On the one hand, it indicates that the Court has made considerable use of its review power. On the other hand, the laws struck down by the Court constitute a very small fraction of the laws that Congress has adopted. And when the Court rules on whether a federal statute is unconstitutional, about five times out of six it upholds the statute.[5]

A closer look at the decisions striking down federal laws provides a better sense of how the Court has used judicial review.[6] One question is the importance of the statutes that the Court overturns. The Court has struck down some statutes of major importance. One example was the Missouri Compromise of 1820, limiting slavery in the territories, which the Court declared unconstitutional in the *Dred Scott* case in 1857. Another was the New Deal economic legislation that the Court overturned in several decisions in 1935 and 1936.[7] In contrast, many of the Court's decisions declaring

TABLE 5-2
Number of Federal Statutes and State and Local Statutes Held Unconstitutional by the Supreme Court, 1790–2014

Period	Federal statutes	State and local statutes
1790–1799	0	0
1800–1809	1	1
1810–1819	0	7
1820–1829	0	8
1830–1839	0	3
1840–1849	0	10
1850–1859	1	7
1860–1869	4	24
1870–1879	7	36
1880–1889	4	46
1890–1899	5	36
1900–1909	9	40
1910–1919	6	119
1920–1929	15	139
1930–1939	13	92
1940–1949	2	61
1950–1959	4	66
1960–1969	18	151
1970–1979	19	195
1980–1989	16	164
1990–1999	24	62
2000–2009	16	38
2010–2014	13	16
Total	177	1,321

Source: Congressional Research Service, *The Constitution of the United States of America: Analysis and Interpretation* (Washington, DC: Government Printing Office, 2014); updated by the author.

Note: State and local laws include those that the Supreme Court held to be preempted by federal statutes.

statutes invalid were unimportant to the policy goals of Congress and the president, either because the statutes were minor or because they were struck down only as they applied to particular circumstances.

A related question is the timing of judicial review. The Court's decisions striking down federal statutes fall into three groups of nearly equal size: those that came within four calendar years of a statute's enactment, those that came five to twelve years after enactment, and those that occurred more than twelve years later. Congress sometimes retains a strong commitment to a statute from an earlier period. But often few members of Congress care much when an older law is overturned, because the statute has become less relevant over time or because Congress collectively has become less favorable to the provision that was struck down.

For these reasons the Court's frequent use of its power to invalidate congressional acts is somewhat misleading. Any decision that strikes down a federal statute might seem likely to produce major conflict between the Court and Congress, but that is not necessarily the case. Conflict is most likely when the Court invalidates an important congressional policy within a few years of its enactment, but most decisions striking down statutes do not meet both those criteria. Some decisions overturning legislation receive little attention, and some others are actually welcomed by presidents and members of Congress.[8]

As Table 5-2 shows, the Court has not overturned federal statutes at a constant rate. It struck down only two statutes before 1865. It then began to exercise its judicial review power more actively, overturning thirty-five federal laws between 1865 and 1919. Two more increases, even more dramatic, followed: the Court struck down fifteen federal laws during the 1920s and twelve from 1934 through 1936.

The period between 1918 and 1936 featured the highest level of conflict between the Court and Congress. The Court overturned twenty-nine federal laws, many of them quite significant. Between 1918 and 1928 the Court invalidated two child labor laws and a minimum wage law, along with several less important statutes. Then, between 1933 and 1936 a majority of the Court engaged in a frontal attack on the New Deal program, an attack that ended with the Court's 1937 shift to a broader interpretation of federal power.

The Court used its judicial review power sparingly in the quarter-century after 1936, but it then overturned 106 statutes in the forty-two years from 1963 through 2014. That number is far greater than in any previous period of the same length, and it constitutes three-fifths of the total for the Court's entire history. This recent period can be divided into three parts.

Among all the statutes that the Court declared unconstitutional between 1963 and 1994, most were of limited significance. As a result, the decisions striking them down received little attention from the mass media or the general public. However, a few of those statutes were quite important. *Buckley v. Valeo* (1976) and several later decisions invalidated major provisions of the federal campaign funding laws of the 1970s on First Amendment grounds and thereby made it impossible for Congress to regulate campaign finance comprehensively. In *Immigration and Naturalization Service v. Chadha* (1983), the Court struck down a relatively minor provision of an immigration law. But its ruling indicated that the legislative veto, a mechanism widely used for congressional control of the executive branch, violated the constitutional separation of powers.

Between 1995 and 2002 the Court invalidated thirty-two federal laws, a record number for an eight-year period. During that period too, most of these laws were relatively minor. The biggest exception was the statute that gave presidents the power to veto individual items in budget bills, a major addition to presidential power, which the Court struck down in *Clinton v. City of New York* (1998).

Over those eight years, the Court also handed down ten decisions that limited the power of Congress to regulate state governments. In these decisions the Court gave narrow interpretations to the commerce clause and the Fourteenth Amendment as bases for federal power, while giving a broad interpretation to the Eleventh Amendment as a limit on lawsuits against states. In *Board of Trustees v. Garrett* (2001), for example, the Court ruled that Congress could not authorize people with disabilities to seek monetary damages from states in lawsuits for discrimination. This set of decisions constituted a substantial change in the federal-state balance. But it did not create serious conflict with Congress, because the Republican majorities in Congress during that period did not want to assert federal power against the states in the areas in which the Court limited that power.

The frequency of overturnings declined considerably after 2002. In the dozen years that followed, the Court issued only eighteen decisions striking down federal laws. But several of these decisions were quite consequential. In *United States v. Booker* (2005), the Court invalidated a provision that made the federal sentencing guidelines mandatory, thereby upsetting the sentencing system that had operated in the federal courts for nearly two decades. In *United States v. Windsor* (2013), the Court struck down the

Former Florida governor Jeb Bush in 2015, during a tour of South Carolina that included several events to raise money for his prospective presidential campaign. Supreme Court decisions have struck down major provisions of federal statutes that regulate the funding of presidential and congressional campaigns.

prohibition on recognition of same-sex marriages by the federal government. Another 2013 decision, *Shelby County v. Holder,* struck down one section of the Voting Rights Act and thereby made inoperative another section that required federal approval of election law changes in certain states and localities. And a series of five decisions between 2003 and 2014 held that various provisions of the Bipartisan Campaign Reform Act of 2002 were unconstitutional. Taken together, these decisions largely blunted the second major effort by Congress to regulate funding of political campaigns.[9]

Overturning State and Local Laws

The Supreme Court's exercise of judicial review over state and local laws has less of an activist element than its use of that power over federal laws. When the Court strikes down a state law, it does not put itself in conflict with the other branches of the federal government. Indeed, it may be supporting their powers over those of the states. Still, the Court is invalidating the action of another policymaker. For that reason, this form of judicial review is significant.

From 1790 to 2014, by one count, the Court overturned 1,080 state statutes and local ordinances as unconstitutional. It ruled that another 241 state and local laws were invalid because they were preempted by federal law under the constitutional principle of federal supremacy. The total of 1,321 state and local laws struck down is more than seven times the number for federal statutes. The disparity is even greater than that figure suggests, because many decisions that overturned specific state and local laws also applied to similar laws in other places.

As with federal laws, the rate at which the Court overturns state and local laws has tended to increase over time, and it was far higher in the twentieth century than in the nineteenth. The rate of invalidations was very high between 1909 and 1937, and that rate was even higher from the 1960s through the 1980s. In that period the Court struck down an average of seventeen state and local laws per year. The rate of invalidations has been much lower since 1990, and in the first fifteen years of the twenty-first century it returned to the pace of the late nineteenth century.

Although the Court struck down relatively few state laws before 1860, its decisions during that period were important because they limited state powers under the Constitution. For example, under Chief Justice John Marshall (1801–1835) the Court weakened the states with decisions such as *McCulloch v. Maryland* (1819), which denied the states power to tax federal agencies, and *Gibbons v. Ogden* (1824), which reduced state power to regulate commerce. During the late nineteenth century and the first one-third of the twentieth, the Court struck down a great deal of state economic legislation, including many laws regulating business practices and labor relations. The net effect was to slow a major tide of public policy.

Some of the Court's decisions since the mid-1950s have also impinged on major elements of state policy. A series of rulings helped to break down the legal bases of racial segregation and discrimination in the southern states. In 1973 the Court overturned the broad prohibitions of abortion that existed in most states, thereby requiring a general legalization of abortion; later decisions struck down several new laws regulating abortion and indirectly invalidated many other abortion laws. In 2015 the Court ruled that the prohibitions of same-sex marriage that existed in most states were unconstitutional. And through a long series of decisions, the Court has limited state power to regulate the economy in areas that Congress has preempted under its constitutional supremacy. To a degree, however, the impact of those decisions has been balanced by the Court's rulings since 1995 that struck down federal laws on the ground that they infringed on state powers.

Other Targets of Judicial Review

The Supreme Court can declare unconstitutional any government policy or practice, not just laws enacted by legislatures. The number of nonstatutory policies and practices that the Court has struck down is probably much larger than the number of statutes it has overturned. On constitutional grounds the Court has overruled actions taken by policymakers such as federal cabinet departments, local school boards, and state courts.

The Court is especially active in overseeing criminal procedure under the Constitution, and it frequently holds that actions by police officers or trial judges violate the rights of defendants. In *Riley v. California* (2014), for instance, it ruled that police officers had violated the Fourth Amendment prohibition of unreasonable searches and seizures by searching digital information on a cell phone they had taken from an arrestee without a warrant for that search.

Of particular interest is the Court's review of presidential orders and policies. Decisions of presidents or officials acting on their behalf can be challenged on the grounds that they are unauthorized by the Constitution or that they violate a constitutional rule. It is impossible to specify how frequently the Court strikes down presidential actions as unconstitutional, because it is often unclear whether an action by the executive branch should be considered "presidential." But such decisions by the Court seem to be relatively rare, though the Court arguably has become more willing to challenge presidential policies in the past few decades.[10]

Over its history, the Court has invalidated a few major actions by presidents. In *Ex parte Milligan* (1866), it held that President Abraham Lincoln had lacked the power to suspend the writ of habeas corpus for military prisoners during the Civil War. In *Youngstown Sheet and Tube Co. v. Sawyer* (1952), it declared that President Harry Truman had acted illegally during the Korean War when he ordered the federal government to seize and operate major steel mills because their workers were preparing to go on

strike. Between 2004 and 2008 the Court issued four decisions that established procedural protections for Guantánamo detainees. Those decisions did not hold that any decisions by President George W. Bush were
unconstitutional, but they overruled some of the president's policies relating to terrorism.[11] Most recently, the Court invalidated some "recess
appointments" that President Obama had made to executive branch positions in *National Labor Relations Board v. Noel Canning* (2014), though the
Court's interpretation of the recess appointment power was favorable to
presidents in some important ways.

Judicial Review: The General Picture

The Supreme Court's record of judicial review is complicated. The Court
has engaged in more activism in some eras than in others. The overall
level of activism has increased over time, in part because of growth in the
amount of government activity that is available to challenge. The Court
has struck down far more state and local policies than federal policies.

Altogether, the justices have made considerable use of the power of judicial review. Yet the justices also have been quite selective in using their
power to strike down laws. Partly as a result, the great majority of public
policies at all levels of government have continued without interference
from the Court. Thus, important as judicial review has been, it has not given
the Court anything like a dominant position in the national government.

Statutory Interpretation

Historically and currently, most of the Supreme Court's decisions interpret
federal statutes rather than constitutional provisions. Statutory interpretation may seem routine, but it can involve activism. For one thing, the Court's
statutory decisions often are about whether an administrative agency has
interpreted a statute correctly in the process of implementing it. If the Court
concludes that an agency has erred, it strikes down the agency's action as
contrary to the statute. More broadly, the Court often puts its own stamp on
a statute through its interpretations of that statute over the years. It has done
so in fields such as antitrust, labor relations, and environmental protection.

This process is exemplified by Title VII of the Civil Rights Act of 1964,
the most important of the federal statutes that prohibit employment discrimination. As with many other statutes, Congress laid out the broad
outlines of the law and left it to the other branches to fill in the gaps. Over
the years the Court has resolved many major issues arising under Title VII.
For example, it has established and revised the guidelines that trial courts
use to determine whether an employer has engaged in discrimination. It
ruled that a company's policies could violate Title VII on the basis of their
impact, even if the employer did not intend to discriminate.[12] It held that
sexual harassment may constitute sex discrimination under Title VII and

Cecil Stoughton, White House Press Office

President Lyndon Johnson signing the Civil Rights Act of 1964. The Supreme Court's decisions interpreting the section of the act that prohibits discrimination in employment have powerfully shaped the meaning and impact of this section.

set up rules to determine when an employer is legally responsible for harassment.[13] And it limited the use of class action lawsuits to challenge a company's employment practices.[14] Through these and other rulings, the Court has shaped federal policy on employment discrimination.

The Content of Policy

So far, I have examined the areas in which the Supreme Court concentrates its efforts and the extent of its activism. A third aspect of the Court's role as a policymaker is the content of its policies. This content can best be understood in terms of the ideological direction of the Court's policies and which segments of society they benefit. Dividing the Court's history into eras is arbitrary. But it is useful to think of the period since the late nineteenth century as containing three eras, each with its own themes in the content of the Court's policies.

The 1890s to the 1930s

Over several decades the Supreme Court is certain to shift its position on some broad issues. That was true of the period that began in the 1890s and ended in the 1930s. But in ideological terms the Court of that era was predominantly conservative. Most of its activism was on behalf of advantaged interests such as business corporations. In contrast, it did little to protect disadvantaged interests such as racial minority groups.

Scrutinizing Economic Regulation. In 1915 the Supreme Court decided *South Covington & Cincinnati Street Railway Co. v. City of Covington.* The company, which ran streetcars between Covington, Kentucky, and Cincinnati, Ohio, challenged several provisions of a Covington ordinance regulating its operations. The Court struck down some provisions on the ground that they constituted a burden on interstate commerce between Ohio and Kentucky. The Court also declared invalid a regulation stipulating that the temperature in the cars never be permitted to go below 50 degrees Fahrenheit—"We therefore think . . . this feature of the ordinance is unreasonable and cannot be sustained"—apparently on the ground that the regulation violated the Fourteenth Amendment by depriving the company of its property without due process of law.[15]

The *South Covington* case illustrates some important attributes of the Court's decisions from the 1890s to the late 1930s. During that period the Court dealt primarily with economic issues. Most important, it frequently addressed challenges to the growing body of government regulations of business practices.

In those cases the Court often ruled in favor of government, rejecting most challenges to federal and state policies and giving broad interpretations to some government powers.[16] But the Court limited government regulatory powers in important respects, and over time its limits on regulation tightened. This development is reflected in the number of laws involving economic policy that the Court struck down each decade: 43 from 1900 to 1909, 114 from 1910 to 1919, and 133 from 1920 to 1929.[17] The Court's attacks on government regulation peaked in the mid-1930s, when it struck down most of the major statutes in President Franklin Roosevelt's New Deal program to deal with the Great Depression.

The theme of limiting government regulatory powers was reflected in the Court's constitutional doctrines. At the national level the Court gave narrow interpretations to congressional powers to tax and to regulate interstate commerce. In contrast, the Court gave a broad reading to the general limitation on federal power in the Tenth Amendment, using that provision to prohibit some federal actions on the ground that they interfered with state prerogatives. At the same time the Court limited state powers in the economic sphere. It ruled in 1886 that corporations were "persons" with rights protected by the Fourteenth Amendment.[18] It also interpreted the Fourteenth Amendment requirement that state governments provide due process of law as an absolute prohibition of regulations that interfered unduly with the liberty and property rights of businesses. The Court's ruling against the streetcar temperature regulation was one of many such decisions.

The Court's Beneficiaries. The Court's mixed record in economic cases meant that there was no dominant beneficiary of its decisions. But to the extent that the Court limited government regulatory powers, the business community—especially large businesses—benefited from the Court's policies during this period. Of the regulatory legislation that the Court overturned or limited, much was aimed at the activities of large businesses. The railroads were the most prominent example. Although the Court allowed a good deal of government control over railroads, it also struck down a large body of railroad regulation.[19] In the decade from 1910 to 1919, the Court overturned forty-one state laws in cases brought by railroad companies. Major corporations such as railroads might be considered the primary clientele of the Court from the 1890s to the 1930s.

Large corporations did not simply benefit from the Court's policies; they helped to bring them about.[20] Beginning in the late nineteenth century, the corporate community employed much of the best legal talent in the United States to challenge the validity of regulatory statutes. The effective advocacy of these attorneys helped lay the groundwork for the Court's policies favoring business.

Corporate interests came to the judiciary because of their defeats elsewhere in government. On the whole, Congress and the state legislatures were friendly to business interests, but they did enact a good many regulations of private enterprise. In scrutinizing these regulations closely, the Court served as a court of last resort for corporations politically as well as legally.

Civil Liberties: A Limited Concern. Some of the Court's decisions limiting government regulation of business were based on constitutional protections of civil liberties. The Court decided relatively few cases involving the liberties of individuals in that era, but it gave some attention to that field.[21] Overall, the justices provided less protection for individual liberties than for the economic rights of businesses. The Court's limited support for racial equality was exemplified by *Plessy v. Ferguson* (1896), in which it promoted racial segregation by ruling that state governments could mandate "separate but equal" facilities for different racial groups. The Court reached some decisions that favored the rights of criminal defendants, but it held that only a small subset of the procedural rights for criminal defendants in the Bill of Rights was incorporated into the due process clause of the Fourteenth Amendment and thus was applicable to proceedings in state courts.[22] Late in that era the Court ruled that the due process clause protected freedom of speech and freedom of the press from state violations. But in a series of decisions it held that the federal government could prosecute people whose expressions arguably endangered military recruitment and other national security interests.[23]

A Long-Standing Position. The Court's conservatism during that period was not new; the dominant themes of the Court's work in earlier periods were also conservative. The Court provided considerable support for the rights of property holders and much less support for civil liberties outside the economic sphere.

Because of this history, observers of the Supreme Court in the New Deal period had reason to conclude that the Court was a fundamentally conservative body. Indeed, this was the position of two distinguished observers in the early 1940s. The historian Henry Steele Commager argued in 1943 that, with one possible exception, the Court had never intervened on behalf of the underprivileged; in fact, it frequently had blocked efforts by Congress to protect the underprivileged.[24] Two years earlier, Attorney General Robert Jackson, a future Supreme Court justice, reached this stark conclusion: "Never in its entire history can the Supreme Court be said to have for a single hour been representative of anything except the relatively conservative forces of its day."[25] Jackson may have exaggerated for effect, but he captured an important theme in the Court's history.

1937 to 1969

Even before Commager and Jackson described this record of conservatism, however, the Court was beginning a shift in its direction, which one historian called "the Constitutional Revolution of 1937." That revolution, he said,

> altered fundamentally the character of the Court's business, the nature of its decisions, and the alignment of its friends and foes. From the Marshall Court to the Hughes Court, the judiciary had been largely concerned with questions of property rights. After 1937 the most significant matters on the docket were civil liberties and other personal rights. . . . While from 1800 to 1937 the principal critics of the Supreme Court were social reformers and the main supporters people of means who were the principal beneficiaries of the Court's decisions, after 1937 roles were reversed, with liberals commending and conservatives censuring the Court.[26]

Acceptance of Government Economic Policy. In the first stage of the revolution, the Court abandoned the limits it had placed on government intervention in the economy. That step came quickly. In a series of decisions beginning in 1937, majorities accepted the constitutional power of government—especially the federal government—to regulate and manage the economy. This shift culminated in *Wickard v. Filburn* (1942), in which the Court held that federal power to regulate interstate commerce extended so far that it applied to a farmer who grew wheat for his own livestock.

This collective change of heart proved to be long-lasting. The Court consistently upheld major economic legislation against constitutional challenges, striking down only one minor provision of the federal laws regulating business from the 1940s through the 1960s.[27] Supporting federal supremacy in economic matters, the Court invalidated many state laws on the ground that they impinged on the constitutional powers of the federal government or that they were preempted by federal statutes. But in other respects it gave state governments more freedom to make economic policy.

The Court continued to address economic issues involving interpretations of federal statutes. In some instances it overrode decisions of regulatory agencies such as the National Labor Relations Board, holding that those decisions misinterpreted the statutes they applied. Some of these interventions were significant, but the Court did not challenge the basic economic programs of the federal government.

Support for Civil Liberties. In a 1938 decision, *United States v. Carolene Products Co.,* the Court signaled that there might be a second stage of the revolution. The case was one of many in which the Court upheld federal economic policies. But in what would become known simply as "footnote 4," Justice Harlan Fiske Stone's opinion for the Court argued that the Court was justified in taking a tolerant view of government economic policies while it gave "more exacting judicial scrutiny" to policies that infringed on civil liberties.

This second stage took a long time to develop. The Court gave more support to civil liberties in the 1940s and 1950s than it had in earlier eras, but it did not make a strong and consistent commitment to the expansion of individual liberties. This stage of the revolution finally came to full fruition in the 1960s. Civil liberties issues dominated the Court's agenda for the first time. The Court's decisions expanded liberties in many areas, from civil rights of racial minority groups to procedural rights of criminal defendants to freedom of expression.

As in the preceding era, the Court's policy position was reflected in the constitutional doctrines it adopted. Departing from its earlier view, the Court of the 1960s ruled that nearly all the rights of criminal defendants in the Bill of Rights were incorporated into the Fourteenth Amendment and therefore applied to state proceedings. In interpreting the equal protection clause of the Fourteenth Amendment, the Court held that it would give government policies "strict scrutiny" if the groups that the policies disfavored were especially vulnerable or if the rights involved were especially important.

The Court's sympathies for civil liberties were symbolized by *Griswold v. Connecticut* (1965), which established a new constitutional right to privacy. A majority of the justices discovered that right in provisions of the Bill of Rights nearly two centuries after those provisions were written.

The Court's direction after 1937 is illustrated by the pattern of decisions declaring laws unconstitutional. Figure 5-1 shows the number of economic statutes and statutes limiting civil liberties that the Court overturned in each decade of the twentieth century and the first fifteen years of the twenty-first. The number of economic laws the Court struck down declined precipitously between the 1920s and the 1940s and fell even lower in the 1960s. In contrast, the number of statutes struck down on civil liberties grounds became substantial in the 1940s and 1950s and rose sharply in the 1960s. The reversal of these trends in the 1980s is also noteworthy, and I will discuss its implications later in this section.

The Court's Beneficiaries. The groups that the Court's policies benefited most were those that gained from expansions of legal protections for civil liberties. Among them were socially and economically disadvantaged groups, criminal defendants, and people who took unpopular political stands. In 1967, during the Court's most liberal period, an unsympathetic

FIGURE 5-1
Number of Economic and Civil Liberties Laws (Federal, State, and Local)
Overturned by the Supreme Court by Decade, 1900–2014

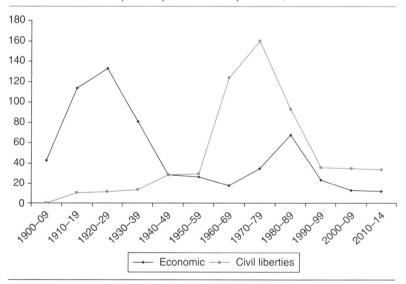

Source: Congressional Research Service, *The Constitution of the United States of America: Analysis and Interpretation* (Washington, D.C.: Government Printing Office, 2014); updated by the author.

Notes: The civil liberties category does not include laws supportive of civil liberties. The numbers of laws struck down in 2010–2014 were doubled to make them equivalent to the numbers for full decades.

editorial cartoonist depicted the Court as a Santa Claus whose list of gift recipients included communists, pornographers, extremists, drug pushers, criminals, and perverts.[28] Whatever may be the accuracy of that characterization, it underlines the change in the Court. Like the Court's policies favoring corporations in an earlier era, this support reflected effective litigation campaigns—in this era, by groups such as the NAACP Legal Defense Fund and the American Civil Liberties Union (ACLU).

The segment of the population that the Court supported most strongly was African Americans—especially in the fields of education and voting rights. The Court also made efforts to protect the civil rights movement when southern states attacked it in the late 1950s and 1960s.

The Court was generally more favorable to liberties than were the other branches of government. Congress did not adopt a strong statute attacking racial discrimination until 1964, ten years after *Brown v. Board of Education*. The Court's support for some other liberties diverged even more from the positions of the other branches. The procedural rights of criminal defendants had few advocates in the executive and legislative branches. Congress did much to restrict and punish leftist political groups such as the Communist Party. As it had done when it favored business interests, the Court provided relief for groups that fared less well elsewhere in government.

The Era since 1969

It is even more difficult to characterize the Supreme Court's policies in the recent past than in more distant eras, and that certainly is true of the period since the end of the Warren Court in 1969. Perhaps the best characterization is that the Court has moved slowly, unevenly, but substantially in a conservative direction.

Mixed Positions on Civil Liberties. To some extent in the Burger Court, and to a greater extent since then, the Court has narrowed legal protections for individual liberties. The Court's shift is reflected in the rate of success for parties bringing civil liberties claims. Comparisons over time are inexact, because the kinds of cases that the Court hears evolve, but those comparisons provide a general sense of changes in the Court's position. As discussed in Chapter 4, the proportion of decisions that favored civil liberties claims dropped precipitously between the 1960s and the 1970s, and it has remained at that lower level since then. Figure 5-1 shows that the number of laws struck down on the ground that they violated constitutional protections of civil liberties increased in the 1970s but declined dramatically after that.

The reduction in support for civil liberties came most quickly on the rights of criminal defendants. Beginning in the early 1970s, the Court has narrowed the *Miranda* rules for police questioning of suspects and the *Mapp* rule disallowing the use of evidence obtained through illegal searches. The Court's policies on capital punishment have been complicated: the Court struck down existing death penalty laws in *Furman v. Georgia* (1972), upheld a new set of laws in *Gregg v. Georgia* (1976), and since then has had a mixed record on when the death penalty can be imposed. In conjunction with Congress the Court limited the use of habeas corpus petitions as a means for criminal defendants to challenge their convictions after their original appeals ran out.

On issues of equality, the Court moved in a conservative direction more slowly and unevenly. The Burger Court was the first to strike down laws under the equal protection clause on the ground that they discriminated against women. It also held that northern-style school segregation, in which schools were not explicitly segregated by law, could violate equal protection. It generally gave broad interpretations to federal laws against discrimination but ruled against constitutional challenges to discrimination in private institutions that are connected to government. The Rehnquist and Roberts Courts have interpreted federal antidiscrimination laws more narrowly. The Rehnquist Court also approved the termination of court orders that maintained racial integration of public schools and limited the power of the federal government to enforce antidiscrimination laws against state governments. However, the Rehnquist Court continued to strengthen legal protections against sex discrimination in some important respects.

Freedom of expression is the only field in which the Court has directly overruled major Warren Court decisions favoring civil liberties—specifically, on the definition of obscenity.[29] The Burger and Rehnquist Courts narrowed some other First Amendment protections as well. But this is the field in which the Court in the current era has given the greatest support to civil liberties. One example is its protections for commercial speech such as advertising. The Court also struck down several major provisions of two federal statutes regulating campaign finance on First Amendment grounds.

Conservatism on Economic Issues. The Court since 1969 has not reversed its expansion of government powers to regulate the economy, though it has narrowed federal power to regulate interstate commerce in some respects. Most recently, in *National Federation of Independent Business v. Sebelius* (2012), five justices agreed that the commerce power did not extend to a mandate that people buy health insurance, though the Court upheld that mandate under the federal power to levy taxes.

But in its interpretations of federal statutes, the Court has taken positions that are markedly, and increasingly, more conservative in the sense that they favor groups with relatively great economic power over those with less power. The proportion of economic decisions that were classified as liberal by one set of criteria was 74 percent in the 1962–1968 terms. That proportion dropped to 52 percent in the Burger Court (1969–1985 terms), 47 percent in the Rehnquist Court (1986–2004 terms), and 41 percent in the first nine terms of the Roberts Court.[30]

This decrease reflects policy changes in several economic fields—changes that are clearest in the Roberts Court. Since 1969 the Court has narrowed the application of antitrust laws to business practices, and it has given more support to employers in labor law. It has limited the amount of punitive damages that winning parties can be awarded, a limitation that affects primarily plaintiffs who are individuals. It has also reached a number of decisions in which it barred individuals' lawsuits against businesses or the enforcement of state regulations of business practices on the ground that they are preempted by federal laws in the same fields and thus invalid. In *Mutual Pharmaceutical Company v. Bartlett* (2013), for instance, the Court held that a lawsuit against a drug manufacturer under state law for not providing a warning of a drug's potential side effect was preempted by the federal Food, Drug, and Cosmetic Act.

The Court's economic conservatism extends to procedural issues. In several decisions it has upheld the enforcement of contract provisions that require consumers to bring their disputes against companies to arbitration rather than going to court. In another set of decisions, the Court has limited the ability of consumers and employees to bring class action suits against businesses.

The Court's Beneficiaries. By definition, the Court's economic conservatism in the current era has favored the interests of the business community where they conflict with the interests of employees and consumers. Since the 1990s, the business community has also benefited from the Court's decisions in some fields of civil liberties. Some of the Court's expansions of protection for freedom of expression have come in cases brought by businesses, and corporations have been major beneficiaries of the Court's decisions limiting government regulation of electoral campaign funding. And just as the campaign funding decisions reinforced the Court's position that corporations have free speech rights, its decision in *Burwell v. Hobby Lobby Stores* (2014) established that at least some corporations have the right to religious freedom under the federal Religious Freedom Restoration Act.

As in an earlier era, this favorable record is largely a product of the Court's membership but also reflects effective litigation by businesses and business groups. The U.S. Chamber of Commerce developed a strong litigation arm to advocate for business interests, and it has been especially successful in using amicus briefs to support businesses that seek hearings in the Court. The lawyers in the private sector who have become regular and skilled advocates in the Supreme Court serve primarily business clients.

The Court has not been uniformly favorable to business in the current era. As a result, its record can be interpreted in different ways, and not everyone agrees with a headline's characterization of the Roberts Court as "Friend of the Corporation."[31] Still, it seems clear that the Court has become more supportive of business interests since the 1970s than in any other period since its shift in direction in the 1930s. Indeed, the breadth of the Court's support for the business community may exceed that of the late nineteenth and early twentieth centuries.

Explaining the Court's Policies

In the preceding sections I described the Supreme Court's agenda, the extent of its activism, and the content of its policies in three historical periods. Each is summarized in Table 5-3.

The substantial changes in these aspects of the Court's policies over time underline the need to explain them. What forces can account for patterns in Supreme Court policies—especially their ideological content? Elaborating on ideas presented earlier in the book, I will suggest some explanations for those patterns.

The Court's Environment

Freedom from External Pressures. The life terms of Supreme Court justices give them considerable freedom from the rest of government and the general public, a freedom that distinguishes the Court from the other

TABLE 5-3
Summary of the Supreme Court's Policies during Three Historical Periods

Period	Predominant area on agenda	Extent of activism	Content of policy
1890s to 1930s	Economic regulation	Variable, increasing over time	Mixed, primarily conservative
1937 to 1969	Economic regulation, then civil liberties	Initially low, then increasing; very high in 1960s	Generally liberal, very liberal in the 1960s
1969 to 2015	Civil liberties	High, declining in some respects after the 1970s	Initially moderate, then increasingly conservative

Note: Characterizations of each period are approximate and subject to disagreement. The extent of activism is gauged primarily by the striking down of government policies.

branches of government. The Court's freedom is reflected in some of the positions that it takes in individual decisions. Political realities would not allow a legislature to support the right to burn the American flag as a form of political protest or to prohibit student-led prayers at football games. But the Court did make those decisions.[32]

More important, the Court has adopted some broad lines of policy that clearly conflicted with the majority view in the general public and elsewhere in government. Perhaps the most striking was the Court's major expansion of the procedural rights of criminal defendants in the 1960s. No elected body could have adopted so many rules favoring a segment of society that was so unpopular.

Influence from the Other Branches. The Court is not entirely free from external pressure. For one thing, Congress and the president have substantial powers over the Court and its decisions. The other branches frequently act to override Court decisions or to limit their impact. They seldom take action against the Court itself, but threats of such action—especially bills to limit the Court's jurisdiction—are common. The existence and use of these powers give the justices some incentive to avoid or minimize conflicts with the other branches.

It is difficult to ascertain the effect of this incentive on the Court's policies. On the whole, it appears, the justices have felt free to go their own way. But there are some specific episodes in which the other branches appeared to influence the course of Court policy. Examples include the Court's retreat from some of its expansions of civil liberties in the late 1950s and its refusal to decide whether American participation in the Vietnam War was unconstitutional.

More broadly, the Court has shown some caution about using judicial review to strike down significant national policies that enjoyed strong support in the other branches. It is noteworthy that the Court has struck down far more state laws than federal laws. The activism of the Warren Court in civil liberties was directed primarily at the states, and on the whole, that Court was sympathetic to the federal government.[33] Justices in the Rehnquist Court may have felt free to adopt new limitations on federal power because members of Congress during that period were largely sympathetic to those limitations.[34]

Societal Influence. It may be that the state of public opinion on particular issues exerts a subtle impact on justices. More important, however, are broader developments in society. Those developments affect justices' attitudes toward issues such as women's rights and terrorism, just as they affect the attitudes of the public as a whole. They can also exert a direct influence on the Court.

One form of influence involves what can be called a requirement of minimum support: The Court is unlikely to take a sustained policy position that lacks significant support outside the Court, especially support from the segments of society whose judgment is most important to its members. Justices may perceive that taking such positions would damage the Court's institutional position. More fundamentally, they may see positions with little support as unreasonable in themselves. Further, the Court acts on the cases that come to it. The justices cannot reshape their agenda without action by litigants and by the interest groups that support litigation. In turn, those groups develop from broad social movements.

These influences are reflected in the two most distinctive patterns in the Court's policies during the twentieth century. The Court's resistance to government regulation of the economy before 1937 may have conflicted with the majority view in society, but most of the business community and much of the legal community strongly approved that position. Corporations and their representatives engaged in a concerted litigation campaign, bringing to the Court a steady flow of litigation and strong legal arguments against government economic policies.

The Court's expansions of civil liberties from the 1940s to the 1970s also benefited from social support. If these expansions were not always popular, they had significant support within society as a whole and within political and legal elite groups.[35] Social changes and the work of organizations such as the NAACP and the ACLU allowed civil liberties to take a more prominent place on the Court's agenda and allowed the Court to broaden its interpretations of constitutional rights.[36]

To a degree, the Court's increased conservatism since the 1970s reflects changing attitudes in the general public and a growth in litigation by conservative groups. Yet there is probably too little support for the Court to fully reverse its earlier expansions of government regulatory power and protections for civil liberties. The Court has considerable freedom from societal opinion and social trends, but its freedom is not total.

Policy Preferences and the Appointment Power

The freedom that justices do have generally allows them to make their own judgments about the issues they face. Those judgments are based in part on the justices' assessments of the legal merits of cases. But because the questions before the Court seldom have clear legal answers, justices' policy preferences are the primary basis for the positions they take.

The importance of policy preferences suggests that a great deal about the Court's policies can be explained simply and directly: During any given period in the Court's history, its policies have largely reflected the collective preferences of its members. Most of the justices who served from the 1890s through the early 1930s were political conservatives who questioned the desirability of government regulation of business enterprises. In contrast, the justices who came to the Court from the late 1930s through the mid-1960s were predominantly liberals who supported government management of the economy and, in most instances, broader protections of civil liberties.

Collectively, the justices joining the Court since 1969 have been more conservative on civil liberties and economic issues than the justices of the preceding period. In 2007 Justice John Paul Stevens underlined how much the Court's membership had changed in ideological terms: "Including myself, every judge who's been appointed to the Court since Lewis Powell [selected in 1971] has been more conservative than his or her predecessor. Except maybe Justice Ginsburg. That's bound to have an effect on the court."[37]

An explanation of the Court's direction that focuses on the justices' policy preferences is not entirely satisfying, because it does not show why certain preferences predominated in the Court during particular periods. One reason is that some values were dominant in the nation during the periods in which justices were developing their attitudes. Another is that the justices came from backgrounds that instilled particular values in them. Most important, the higher-status backgrounds that predominated during most of the Court's history fostered sympathy for the views and interests of higher-status segments of society. Further, the prevailing ideology in elite segments of the legal profession shapes the views of its members, including future Supreme Court justices.

The most direct source of the Court's collective preferences, however, is the decisions that presidents make in appointing justices. Indeed, the predominant pattern of Supreme Court policy at any given time tends to reflect the identities of the presidents who selected the justices. If a series of appointments is made by conservative presidents, the Court is likely to become a conservative body. And because vacancies occur in the Court fairly often—historically, about every two years on average—most presidents can affect the Court's direction significantly.

Robert Dahl argued that for this reason "the policy views dominant on the Court are never for long out of line with the policy views dominant among the lawmaking majorities of the United States."[38] In Dahl's judgment, the president's power to make appointments, with Senate confirmation of nominees, limits the frequency with which the Court overturns major federal statutes: Justices generally have the same views about policy as the president and members of Congress, so they seldom upset the policies of these branches. I think there is much to Dahl's argument. But because of several complicating factors, the appointment power produces only imperfect control by "lawmaking majorities."

One factor is time lag. Most justices serve for many years, and this is especially true in the current era. As a result, the Court usually reflects the views of past presidents and Senates more than those of the current president and Senate. The lag varies in length, chiefly because presidents have differing opportunities to make appointments. Richard Nixon selected four justices during his six years in office, but Bill Clinton and George W. Bush each chose only two justices in eight years. Jimmy Carter did even worse. The absence of vacancies during his term, combined with his failed reelection bid in 1980, made him the only president to serve at least four years without appointing any justices. As a result, every appointment to the Court between 1969 and 1992 was made by a Republican president.

Further, a president's influence on the Court depends in part on its ideological configuration and on which members leave it. Barack Obama appointed two new justices in his first two years in office. But each replaced one of the Court's most liberal justices, so the two appointments had little impact on the Court's ideological position.

Another complicating factor is deviation of justices from presidential expectations. Presidents usually get most of what they want from their appointees, but that is not a certainty. The unprecedented liberalism of the Court in the 1960s resulted largely from Dwight Eisenhower's miscalculations in nominating Earl Warren and William Brennan. The Rehnquist Court was not as conservative as it could have been because Sandra Day O'Connor, Anthony Kennedy, and especially David Souter diverged from the expectations of the Republican presidents who chose them. Such unexpected results are much less likely today than in most past eras, because of the ideological gulf between the two parties and the greater care that presidents take in choosing justices. But they are still possible.

The role of chance in shaping the Court's general direction should be underlined. Chance plays a part in the timing of Court vacancies and in the performance of justices relative to their appointers' expectations. For that matter, the identity of the president who fills vacancies in the Court sometimes reflects chance. The close electoral victories of John Kennedy in 1960 and Richard Nixon in 1968 were hardly inevitable. The election of George W. Bush in 2000 was even closer. The Kennedy and Nixon appointments had a major impact on the Court's policies, and Bush's appointments also had an effect.

The policy orientations of the Supreme Court between the 1890s and the 1960s reflected the existence of strong lawmaking majorities during two periods: the conservative Republican governments that dominated much of the period from the Civil War to the Great Depression and the twelve-year tenure of Franklin Roosevelt that was accompanied by heavily Democratic Senates. These orientations also reflected patterns of resignations and deaths, unexpected behavior on the part of justices, and other

factors that were a good deal less systematic. And if these factors had operated differently since 1969, the current Court might be less conservative—
or even more so—than the one that actually exists. The forces that shape
the Court's policy positions, like so much about the Court, operate in
complex ways.

Conclusion

In this chapter I have examined several issues relating to the Supreme
Court's policy outputs. A few conclusions merit emphasis.

First, in some periods the Court's policymaking has had fairly clear
themes. During the first part of the twentieth century, the dominant
theme was scrutiny of government economic policies. Later in that century the primary theme was scrutiny of policies and practices that impinged
on individual liberties. In each instance the theme was evident in both the
Court's agenda and the content of its decisions.

Second, these themes and the Court's work as a whole reflect both the
justices' policy preferences and the influence of the Court's environment.
The Court's policies are largely what its members would like them to be. But
the Court is subject to some external influences that shape its policies in
direct and indirect ways. And the president's appointment power creates a
link between the justices' policy preferences and their political environment.

Finally, the Court's role as a policymaker, significant though it is, has
major limits. The Court gives considerable attention to some areas of
policy but scarcely touches others. Some critical matters, such as foreign
policy, are left almost entirely to the other branches of government. Even
in the areas to which the Court gives the most attention, it seldom disturbs
the basic features of national policy.

To a considerable degree, the significance of the Supreme Court as a
policymaker depends on the impact of its decisions, the subject of Chapter 6.
After examining the effect of the Court's decisions, I can make a more
comprehensive assessment of the Court's role in the policymaking process.

NOTES

1. The discussion of agenda change in this section is drawn in part from Richard
   L. Pacelle Jr., *The Transformation of the Supreme Court's Agenda: From the New Deal
   to the Reagan Administration* (Boulder, Colo.: Westview Press, 1991); Richard L.
   Pacelle Jr., "The Dynamics and Determinants of Agenda Change in the
   Rehnquist Court," in *Contemplating Courts*, ed. Lee Epstein (Washington,
   D.C.: CQ Press, 1995), 251–274; and Drew Noble Lanier, *Of Time and Judicial
   Behavior: United States Supreme Court Agenda-Setting and Decision-Making, 1888–
   1997* (Selinsgrove, Pa.: Susquehanna University Press, 2003), chap. 3. Numbers
   of cases in broad policy areas and involving particular issues were calculated

from data collected and presented by Pacelle in his publications and from data in the Supreme Court Database: http://scdb.wustl.edu.

2. These and other data in this paragraph are taken from Pacelle, *Transformation of the Supreme Court's Agenda*, 56–57. The civil liberties category includes cases classified by Pacelle as due process, substantive rights, and equality.

3. *National Federation of Independent Business v. Sebelius* (2012); *King v. Burwell* (2015).

4. Because of ambiguities, different people have counted different numbers of federal and state laws that the Supreme Court struck down. The numbers presented in this chapter are based on data in Congressional Research Service, *The Constitution of the United States of America: Analysis and Interpretation, 2014 Edition* (Washington, D.C.: Government Printing Office, 2014), with my updating. There are some errors and inconsistencies in the Congressional Research Service data, but the broad patterns shown in Table 5-2 are clearly accurate.

5. Linda Camp Keith, *The U.S. Supreme Court and the Judicial Review of Congress* (New York: Peter Lang, 2008), 26.

6. The distinctions made in the paragraphs that follow are drawn chiefly from Robert A. Dahl, "Decision-Making in a Democracy: The Supreme Court as a National Policy-Maker," *Journal of Public Law* 6 (Fall 1957): 279–295.

7. Among these decisions were *United States v. Butler* (1936) and *Schechter Poultry Corp. v. United States* (1935).

8. See Keith E. Whittington, *Political Foundations of Judicial Supremacy: The Supreme Court and Constitutional Leadership in U.S. History* (Princeton, N.J.: Princeton University Press, 2007).

9. The decisions were *McConnell v. Federal Election Commission* (2003); *Federal Election Commission v. Wisconsin Right to Life, Inc.* (2007); *Davis v. Federal Election Commission* (2008); *Citizens United v. Federal Election Commission* (2010); and *McCutcheon v. Federal Election Commission* (2014).

10. Robert Scigliano, "The Presidency and the Judiciary," in *The Presidency and the Political System*, 3rd ed., ed. Michael Nelson (Washington, D.C.: CQ Press, 1990), 471–499; David A. Yalof, "The Presidency and the Judiciary," in *The Presidency and the Political System*, 9th ed., ed. Michael Nelson (Washington, D.C.: CQ Press, 2010), 456–459.

11. The decisions were *Rasul v. Bush* (2004); *Hamdi v. Rumsfeld* (2004); *Hamdan v. Rumsfeld* (2006); and *Boumediene v. Bush* (2008).

12. *Griggs v. Duke Power Co.* (1971).

13. *Meritor Savings Bank v. Vinson* (1986); *Burlington Industries v. Ellerth* (1998).

14. *Wal-Mart Stores, Inc. v. Dukes* (2011).

15. *South Covington & Cincinnati Street Railway Co. v. City of Covington*, 235 U.S. 537, 549 (1915).

16. Sandra L. Wood, Linda Camp Keith, Drew Noble Lanier, and Ayo Ogundele, "The Supreme Court, 1888–1940: An Empirical Overview," *Social Science History* 22 (Summer 1998): 215–216; William G. Ross, *A Muted Fury: Populists, Progressives, and Labor Unions Confront the Courts, 1890–1937* (Princeton, N.J.: Princeton University Press, 1994).

17. To obtain these figures and others that are presented later in the chapter, I categorized decisions that struck down laws according to whether they pertained to economics, civil liberties, or other subjects. The criteria that I used were necessarily arbitrary; other criteria would have resulted in somewhat different totals, though the general patterns would not have changed.

18. *Santa Clara County v. Southern Pacific Railroad Co.* (1886).

19. James W. Ely Jr., *Railroads and American Law* (Lawrence: University Press of Kansas, 2001); Richard C. Cortner, *The Iron Horse and the Constitution: The Railroads and the Transformation of the Fourteenth Amendment* (Westport, Conn.: Greenwood Press, 1993).

20. Benjamin Twiss, *Lawyers and the Constitution* (Princeton, N.J.: Princeton University Press, 1942).

21. This discussion draws from John Braeman, *Before the Civil Rights Revolution: The Old Court and Individual Rights* (Westport, Conn.: Greenwood Press, 1988).

22. *Twining v. New Jersey* (1908).

23. See, for example, *Schenck v. United States* (1917). See also David Rabban, *Free Speech in Its Forgotten Years* (New York: Cambridge University Press, 1997).

24. Henry Steele Commager, "Judicial Review and Democracy," *Virginia Quarterly Review* 19 (Summer 1943): 428. The possible exception was *Wing v. United States* (1896).

25. Robert H. Jackson, *The Struggle for Judicial Supremacy* (New York: Knopf, 1941), 187.

26. William E. Leuchtenburg, *The Supreme Court Reborn: The Constitutional Revolution in the Age of Roosevelt* (New York: Oxford University Press, 1995), 235.

27. *United States v. Cardiff* (1952).

28. Ken Alexander, *San Francisco Examiner*, December 14, 1967, 42.

29. *Miller v. California* (1973).

30. The percentages of liberal decisions are based on analysis of data in the Supreme Court Database, http://scdb.wustl.edu. Economic cases are those in issue areas 7–8 that were decided after oral argument. The unit of analysis is the case citation.

31. Adam Liptak, "Friend of the Corporation," *New York Times*, May 5, 2013, BU1. For divergent views of the Roberts Court's business-related policies, see Lee Epstein, William M. Landes, and Richard A. Posner, "How Business Fares in the Supreme Court," *Minnesota Law Review* 97 (April 2013): 1431–1472; and Jonathan H. Adler, "Business and the Roberts Court Revisited (Again)," The Volokh Conspiracy, May 6, 2013, http://volokh.com/2013/05/06/business-and-the-roberts-court-revisited-again.

32. *Texas v. Johnson* (1989); *Santa Fe Independent School District v. Doe* (2000).

33. Lucas A. Powe Jr., *The Warren Court and American Politics* (Cambridge, Mass.: Harvard University Press, 2000).

34. See Keith E. Whittington, "Taking What They Give Us: Explaining the Court's Federalism Offensive," *Duke Law Journal* 51 (2001): 477–520.

35. See Powe, *Warren Court and American Politics*, 485–501.

36. Charles R. Epp, *The Rights Revolution: Lawyers, Activists, and Supreme Courts in Comparative Perspective* (Chicago: University of Chicago Press, 1998), chaps. 3, 4.

37. Jeffrey Rosen, "The Dissenter," *New York Times Magazine*, September 23, 2007, 52–53.

38. Dahl, "Decision-Making in a Democracy," 285.

Chapter 6

The Court's Impact

W hen the Supreme Court announces its ruling on a major case, the decision is reported in headlines. Afterward, attention usually moves on to other issues and events. But what happens after a Court decision can be as important as the decision itself. Actions by lower courts and the other branches of government help determine the impact of a decision on government policy. People outside of government shape the effects of a Supreme Court decision on society as a whole.

The results can be striking. A decision by the Court that seems monumental may turn out to have more limited effects than originally expected. For that matter, a decision that attracts little notice when the Court issues it may make considerable difference. Thus, it is impossible to understand the role of the Supreme Court in American life without taking into account the actual effects of the decisions it reaches and the policies it makes in those decisions.

This chapter examines the impact of the Court's decisions and the forces that shape their impact. I begin by looking at what happens to litigants after the Court decides their cases. In the remainder of the chapter I discuss the broader effects of the Court's policies: their implementation by judges and administrators, the responses of legislatures and chief executives, and their effects on society as a whole.

Outcomes for the Litigants

Whatever else it does, a Supreme Court decision affects the parties in the case. But the Court's ruling does not always determine the final outcome for the two sides. Indeed, a great deal can happen to the parties after the Court rules in their case.

If the Court affirms a lower-court decision, that decision usually becomes final. If the Court reverses, modifies, or vacates a decision, it usually remands

Justice at Stake

Hugh Caperton's 2009 Supreme Court victory in a dispute with a coal company was only one step in a long legal dispute that still had no final resolution as of 2015.

(sends back) the case to the lower court for "further proceedings consistent with this opinion" or similar language. When it remands a case, the Court sometimes gives the lower court little leeway on what to do, and in that situation the judges on that court almost always follow the Supreme Court's lead. But often the lower court has wide discretion on how to apply the Court's ruling, and sometimes it rules in favor of the party that had lost in the Supreme Court. The Court ruled in 2013 that the federal Fifth Circuit Court of Appeals had not used a strict enough standard under the Fourteenth Amendment when it upheld an affirmative action program for admissions to the University of Texas. The court of appeals then applied the stricter standard but upheld the program again.[1]

When the Court overturns a criminal conviction on procedural grounds, the defendant is often retried after correction of the procedural problem, and the retrial sometimes produces a second conviction. To take one prominent example, Ernesto Miranda was convicted a second time after the Court reversed his conviction in *Miranda v. Arizona* (1966). Although his statements to the police could not be used in the retrial, other evidence was sufficient to produce a conviction.

The conflict that resulted in a Supreme Court decision may continue after the decision, radiating beyond the court to which the Court remanded the case. Three months after the Court's 2013 ruling in a child custody case under the Indian Child Welfare Act, according to one reporter, "here's who else has had a say: two South Carolina courts, three Oklahoma courts, the Supreme Court of the Cherokee Nation, a battalion of lawyers, two governors and someone from the United Nations."[2] It took another year to resolve the case.

Resolution of a case sometimes takes considerably longer. In 2009 the Supreme Court overturned a West Virginia Supreme Court decision. The chair of the Massey Coal Company had spent $3 million to help elect one of the West Virginia justices. That justice then voted on the majority side of his court's 3–2 decision in favor of the company's appeal from a jury verdict that had required it to pay $50 million to a rival coal company operator. The Supreme Court held that participation in the decision by a justice who had been the beneficiary of so much campaign spending by the company chair violated the due process rights of Hugh Caperton, the rival operator.

When it heard the case on remand from the Supreme Court, with a substitute for the justice in question, the West Virginia court adhered to its original judgment. After that ruling Caperton was able to move his case to Virginia. He then won $5 million in damages in a 2014 trial, but he asked for a new trial on the ground that the damages awarded were inadequate. His request for a new trial was granted in 2015, so the legal dispute continued six years after the Supreme Court's decision and eighteen years after the dispute had begun.[3]

Implementation of Supreme Court Policies

More important than the outcome of a case for the litigants are the broader effects of the legal rules that the Court lays down in its opinions. Like statutes or presidential orders, these rules have to be implemented by administrators and judges. Judges are obliged to apply the Court's interpretations of the law whenever they are relevant to a case. For their part, administrators at all levels of government, such as cabinet officers and police officers, are expected to follow Court-created rules that are relevant to their work. The ways that judges and administrators apply Supreme Court decisions do a great deal to determine the ultimate impact of those decisions.

The responses of judges and administrators to the rules of law that the Court issues can be examined in terms of their compliance or noncompliance with these rules. But the Court's decisions may evoke responses ranging from complete rejection to enthusiastic acceptance and extension, and the concept of compliance does not capture all the possible variations.

The Effectiveness of Implementation

When judges and administrators address issues on which the Supreme Court has ruled, most of the time they readily apply the Court's ruling. They often do so even when that requires them to depart from positions on legal policy they had adopted before the Court's decision. These actions typically get little attention because they accord with most people's assumption that judges and administrators will follow the Court's lead and carry out its decisions fully.

Contrary to this assumption, however, implementation of the Court's policies is often quite imperfect. For Supreme Court decisions, like congressional statutes, the record of implementation is mixed. Some Court rulings are carried out more effectively than others, and specific decisions often are implemented better in some places or situations than in others.

Implementation of the Court's decisions is most successful in lower courts, especially appellate courts. When the Court announces a new rule of law, judges generally do their best to follow its lead. And when a series of decisions indicates that the Court has changed its position in a field of policy, lower courts tend to follow the new trend. For this reason, Court decisions that require only action by lower courts tend to be carried out more effectively than decisions that involve other policymakers.[4]

But even appellate judges sometimes diverge from the Court's rulings. Seldom do they explicitly refuse to follow the Court's decisions. More common is what might be called implicit noncompliance, in which a court purports to follow the Supreme Court's lead but actually evades the implications of the Court's ruling. To take one example, the Court ruled in *Boumediene v. Bush* (2008) that prisoners at the Guantánamo Bay Naval Station had a right to seek their release through writs of habeas corpus. Guantánamo prisoners had to bring their cases to the federal district court in the District of Columbia, and the federal Court of Appeals for the District of Columbia Circuit adopted standards that made it exceedingly difficult for prisoners to win their cases. The judge who dissented from a 2011 decision by the court of appeals complained that "it is hard to see what is left of the Supreme Court's command in *Boumediene* that habeas review be 'meaningful.'"[5]

The Court enjoys considerable success in getting compliance from administrative bodies, and this is especially true of federal administrative agencies. Yet implementation problems are more common among administrators than among judges. For instance, a series of Court decisions since 1962 has limited organized religious observances in public schools, but many schools maintain practices that directly violate the Court's limits.[6] And there has been widespread noncompliance with the Supreme Court's ruling in *Brady v. Maryland* (1963) that prosecutors must provide the defense with evidence that favors the defendant and that is relevant to the issue of guilt or innocence. In 2013 the chief judge of a federal court of appeals referred to "an epidemic of *Brady* violations."[7]

Explaining the Effectiveness of Implementation

How well Supreme Court decisions are implemented depends on several conditions. The most important of these conditions relate to communication of policies to relevant officials, the motivations of those officials to follow or resist the Court's policies, the Court's authority, and the sanctions it can use to deter noncompliance.

Communication. Judges and administrators can carry out Supreme Court decisions well only if they know what the Court wants them to do. The communication process begins with the Court's opinions. Ideally, an opinion would state the Court's legal rules with sufficient precision and specificity that an official who reads the opinion would know how to apply those rules to any other case or situation. But that goal is often difficult to achieve.

The Court can reduce its ambiguity by deciding a series of cases that fills in needed detail. But even a series of decisions may fail to provide clarity. Under federal sentencing law, it can make considerable difference whether a criminal defendant had a prior conviction for a violent crime. But the sentencing statute is not at all clear about how to determine whether a crime is violent, and a series of Supreme Court decisions has not overcome that problem. In 2014, one legal scholar referred to this series of decisions as an "ugly mess."[8] In *Johnson v. United States* (2015), the Court resolved the problem by ruling that the statute's lack of clarity made it unconstitutional.

Sometimes the Court does not follow up on an ambiguous decision. It ruled in *District of Columbia v. Heller* (2008) that the Second Amendment protects gun ownership by individuals from violation by the federal government, and in *McDonald v. Chicago* (2010) it extended that ruling to state violations. But the Court has decided no additional cases to determine which kinds of gun regulations are acceptable under *Heller* and *McDonald,* so lower-court judges have been left on their own to make those judgments.

Ambiguity does more than create difficulties for judges and administrators; it also leaves them with more freedom to reach judgments that accord with their own views. If they disagree with a Supreme Court decision, they may use their freedom to limit the impact of that decision.

Whether the Court's position on an issue is clear or ambiguous, its decisions must be transmitted to relevant judges and administrators. The transmission of decisions is not usually automatic. Even judges seldom monitor the Supreme Court's output systematically to identify relevant decisions. Instead, decisions come to the attention of officials through other channels.

One channel is the mass media. A few Supreme Court decisions are sufficiently interesting to receive heavy publicity in newspapers and on television. But most decisions garner little or no coverage in the mass media, and what the media report is sometimes misleading.

Attorneys communicate decisions to some officials. Through their arguments in court proceedings and administrative hearings, lawyers bring favorable precedents to the attention of judges and administrators. Staff lawyers in administrative agencies often inform agency personnel of relevant decisions. But administrators such as teachers and public welfare workers usually lack that source of information.

Another channel of information is professional hierarchies. State trial judges often become aware of the Court's decisions when they are cited by state appellate courts. Police officers learn of decisions from superiors in their departments. There is considerable potential for misinformation in this process, especially when the communicator disagrees with a decision. Some state supreme courts and many police officials conveyed negative views of decisions by the Warren Court that expanded the rights of criminal defendants when they informed their subordinates of those decisions.

Awareness of Supreme Court decisions is likely to fade over time. When the Court in 1989 struck down a Texas statute that made it a criminal offense to burn flags under most circumstances, its decision and a follow-up decision the next year received enormous attention and generated great controversy. But some states left similar statutes on their books, and occasionally prosecutions are brought under those statutes. In a 2014 case that involved such a prosecution in Missouri, both the arresting police officer and the prosecuting attorney said they had not known about the 1989 and 1990 decisions.[9]

Effective communication of decisions depends on the receivers as well as the channels of transmission. Legally trained officials are the most capable of understanding the Court's decisions and their implications. Police officers and other nonlawyers who work regularly with the law also have some advantage in interpreting decisions. On the whole, administrators who work outside the legal system have the greatest difficulty in interpreting what they learn about Supreme Court rulings.

These problems have an obvious impact. Policymakers who do not know of a decision cannot implement it, and those who misunderstand the Court's requirements will not follow them as intended. Successful implementation of the Court's policies requires both clarity in those policies and their effective transmission to the people who are responsible for carrying them out.

Policy Preferences and Self-Interest. If policymakers know of a Supreme Court decision that is relevant to a choice they face, they must decide what to do about that decision. Officials are likely to carry out the Court's interpretation of the law faithfully if they think it constitutes desirable policy and think they will benefit from adopting it. But if the Court's interpretation conflicts with their policy preferences or their self-interest, they may resist the Court's lead. When appellate judges do not implement decisions fully, the most common reason is a conflict between those decisions and their policy preferences. Trial judges and administrators may also disagree with decisions on policy grounds, as many teachers and administrators did with the Court's rulings on school religious observances, but their self-interest often comes into play as well.

One example of enthusiastic implementation by policymakers who approve of the Court's ruling is the response of federal judges to *United States v. Windsor* (2013), in which the Court struck down the statutory provision that barred the federal government from recognizing same-sex marriages. The application of *Windsor* to state prohibitions of same-sex marriage was uncertain. But most judges who heard challenges to those prohibitions ruled that they were unconstitutional, often using *Windsor* as a basis for their rulings. In doing so, they not only accepted the Court's ruling but extended it by a big step.

In contrast, some judges strongly disagreed with the Court's decision in *Graham v. Florida* (2010), which prohibited life sentences with no possibility of parole for juveniles who were convicted of offenses other than homicide. Those judges followed that prohibition literally, but they skirted the Court's intent by imposing long sentences—in one instance, replacing a life sentence with one of 170 years.[10] Whether such sentences comply with the Court's requirement in *Graham* that defendants be given "some meaningful opportunity to obtain release" has not been determined.

Disagreement about judicial policy tends to follow ideological lines. The Ninth Circuit Court of Appeals on the West Coast has long been the most liberal federal appellate court, distinctly more liberal than the Supreme Court. As a result, judges on the Ninth Circuit sometimes give narrow interpretations to conservative decisions by the Court.

Supreme Court policies conflict with officials' self-interest if they threaten practices that serve important purposes. In *Bearden v. Georgia* (1983), the Court ruled that a defendant's probation could not be revoked because of inability to pay a fine and restitution. Almost surely, the Court's rationale applies to any fees imposed on defendants. But local governments have increasingly imposed a variety of fees and fines on defendants as a means to raise money, and they use the threat of jail as a way to pressure defendants to find the money to pay these costs. As a result, a great many people with limited economic resources are jailed in violation of *Bearden*.[11] Full compliance with the *Brady* rule that prosecutors give defense attorneys evidence favorable to their clients would lead to acquittals and dismissals in some cases, and that consequence explains the widespread noncompliance with *Brady*.

Decisions that expand the procedural rights of criminal defendants in court proceedings may also encounter resistance if they would be costly to implement or if they would slow the processing of cases. For both reasons, trial courts sometimes do not comply with the Court's rulings that extended the right of indigent defendants to be provided an attorney to some misdemeanor cases. Similarly, juvenile defendants are not always accorded the procedural rights that the Court has said they are entitled to. In a 2012 report, for instance, the U.S. Department of Justice described a substantial gap between those rights and the practices of the juvenile court in Memphis.[12]

Elected judges and administrators have some incentive to avoid carrying out Supreme Court decisions that are highly unpopular with their constituents. This is true, for instance, when following the Court's rules would require ruling in favor of criminal defendants who are charged with serious crimes. Federal judges with life terms need not worry about keeping their decisions, but they may want to avoid incurring public wrath on highly visible issues.

The Court's Authority. A lawsuit charged that army officers in Hawaii violated army regulations in 2006 by refusing to give light duty to a soldier with a high-risk pregnancy. Her baby died shortly after his premature birth, and her husband sued the army for the death. But a federal district court dismissed the case on the basis of *Feres v. United States* (1950), in which the Supreme Court established a general rule barring lawsuits against the federal government for injuries arising out of military service. In *Ritchie v. United States* (2014), the U.S. Court of Appeals for the Ninth Circuit affirmed the dismissal of the case. Two of the three judges on the panel wrote opinions that denounced *Feres* and its impact on the *Ritchie* case, but they reluctantly concluded that they had no choice but to follow *Feres* and dismiss the case.

In reaching this judgment, the Ninth Circuit judges were accepting both the Supreme Court's authority to make conclusive judgments about the law and their own obligation to comply with the Court's decisions. This acceptance, broadly shared among judges and administrators, fosters faithful implementation of Supreme Court decisions.

The Court's authority is strongest for judges, who have been socialized to accept the leadership of higher courts and who benefit from acceptance of judicial authority. It is highly unusual for a judge to reject the Court's authority directly. More often, judges give narrow interpretations to Court decisions with which they disagree, thereby limiting the impact of those decisions while acknowledging the Court's authority. In some instances, these narrow interpretations seem inconsistent with the Court's decisions. But because most judges fully accept their duty to follow the Court's lead, even that indirect noncompliance is the exception to the rule.

The Court's authority extends to administrators, and it helps to foster faithful implementation of decisions by administrative bodies. To take one important example, some public school officials have eliminated religious observances they would prefer to maintain because they accept their duty to follow Supreme Court rulings.[13] On the whole, however, the Court's authority is weaker for administrators than for judges. Administrative bodies are somewhat removed from the judicial system and its norm of obedience to higher courts, and most administrators have not had the law school training that supports this norm. As a result, administrative officials find it easier to justify deviation from Supreme Court policies than judges do.

The Court's authority tends to decline as organizational distance from the Court increases. State trial judges typically orient themselves more closely to appellate courts in their state than to the Supreme Court, which is several steps away from them in the judicial hierarchy. For administrators at the grassroots level, both state courts and administrative superiors may seem far more relevant to their policy choices than the Supreme Court does.

Sanctions for Disobedience. Alongside its authority, the Court has more concrete sanctions with which to secure effective implementation of its rulings. For judges, the most common sanction is reversal. If a court does not follow an applicable Supreme Court policy, the losing litigant may appeal the case and secure a reversal of the judge's decision. The Court sometimes uses reversals as a means to get lower courts in line, as it did with three reversals of state court decisions that the justices deemed inconsistent with the Court's decisions on arbitration of disputes.[14] And the Court has reversed decisions of the U.S. Court of Appeals for the Federal Circuit several times in recent years in an effort to rein in that court's interpretations of patent law.

The threat of reversal does not always secure compliance. The primary reason is that reversal has its limits as a sanction. Judges who feel strongly about an issue may be willing to accept reversals on that issue as the price for following their personal convictions. Judges on the Federal Circuit have been slow to change their patent policies despite the reversals that stem from those policies. In one Federal Circuit decision, a dissenting judge complained that "the majority resists the Supreme Court's unanimous directive to apply the patentability subject matter test with more vigor."[15] But the full membership of the Federal Circuit reheard the case and ruled in the other direction, and the Supreme Court affirmed its decision in 2014—in effect, telling the lower court that this time it got things right.[16]

For that matter, failure to follow the Supreme Court's lead does not always lead to reversal. The Court reviews a very small proportion of decisions by federal courts of appeals and state supreme courts. Further, the great majority of judges are reviewed by a court other than the Supreme Court, and the reviewing court may share their opposition to the Court's policies.

For administrators, the most common sanction is a court order that directs compliance with a decision. If an agency fails to follow an applicable Supreme Court policy, someone who is injured by its failure may bring a lawsuit to compel compliance with the Court's decision. Administrative agencies find any suit unwelcome because of the trouble and expense it entails. A successful suit is even worse, because an order to comply with a Supreme Court rule puts an agency under judicial scrutiny and can embarrass agency officials. The agency may also be required to pay monetary damages to the person who brought the lawsuit.

But this sanction has weaknesses. Most important, it can be used only if people sue agencies, and often agency noncompliance does not lead to any lawsuits. Most school religious observances that violate the Court's decisions are not challenged in court, either because nobody in the community disagrees with those observances or because the negative consequences of bringing a lawsuit—including hostile reactions from people in the community—deter such challenges. If a lawsuit is threatened or actually brought, whether on school religion or another issue, agencies can usually change their practices in time to avoid serious costs. And sanctions lose some of their efficacy in situations in which noncompliance is difficult to ascertain.

Still, to follow a policy that conflicts with a Supreme Court ruling carries risks that officials usually prefer to avoid. This attitude helps to account for the frequency with which administrative organizations take the initiative to eliminate practices that the Court prohibits. Administrators whose actions require court enforcement such as some regulatory officials have even more reason to avoid noncompliance, since it may cost them the judicial support they need.

Police practices in searches and seizures illustrate both the strength and the limitations of sanctions.[17] Under *Mapp v. Ohio* (1961), noncompliance with constitutional rules for searches generally prevents the use of the seized evidence in court. Largely for this reason, officers frequently comply with rules they would prefer to ignore. But officers seldom receive any personal sanctions for noncompliant practices that cause evidence to be thrown out, and they do not necessarily care a great deal about convictions of the people they arrest. Moreover, illegal searches may not prevent convictions. Most defendants plead guilty, and by doing so they generally waive their right to challenge the legality of searches. Trial judges usually give the benefit of the doubt to police officers when searches are questioned. And evidence that is ruled illegal may not be needed for a conviction. Thus, police officers have an incentive to avoid illegal searches but not so strong an incentive that they always try to follow the applicable rules.

This discussion points to two conditions that affect the implementation process. First, interest groups that are involved in litigation help secure enforcement of Supreme Court decisions by challenging noncompliance that might go on undisturbed without groups' initiative. Second, the Court's decisions are easiest to enforce when the affected policymakers are small in number and highly visible. It is relatively simple for the Court to oversee the fifty state governments that must carry out its decisions on the drawing of legislative districts. It is far more difficult for the Court to oversee the day-to-day activities of all the police officers who investigate crimes.

In general, the sanctions available to the Court are fairly weak. For that reason, help from Congress and the president can make a great deal of difference when the Court faces widespread noncompliance.

Two Case Studies of Implementation

The implementation process can be illuminated with two case studies. School desegregation and police questioning of suspects highlight the difficulties of implementation and the variation in its success.

School Desegregation. Before the Supreme Court's 1954 decision in *Brown v. Board of Education,* separate public schools for black and white students existed throughout the South and in most districts of border states such as Oklahoma and Maryland. The Court's decision required that these dual school systems be eliminated. In the border states compliance was slow and imperfect, but there was a gradual movement toward desegregation. In contrast, policies in the South changed very slowly. As late as 1964–1965, there was no southern state in which even 10 percent of the black students went to school with any white students, a minimal definition of desegregation.[18]

The difference between the two regions reflected differences in the level of commitment to segregated schools. Southern judges and school officials responded to *Brown* in an atmosphere that was quite hostile to desegregation. Most white citizens were strongly opposed to desegregation. The opinions of black citizens had only a limited impact, in part because a large proportion of them were prevented from voting. For their part, public officials encouraged resistance to the Supreme Court.

Because of this political atmosphere and their own opposition to *Brown,* most school administrators did everything possible to preserve segregation. Those administrators who wanted to comply with the Court's ruling were deterred from doing so by pressure from state officials and local citizens.

In places where the schools did not comply on their own, parents could file lawsuits in the federal district courts to challenge the continuation of segregated systems. In many districts no suits were ever brought, in part because of fear of retaliation.

Even where suits were brought, their success was limited. In its second decision in *Brown* in 1955, the Supreme Court gave federal district judges great freedom to determine the appropriate schedule for desegregation in a school district. Many judges themselves disagreed with *Brown,* and all felt local pressure to maintain segregation. As a result, few judges demanded speedy desegregation of schools, and some actively resisted desegregation. Some judges did support the Court wholeheartedly, but they found it difficult to overcome delaying tactics by school administrators and elected officials.

After a long period of resistance, officials in the southern states began to comply. In the second decade after *Brown,* most dual school systems in the South were finally dismantled. Although school segregation was not eliminated altogether, the proportion of black students attending school with whites increased tremendously. Table 6-1 shows that change.

The major impetus for the change came from Congress. The Civil Rights Act of 1964 allowed federal funds to be withheld from institutions that practiced racial discrimination. In carrying out that provision, President Lyndon Johnson's administration required that schools make a "good-faith start" toward desegregation to receive federal aid. Faced with a threat to important financial interests, school officials felt some compulsion to go along. The 1964 act also allowed the Justice Department to bring desegregation suits where local residents were unable to do so, and that provision greatly increased the potential for litigation against school districts that refused to change their policies. The Court reinforced the congressional action with decisions in 1968 and 1969 that demanded effective desegregation without further delay.[19]

In the 1970s the Court turned its attention to the North. In many northern cities, housing patterns and school board policies had combined to create a situation in which white and nonwhite students generally went to different schools. In a Denver case, *Keyes v. School District No. 1* (1973), the Court held that segregation caused by government in such cities violated the Fourteenth Amendment and required a remedy. In a line of decisions over the next decade, the Court spelled out rules with which to identify segregation that violated the Constitution and to devise remedies for that segregation.

More favorable to desegregation than their southern counterparts, federal district judges in the North gave much more support to the Court's mandates. Many ordered sweeping remedies for segregation in the face

TABLE 6-1
Percentage of Black Elementary and Secondary Students Going to School with Any Whites, in Eleven Southern States, 1954–1973

School year	Percentage	School year	Percentage
1954–1955	0.001	1964–1965	2.25
1956–1957	0.14	1966–1967	15.9
1958–1959	0.13	1968–1969	32.0
1960–1961	0.16	1970–1971	85.6
1962–1963	0.45	1972–1973	91.3

Sources: For 1954–1967, Southern Education Reporting Service, *A Statistical Summary, State by State, of School Segregation-Desegregation in the Southern and Border Area from 1954 to the Present* (Nashville, Tenn.: Southern Education Reporting Service, 1967); for 1968–1973, U.S. Bureau of the Census, Statistical Abstract of the United States (Washington, D.C.: Government Printing Office, 1971 and 1975).

Note: The states are Alabama, Arkansas, Florida, Georgia, Louisiana, Mississippi, North Carolina, South Carolina, Tennessee, Texas, and Virginia.

of strong local opposition to those remedies—especially busing of students. One judge ordered the imposition of higher property taxes to pay for school improvements that might facilitate desegregation in Kansas City, Missouri. Another held a city in New York State and some of its council members in contempt for failing to approve new public housing for a similar purpose.[20] Ironically, the Court found some of these remedies *too* sweeping.

Few northern school districts took significant steps to reduce segregation until they were faced with a court order or pressure from federal administrators. But most northern districts complied with desegregation orders. One reason was the willingness of some district judges to supervise school desegregation closely. Congress and some presidents took steps to limit northern desegregation, but their actions were mostly symbolic and had little impact.

When desegregation plans were put in place, it was uncertain whether and when such plans could be terminated. In a pair of decisions in 1991 and 1992, the Court indicated that these plans need not remain permanent even if ending them would produce high levels of racial segregation within a school district.[21] With support for desegregation declining, administrators in many districts have accepted this invitation and returned to systems in which students are assigned to schools based on where they reside.

In contrast, administrators in Seattle and Louisville designed school assignment plans to reduce segregation, and lower federal courts upheld those plans. But the Supreme Court struck down these plans in *Parents Involved v. Seattle School District No. 1* (2007) on the ground that they impermissibly took race into account. The ultimate impact of that ruling on school district policies remains uncertain. That was the Court's only decision on school segregation in the last two decades, as it has left intact the rules it laid down in the period from the mid-1950s to the early 1990s.

Police Questioning of Suspects. In *Miranda v. Arizona* (1966), one of the Supreme Court's best known decisions, the Court required that suspects who were in custody be given certain rights and warnings notifying them of those rights before police questioned them if their statements were to be used as evidence in court. *Miranda* had to be interpreted by lower appellate courts, applied to specific cases by trial judges, and followed by law enforcement officers who question suspects.

Lower-court responses to *Miranda* have been mixed. Some state supreme courts criticized the decision and interpreted it narrowly. Many trial judges who sympathize with the police are reluctant to exclude evidence on the basis of Supreme Court rules. But some lower-court judges have applied *Miranda* vigorously, and the Court's rules have had considerable effect on the pattern of decisions on police questioning in other appellate courts.[22]

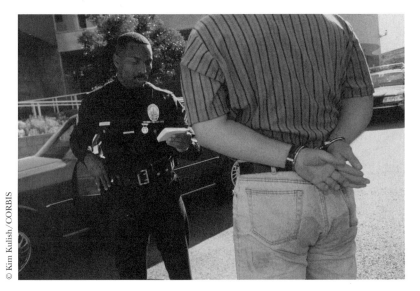

Following what has become standard practice, a Los Angeles police officer in training reads the Miranda rights to a police employee playing a suspect.

Although the basic rules of *Miranda* remain standing, since the 1970s the Court has narrowed its protections of suspects in some respects. That process began with *Harris v. New York* (1971), in which the Court ruled that statements obtained from suspects in violation of *Miranda* could be introduced into evidence to attack the credibility of a defendant's testimony at trial. To take a more recent example, in *Berghuis v. Thompkins* (2010) and other decisions, the Court has said that suspects must explicitly invoke their rights. For instance, a suspect's remaining silent for a lengthy period does not prevent officers from continuing to ask questions and ultimately getting answers that can be admitted in court. This narrowing has made it easier for lower-court judges who want to limit the impact of *Miranda* through their decisions to do so.

Miranda was unpopular in the law enforcement community, because police officers and administrators anticipated that suspects who were warned of their rights would refuse to talk to police.[23] As a result, they feared, their ability to obtain confessions would be severely damaged and the rate of convictions would decline substantially. But the effects of *Miranda* have been more limited than expected. Informing suspects of their rights does not deter most of them from talking with the police. In part, this is because there is an inherently coercive atmosphere when police officers question suspects in custody, so people tend to answer questions even after hearing the *Miranda* warnings.

This reality has reduced the tension between police officers' goal of getting incriminating information from suspects and their goal of having that information be admissible in court. For that reason, it has become standard practice in most places for officers to issue the required warnings to suspects. Still, officers do not always comply with the spirit of *Miranda*. They have found ways to reduce the likelihood that suspects will invoke their rights and refuse to talk, such as treating the warnings as a formality with no meaning. They can avoid providing the warnings by telling suspects they are free to go, so *Miranda* does not apply. In one borough of New York City, the prosecutor's office adopted a practice of preceding the *Miranda* warnings with a statement implying that by talking, suspects could get the office to seek evidence favorable to them.[24]

There is some direct noncompliance with *Miranda*. In some California police departments, for example, officers have told suspects who invoke their *Miranda* rights that they want to ask questions off the record and that nothing the suspect says can be used in court. Most suspects do not realize that under the *Harris* decision, what they tell the police can be used to discredit what they say if they choose to testify on their own behalf in court.[25]

This does not mean that *Miranda* has no impact on the results of police questioning. There is some evidence that confession rates went down after the Court's decision. But that impact probably lessened over time as police officers adapted to the *Miranda* requirements.[26] To a considerable degree, police officers have learned to live with *Miranda*, complying at least partially with its requirements and continuing to get the information they seek from most suspects. Indeed, *Miranda* serves them well in one important respect, because of the practice of asking suspects to say that they are waiving their *Miranda* rights. As one scholar put it, "If warnings were delivered by the police and a waiver was given or signed, it is almost impossible to persuade a judge that the resultant confession or admission is 'involuntary.'"[27] For this reason, although many officers still resent *Miranda*, police condemnation of the decision is far from universal.[28]

Responses by Legislatures and Chief Executives

Congress, the president, and their state counterparts also respond regularly to Supreme Court decisions. Their responses shape the impact of the Court's decisions, and some responses by Congress and the president affect the Court itself.

Congress

Congressional responses to the Court's rulings take several forms. Within some limits, Congress can modify or override the Court's decisions.

Congress also affects the implementation of decisions, and it can act against individual justices or the Court as a whole.

Statutory Interpretation. In the world of statutory law, Congress is legally supreme. When the Supreme Court interprets a federal statute, as it does in most of its decisions, Congress can override that interpretation simply by enacting a new statute—so long as the president signs the statute or Congress overrides a veto. Such action is not rare. One study identified 275 decisions that Congress overrode in the forty-seven years from 1967 through 2011, an average of more than ten in each two-year Congress.[29] These overrides affect a small but meaningful proportion of the Court's statutory decisions; a study of tax decisions from 1954 to 2004 found that Congress overrode at least 8 percent of them.[30]

Some overrides represent direct efforts to invalidate recent Supreme Court decisions that have aroused widespread disagreement in Congress. But statutes that are aimed at specific decisions are a distinct minority. More often, Congress updates the law in an area of policy with a new statute, and in the process it overrides one or more decisions. Occasionally, members of Congress are not even aware that they have overridden the Court with a new statute.

Members of Congress themselves initiate some efforts to override decisions, but more often they respond to interest groups. Just as groups that are unsuccessful in Congress frequently turn to the courts for relief, groups whose interests suffer in the Supreme Court frequently turn to Congress. Sometimes the initiative comes from the Court itself. A dissenting justice may urge Congress to negate the decision in question, as Justice Sotomayor did in her dissenting opinion in a 2014 decision on monetary compensation to victims of child pornography.[31] And occasionally, the Court's majority opinion invites members of Congress to override the Court's decision if they think that the Court misinterpreted their intent or that the Court's decision created an undesirable result.

Legislation is typically difficult to enact, and that is true of bills to override Supreme Court decisions. It can help if an override is attached to a broad bill that has majority support. In 2010 Congress overrode a decision before the Court issued it, because members correctly predicted that the Court would reach a decision they disapproved on the right of individuals to bring lawsuits under the False Claims Act. That speedy action was possible only because it was part of the massive bill that restructured the nation's health care system.[32] Whether Congress overrides a particular decision depends in part on its partisan composition. In recent years Democrats in Congress have introduced bills to override some conservative Supreme Court decisions, but with Republican majorities in one or both houses such bills have little chance for success. And the partisan polarization that makes it more difficult to enact controversial legislation of any type helps to account for a reduction in the number of overrides since the 1990s.

Statutes that override the Court's decisions, like any other statutes, are subject to the Court's interpretation in later cases. Sometimes the Court reads an override in a way that limits the impact of that override on the law. This has been the case with some of the congressional overrides of decisions that gave narrow interpretations to statutes prohibiting employment discrimination.[33] Congress could enact another statute to clarify its intent, but often there is not sufficient interest or political support for such action. Thus, despite the legal supremacy of Congress in statutory law, the Court sometimes has the last word on the issues that both branches address.

Constitutional Interpretation. When the Supreme Court interprets the Constitution, its decisions can be overturned only by amending the Constitution. Members of Congress often introduce resolutions to overturn or blunt the effects of decisions with constitutional amendments. In the 113th Congress of 2013–2014, for instance, there were proposals for amendments on regulation of campaign finance, term limits for members of Congress, mandates to buy health insurance, and flag burning. These efforts seldom win the two-thirds majorities needed for Congress to propose an amendment. Congress has proposed an amendment that was aimed directly at Supreme Court decisions only five times. One of these, proposed in 1924 to give Congress the power to regulate child labor, was not ratified by the states. (A few other amendments have had the effect of negating Supreme Court decisions.) Since the child labor proposal, the only amendment that Congress has proposed to overturn a decision was the Twenty-Sixth Amendment, adopted in 1971. In *Oregon v. Mitchell* (1970), the Court ruled that Congress could not regulate the voting age in elections to state office. Congress quickly proposed an amendment overturning the decision, and the states quickly ratified it.

The difficulty of the constitutional amendment route is illustrated by the repeated failures of efforts to overturn two Supreme Court rulings by allowing criminal penalties for flag burning. In 1989 and 1990, the Supreme Court struck down state and federal statutes prohibiting flag burning on the ground that they punished people for political expression. Shortly after the 1989 decision, some members of Congress began working for a constitutional amendment to allow prohibitions of flag desecration. Its passage might seem inevitable, because most members of Congress abhor flag burning and because a member's vote against the amendment could provide an election opponent with a powerful issue. Indeed, the House approved flag desecration amendments in every

Congress from 1995 to 2006, and in 2006 the Senate came within one vote of sending an amendment to the states. But the general reluctance to amend the Constitution was compounded by a special reluctance to limit the protections of the Bill of Rights. Those concerns were just enough to keep any anti-flag-burning amendment from getting through Congress.

Often, however, a constitutional amendment is not needed to limit or even negate the effects of a decision interpreting the Constitution. When the Court upholds some government practice that was challenged under the Constitution, Congress can simply prohibit that practice by statute so long as doing so is within its power to legislate. And when the Court holds that a federal statute is unconstitutional, Congress can sometimes write a new statute in an effort to meet the Court's objection to the old one and thereby reinstate the same policy at least in part. Congress can also enact such a statute to protect other kinds of government practices that the Court has struck down.

Congress frequently takes this kind of action, as it did in response to two recent First Amendment decisions involving military matters. In *Snyder v. Phelps* (2011), the Court ruled that the father of a Marine could not sue the members of a church that demonstrated near his son's funeral while proclaiming highly critical messages about the family. Congress responded the next year with a statute that limited demonstrations at military funerals. And after the Court ruled in *United States v. Alvarez* (2012) that a statute imposing criminal penalties for falsely claiming to have a military honor violated the First Amendment, in 2013 Congress passed a narrower statute that criminalized such false claims if they were made "with intent to obtain money, property, or other tangible benefit."[34]

When Congress enacts such a statute, the Court often hears a case to determine whether the new statute avoids the constitutional problem it was designed to overcome. Sometimes the Court takes a proactive approach when it strikes down a statute, suggesting that Congress revise the statute to avoid the constitutional problem that the Court identified. And in some cases the Roberts Court has gone a step further, indicating in a decision that it is likely to strike down a statute in a later case if Congress does not address a constitutional problem in the statute.[35]

The Court took both proactive approaches in reviewing the federal Voting Rights Act, under which certain states and local governments are required to get "preclearance" from the federal government before making changes in their election laws. In *Northwest Austin Municipal Utility District No. One v. Holder* (2009), Chief Justice Roberts's opinion for the Court implied that if Congress did not change the formula for determining which governments must get federal approval, the Court might strike down the provision with that formula as unjustified by congressional power to enforce the Fifteenth Amendment. Congress did not act, and four years later the Court did strike down the provision in *Shelby County v. Holder* (2013).

Roberts's opinion for the Court in *Shelby County* invited Congress to "draft another formula based on current conditions," though he also indicated that the Court would not automatically accept such a new formula.[36] Roberts surely recognized that because of political realities, it was very unlikely that Congress would revise the formula. Thus, his invitation to Congress may have been intended to deflect blame from the Court among people who favored preclearance of election laws.

Affecting the Implementation of Decisions. By passing legislation, Congress can influence the implementation of Supreme Court decisions by other institutions. Its most important tool is money. Congress can provide funds to carry out a decision or choose not to provide them. It can also affect responses to Court decisions by state and local governments through its control over federal grants to them. Congressional use of this latter power was critical to school desegregation in the South.

In a 2001 education statute, Congress employed the same power in two different ways. The first was related to *Boy Scouts of America v. Dale* (2000), in which the Court held that the First Amendment allows the Boy Scouts to prohibit membership to gay men and boys. In response, some schools ended their ties with the Scouts. One provision of the 2001 law required that no federal funds be provided to schools that "deny equal access" to the Scouts or "discriminate against" them. Another provision required that schools receiving federal money allow "constitutionally protected prayer." By enacting this provision, Congress gave school districts an incentive to adopt narrow interpretations of the Court's limitations on school religious observances.[37]

When a Supreme Court decision requires Congress itself to comply with the decision, Congress generally does so. The legislative veto is a partial exception. In *Immigration and Naturalization Service v. Chadha* (1983), the Court indicated that any statutes allowing Congress as a whole, one house, or a committee to veto proposed actions by executive-branch agencies are invalid. After the decision, Congress eliminated legislative veto provisions from several statutes. But it has maintained others and adopted more than 1,000 new legislative veto provisions—most requiring that specific congressional committees approve action by administrative agencies. Congress does not use its veto power formally. Rather, veto provisions lead to informal accommodations between agencies and committees, accommodations that administrators accept as preferable to more stringent controls by Congress. As a result, the *Chadha* decision, which had appeared to be a highly consequential decision, has had a very limited effect.[38]

Attacks on Justices and the Court. When members of Congress are unhappy with the Supreme Court's policies, they can attack the Court or the justices directly. The easiest way to do so is verbally, and members of Congress sometimes denounce the Court. In a 2013 speech, for instance, Democratic senator Elizabeth Warren of Massachusetts attacked the "corporate capture of the federal courts," including the Supreme Court, and said that "you follow this pro-corporate trend to its logical conclusion, and sooner or later you'll end up with a Supreme Court that functions as a wholly owned subsidiary of Big Business."[39] Speaking privately to his Republican colleagues in the House, Mike Pence of Indiana compared the Court's 2012 decision upholding the key provision in the federal health care law of 2010 to the terrorist attacks on the United States in 2001 (a remark for which he later apologized).[40]

More concretely, Congress can take several types of formal action against the Court or its members.[41] One type is reduction of the Court's jurisdiction. The Constitution allows Congress to alter the Court's appellate jurisdiction and the jurisdiction of other federal courts through legislation. Some scholars argue that there are limits to congressional power over the Court's jurisdiction. But in *Ex parte McCardle* (1869), the Court ruled that Congress had acted properly when it withdrew the Court's right to hear appeals in habeas corpus actions in order to prevent the Court from deciding a pending challenge to the post–Civil War Reconstruction legislation.

Members of Congress often propose to limit jurisdiction in order to keep the Court from addressing a particular issue or to blunt the impact of its decisions, and in a few instances since the 1869 episode those proposals have been successful. In 1932 Congress withdrew the federal courts' power to hear certain kinds of cases in labor law, partly in reaction to Supreme Court decisions that were perceived as antagonistic to labor unions.[42] And after the Court ruled in *Rasul v. Bush* (2004) that prisoners at the Guantánamo Bay Naval Station had the right to seek release through habeas corpus petitions, Congress enacted statutes in 2005 and 2006 to prohibit all federal courts—not just the Supreme Court—from hearing habeas cases brought by those prisoners. The Court overturned that action in *Boumediene v. Bush* (2008) on the basis of the constitutional provision on habeas corpus. In doing so, it underlined one limitation on congressional power over federal court jurisdiction.

Members of Congress have proposed other types of actions against the Court with some frequency. One example is constitutional amendments to limit the justices' terms. There have also been occasional threats to impeach justices whose decisions displease members of Congress or to use the budget power by limiting Court resources or refusing to increase the justices' salaries. (The Constitution prohibits Congress from reducing justices' salaries.)

Proposals to attack the Court in these and other ways have been more common in some eras than in others. The activism of the Court in support of civil liberties since the 1950s has led to high rates of anti-Court proposals during several periods in this era. The early twenty-first century is one of those periods. Despite the Court's relative conservatism in this period, most of the proposals to take action against the Court have continued to come from congressional conservatives.[43]

In light of the range of congressional powers over the Court and the frequency with which members of Congress threaten to use them, it is striking how little Congress has actually employed its powers during the past century. Of the many actions that members of Congress contemplated using against the conservative Court in the early part of the twentieth century, culminating in Franklin Roosevelt's Court-packing plan, almost none were carried out.[44] The same is true of the attacks on the Court for its civil libertarian decisions since the 1950s. Why has Congress been so hesitant to use its powers, even at times when most members are unhappy about the Court's direction?

Several factors help explain this hesitancy.[45] First, there are always some members of Congress who agree with the Court's policies and lead its defense. The mechanisms available to block legislation give defenders of the Court tools to prevent the enactment of measures they oppose. Second, serious forms of attack against the Court, such as impeachment and reducing its jurisdiction, seem illegitimate to many people, even members of Congress who strongly disagree with the Court's decisions. Finally, when threatened with serious attack, the Court occasionally retreats to reduce the impetus for congressional action. For these reasons, the congressional bark at the Supreme Court has been a good deal worse than its bite.

The President

Like members of Congress, presidents frequently comment on the Supreme Court, and they sometimes criticize the Court's decisions. In 2010, for instance, President Obama used his State of the Union address to criticize *Citizens United v. Federal Election Commission* (2010), a week-old decision in which the Court narrowed congressional power to regulate the funding of election campaigns. (Justice Samuel Alito, sitting in the audience, responded to the president's description of the decision's impact by shaking his head and seemed to mouth the words *not true.*)[46]

Presidents can also influence congressional responses to the Court's decisions by proposing action or taking a position on proposals initiated by others. *Ledbetter v. Goodyear Tire & Rubber Co.* (2007) set a tight time limit on lawsuits for discrimination in pay under the Civil Rights Act of 1964. As a presidential candidate in 2008, Barack Obama championed an effort to override the decision by amending the Civil Rights Act. Within two weeks of his 2009 inauguration, he signed an override bill that Congress had speedily enacted.

Using Executive Power. As chief executive, the president can shape the implementation and impact of Supreme Court decisions. Responses to decisions by the Obama administration illustrate the variety of steps that presidents can take. Reacting to decisions that let companies require that employees take legal grievances against them to arbitration rather than going to court, Obama issued an executive order in 2014 that prohibited companies with substantial federal contracts from requiring arbitration for discrimination claims under the Civil Rights Act of 1964.[47] In response to a 2007 decision upholding a Labor Department regulation that exempted certain home health care workers from the minimum wage law, in 2013 the department changed the regulation to eliminate that exemption.[48] After the Court's ambiguous decision on affirmative action in college admissions in *Fisher v. University of Texas* (2013), the Justice and Education Departments sent a letter to college presidents encouraging the continuation of affirmative action programs.[49] And after *Shelby County v. Holder* (2013), which struck down one section of the Voting Rights Act and thereby made another section inoperative, the Justice Department increased its use of voting rights litigation under two other sections of the statute.

Presidential responses to decisions typically attract the most attention when they are aimed at limiting or negating decisions, but presidents can also act to enhance the impact of decisions they favor. After *United States v. Windsor* (2013), in which the Court struck down a statutory provision that prohibited the federal government from recognizing same-sex marriages, the Obama administration moved to give the decision a broad impact. The Treasury Department adopted a rule that couples in same-sex marriages would be treated as married under federal tax law even if they lived in a state that prohibited such marriages, and the president directed the Department of Veterans Affairs to begin providing spousal benefits to veterans in same-sex marriages despite a federal statute prohibiting such action.

Three presidents provided support to the Court after *Brown v. Board of Education*. In 1957, when a combination of state interference and mob action prevented court-ordered desegregation of the schools in Little Rock, Arkansas, President Dwight Eisenhower deployed federal troops in support of desegregation. In 1962 President John Kennedy took similar action, using federal troops to enforce desegregation at the University of Mississippi. Most important, Lyndon Johnson's administration vigorously used both litigation and control over federal funds to break down segregated school systems in the South.

Compliance with Decisions. Occasionally, a Supreme Court decision requires compliance by the president, either as a party in the case or—more often—as head of the executive branch. Some presidents and commentators have argued that the president need not obey an order of the Supreme Court, on the ground that the Court is a coequal body rather than a legal superior. Whether or not that argument is valid, presidents would seem sufficiently powerful to disobey the Court with impunity.

In reality, their position is not that strong. The president's political power is based largely on the ability to obtain support from other policymakers. In turn, this ability depends in part on perceptions of the president's legitimacy. Because disobedience of the Court would threaten this legitimacy, presidents feel some pressure to comply with the Court's decisions.

This conclusion is supported by presidential responses to two highly visible Court orders. In *Youngstown Sheet and Tube Co. v. Sawyer* (1952), the Court ruled that President Harry Truman had acted illegally during the Korean War when he seized steel mills to keep them operating if a threatened strike took place. The Court ordered an end to the seizure, and Truman immediately complied.

Even more striking is *United States v. Nixon* (1974). During the investigation of the Watergate scandal, President Richard Nixon withheld recordings of certain conversations in his offices that were sought by special prosecutor Leon Jaworski. In July 1974 the Supreme Court ruled unanimously that Nixon must yield the tapes.

In oral argument before the Court, the president's lawyer had indicated that Nixon might not comply with an adverse decision. But he did comply. At the least, this compliance speeded Nixon's departure from office. The content of the tapes provided strong evidence of presidential misdeeds, and opposition to impeachment evaporated. Fifteen days after the Court's ruling, Nixon announced his resignation.

In light of that result, why did Nixon comply with the Court order? He apparently did not realize how damaging the evidence in the tapes actually was. Perhaps more important, noncompliance would have fatally damaged his remaining legitimacy. For many members of Congress, noncompliance in itself would have constituted an impeachable offense, one on which there would be no dispute about the evidence. Under the circumstances, compliance may have been the better of two unattractive choices.

Legislatures and Chief Executives in the States

State and local governments have no direct power over the Supreme Court as an institution. But like Congress and the president, state legislatures, governors, and their local counterparts can influence the impact of the Court's decisions. They can try to limit the effects of decisions that restrict practices they favor, they can act to take advantage of decisions that approve such practices, and they can respond in other ways.

When the Court rules that some type of state statute or constitutional provision violates the U.S. Constitution, legislatures often leave those laws on the books. This inaction may simply reflect inertia or the difficulty of amending state constitutions, but sometimes it is a deliberate choice by legislators who disagree with the Court's decision. Retaining these laws creates a problem only if they are actually enforced, which happens from time to time.

State and local governments sometimes respond to a decision that invalidates one type of law by writing a new law in an effort to meet the Court's constitutional objections to the old one. After *McDonald v. Chicago* (2010), in which the Court held that the right of individuals to own guns applied to the states, some local governments modified prohibitions of gun ownership in ways that they hoped the Court would accept. The same kind of response occurred on capital punishment. After the Court struck down existing death penalty laws in *Furman v. Georgia* (1972), by 1975 thirty-one states wrote new laws that were designed to avoid arbitrary use of capital punishment and thus meet the objections raised by the pivotal justices in *Furman*.[50] In a series of decisions that followed, the Court upheld some of the new statutes and overturned others. States whose laws were rejected by the Court then adopted the forms that the Court had found acceptable.

Governors and state legislatures sometimes get involved in the implementation of decisions. In the 1950s and 1960s, they acted to block school desegregation in the South. Governors in Arkansas, Mississippi, and Alabama used their highly visible opposition to desegregation as a means to enhance their popularity with white voters. Some governors and legislatures have played a similar role in opposition to the Court's limitations on religious observances in public schools.

California governor Jerry Brown has been active in shaping the state's response to *Brown v. Plata* (2011). In that decision the Supreme Court upheld an order by a three-judge district court that the state of California reduce its prison population quite substantially in order to bring health care for prisoners up to the standard required by the Eighth Amendment. The state made efforts to improve health care and reduced the number of prisoners considerably. With these changes, Governor Brown argued in 2013 that California had complied with the spirit of the federal court order even though the prison population was still above the number set by the order, and he warned that full compliance with the order would result in the release of dangerous prisoners. After the Supreme Court chose not to intervene a second time, in 2014 the district court extended the deadline for compliance while criticizing the state for its resistance. In early 2015 the state achieved the mandated number of prisoners a year ahead of time, but a predicted increase in the prison population during that year left the outcome of the case uncertain.[51]

Gideon v. Wainwright (1963) and later decisions required that indigent criminal defendants be provided with legal counsel. The Court's decisions spurred state and local governments to increase their commitment to provide attorneys for indigent defendants. This commitment has been reflected in much higher levels of funding—more than $4 billion a year by state and local governments[52]—and low-income defendants are now in a far better position than they were prior to 1963. But funding of counsel has often been inadequate, and studies of the quality of indigent defense in states and local areas regularly report serious deficiencies.

When the Court upholds a government practice, its action may encourage other state and local governments to adopt that practice. A more complex situation arose after the Court's decision in *Shelby County v. Holder* (2013) effectively ended the requirement in the Voting Rights Act that certain state and local governments get clearance from the federal government before they changed their election laws. In response, state legislators in Southern states that were released from preclearance enacted new laws involving matters such as requirements that people show certain kinds of identification in order to vote.[53] These laws could still be challenged in court, but the outcome of those challenges was uncertain, and the laws might operate for a period of time even if they were ultimately held to be illegal.

Occasionally, a Court decision upholding a government practice spurs state and local officials to consider eliminating it. In *Kelo v. City of New London* (2005), the Court upheld broad government power to take private property with compensation through eminent domain. *Kelo* evoked a strong negative reaction, and within eighteen months two-thirds of the states had enacted legislation to limit the use of eminent domain by local governments.[54] Their action was fully consistent with *Kelo,* since such a decision leaves the states free to protect rights that the U.S. Constitution does not.

In states that allow the voters to enact legislation or amend the state constitution on their own, voters sometimes use those powers in response to Supreme Court decisions. In *Grutter v. Bollinger* (2003), the Court rejected a Fourteenth Amendment challenge to an affirmative action program for admissions to the University of Michigan Law School. Opponents of affirmative action then drafted a state constitutional amendment that would prohibit affirmative action programs by public schools and colleges in Michigan. Voters approved the amendment in 2006. That amendment was then challenged on the ground that *it* violated the Fourteenth Amendment, but the Court upheld the measure in *Schuette v. Coalition to Defend Affirmative Action* (2014).

Abortion as a Case Study

Few Supreme Court decisions have triggered as much activity by legislators and chief executives as *Roe v. Wade* (1973). Based on the constitutional right to privacy, *Roe* mandated a general legalization of abortion prior to the time of viability for a fetus, approximately the end of the sixth month of pregnancy. In the period of more than four decades since that decision, both the federal and state governments have responded with a wide range of actions to reduce its impact or, occasionally, to enhance that impact.

The Federal Government. Shortly after the *Roe* decision, members of Congress who strongly disagreed with the decision initiated an effort to propose a constitutional amendment overturning the decision. That effort failed, but it was revived in the early 1980s after the election of President Ronald Reagan and a more conservative Congress. That effort fell short as well. Some members sought to remove the jurisdiction of the Supreme Court and other federal courts over abortion so that they could not invalidate state and federal policies regulating abortion. This initiative was also unsuccessful.

However, opponents of abortion secured limits on federal funding of abortion in several programs. Most important, since 1976 each annual federal budget has included prohibitions of funding of abortions through federal Medicaid money, though with some limited exceptions. The Supreme Court upheld these prohibitions in *Harris v. McRae* (1980), ruling that decisions by government not to fund abortions were consistent with *Roe*.

Presidents have played a role in congressional action on abortion. They have also acted on their own, using executive orders to adopt policies on various issues under their control such as the availability of abortion to members of the military. Once views on abortion began to split along partisan lines in the 1980s, presidential policies have shifted back and forth as Republican and Democratic presidents succeeded each other. For example, President Reagan prohibited U.S. foreign aid to groups that use their own money in support of abortion, President Clinton repealed that prohibition, President George W. Bush reinstated it, and President Obama repealed it once again.

State Governments. When *Roe* was decided, all but four states had statutes that put severe limits on abortion, and two-thirds of the states allowed abortions only under very limited circumstances or not at all. Faced with the Court's sweeping invalidation of their laws, a great many legislators favored adoption of some new limits. Across the country, a wide range of legislation was enacted to regulate or prohibit abortion under certain circumstances. Governors played important roles in some states as advocates for these laws or opponents of them, as has been true throughout the time since *Roe*.

Many of the new laws were challenged in federal court, and the Supreme Court heard several cases on the new legislation beginning in 1976. Like lower courts, over the next decade the Court struck down a number of laws that substantially limited access to abortion. But it upheld other laws that a majority of the justices saw as consistent with *Roe*. For instance, it ruled out a requirement that all girls under eighteen years old have their parents' consent for an abortion, but it upheld laws with a consent requirement that allowed for some exceptions.

A series of appointments to the Court by Republican presidents reduced the Court's collective commitment to *Roe*, and the Court's decision in *Webster v. Reproductive Health Services* (1989) signaled state legislators that the Court might overturn *Roe* in a future case. In response, legislatures considered a variety of measures to limit abortion. Louisiana, Utah, and Guam enacted general prohibitions of abortion, and Pennsylvania adopted new regulations of abortion. But Connecticut and Maryland enacted statutes that effectively put *Roe* into state law so that overturning of *Roe* would not affect those states.

In *Planned Parenthood v. Casey* (1992), contrary to most people's expectations, the Court largely upheld *Roe*. But the Court did adopt a new rule that a regulation of abortion prior to viability would be unconstitutional if it had the intent or effect of putting an "undue burden" on women's choice to have an abortion. After *Casey*, states continued to enact laws that limited abortion. The appointment of Samuel Alito to the Court in 2006 and the Court's decision upholding the prohibition of one method of abortion in *Gonzales v. Carhart* (2007) encouraged new state legislation restricting abortion. Republican successes in state elections in 2010 and 2014 then increased support for restrictive legislation. State legislatures enacted an array of new laws, including procedural requirements that made it difficult for abortion clinics to operate and general prohibitions of abortion after time points that came before viability.

Like earlier laws, the new wave of laws spurred lawsuits challenging their validity. Federal judges struck down some statutes on the ground that they violated the undue burden test, but judges upheld other laws. As of 2015, the Court was continuing its post-*Casey* pattern of hearing very few cases on regulation of abortion and thereby left uncertain what kinds of laws it would find acceptable.

Impact on Society

The impact of the Supreme Court on government policy is important, but the Court's impact on American society as a whole is even more important. How much difference does the Court make for life in the United States? Among scholars and commentators there is considerable disagreement about the extent of the Court's influence.[55]

A General View

Supreme Court decisions can shape society in different ways. Some effects are more direct, and thus easier to ascertain, than others.

When the Court upholds or strikes down a significant government policy, its decision can have a substantial direct effect. The Court's rulings on the federal health care statute of 2010 in *National Federation of Independent Business v. Sebelius* (2012) allowed the heart of the law to go into effect but also allowed state governments to opt out of the expansion of Medicaid without losing all their federal Medicaid funding. Its decision in *King v. Burwell* (2015) allowed subsidies of health insurance coverage in the many states that had federally established programs under the law. All three rulings affected health care for large numbers of people. Similarly, the Court's decision in *Obergefell v. Hodges* (2015) required all states to allow same-sex marriages and thereby affected the marital status of a great many people.

The potential effects of decisions are not quite as direct when they strengthen the legal position of some set of people or institutions, such as consumers, businesses in a particular industry, or state governments. In effect, such a decision tells its beneficiaries that if they go to court or they are taken to court, they will be in a better position to win. If these beneficiaries take advantage of the decision by bringing legal claims or acting with less fear of claims by someone else, their choices can affect the balance between competing groups and interests in society.

One example is the set of decisions by the Court that make it more difficult for workers and consumers to bring class action lawsuits against businesses. Some kinds of legal claims are impractical for people to bring as individuals, because lawyers would receive little money as their share of the potential winnings and thus have no incentive to take a case. Businesses understandably have sought to make the most of the limits on class actions. In *AT&T Mobility v. Concepcion* (2011), the Court decided that companies could rule out class actions in the arbitration procedures that they often require customers to go through, even when state law favors allowing class actions. Between 2012 and 2013, according to one survey, the proportion of companies that had arbitration clauses ruling out class actions more than doubled.[56]

Businesses were slower to take advantage of another favorable decision. In *National Labor Relations Board v. Mackay Radio & Telegraph Company* (1938), the Court interpreted a federal statute to allow employers to hire new employees as permanent replacements for striking workers—in effect, saying that they could do so without fear of a challenge in the National Labor Relations Board or in federal court. For many years companies made little use of the decision. But employers increasingly did so beginning in the 1980s.

Another kind of example is the series of Supreme Court decisions between 1976 and 2014 that struck down various limits on election campaign funding under the First Amendment. Candidates and political parties that seek to raise money for campaigns and groups that want to contribute money to campaigns or to spend it on their own have been quick to take advantage of those decisions.

Decisions that strengthen the legal position of one group or interest can have effects that radiate broadly. Employers' growing use of the power to hire replacement workers helped to weaken the power of organized labor. *Quill Corp. v. Heitkamp* (1992) held that under the commerce clause, states could not require merchants to collect sales tax from consumers in states where the merchants lacked a physical presence. The decision helped to spur the growth of online retailers such as Amazon. *Dent v. West Virginia* (1889), which rejected a constitutional challenge to state laws that required physicians to obtain licenses, helped to bring about the current structure of the medical profession.[57]

Supreme Court decisions might have more diffuse effects. Some critics of the Court's campaign funding decisions argue that these decisions have transformed the political process by magnifying the impact of money and the power of those who are able to spend money on campaigns. Thinking in even broader terms, opponents of the Court's decisions limiting religious observances in public schools have argued that those decisions helped bring about significant social problems. According to one

Tim Shaffer/Reuters

An Amazon.com warehouse. A 1992 Supreme Court decision about the collection of sales tax on out-of-state sales later facilitated the growth of Amazon and other online merchants.

commentator, these problems range from juvenile crime to corrupt public officials.[58]

It is clear that the Court's decisions can have powerful effects. But those effects should not be exaggerated, because the Court never stands alone in shaping social realities. For one thing, the Court works alongside other policymakers, whose action or inaction shapes the impact of its decisions. As the Court pointed out in its *Quill Corp.* decision, Congress could have negated the impact of the decision by enacting legislation that allowed states to collect sales tax from online merchants. President Reagan's 1981 decision to hire replacements for striking air traffic controllers who were federal employees was probably decisive in triggering employers' use of their power to hire replacement workers under the *Mackay* decision. The widespread noncompliance with the Court's decisions limiting religious observances in schools limits the good or bad effects of those decisions. This is not true of the Court's campaign funding decisions, which could be negated only through the very unlikely route of a constitutional amendment, but those decisions were unusual in that respect.

Moreover, government policy is only one influence on society. Almost surely, buying products online would have become attractive to consumers regardless of tax rules and other public policies. Changes in the economy may be the most important reason for the reduced power of organized labor. And phenomena such as the status of women and the crime rate undoubtedly are affected by government, but only as one influence among others. This limitation is common to all public policies, no matter which branch issues them. But it is especially relevant to Supreme Court decisions, which typically operate on the private sector only in indirect ways.

Thus, the reality is mixed. On the one hand, it is striking how much impact some of the Court's individual decisions and lines of decisions have had. On the other hand, the Court's policies stand alongside other public policies and social forces that also shape society, and those other influences can reinforce or narrow the Court's impact. When commentators credit the Court for what they see as desirable changes in society or blame the Court for social ills, they are usually exaggerating the Court's power.

As this discussion makes clear, it can be difficult to separate the Court's influence from that of other policymakers and other forces in society and thus to ascertain how much difference the Court makes in a particular area. It would seem relatively straightforward to determine the impact of the Court's *Citizens United* decision on spending in political campaigns, but analyses of that impact have reached quite different conclusions.[59] The effects of the Court's decisions in some other fields would be considerably more difficult to ascertain.

Two Areas of Court Activity

The Court's impact on society and the forces that shape its impact can be probed by looking at two areas of the Court's activity as a policymaker. Each of these areas illustrates the complexity of the relationship between Supreme Court decisions and social reality.

Abortion. The Court's 1973 decisions in *Roe v. Wade* and *Doe v. Bolton* fundamentally changed the law by requiring the forty-six states that prohibited abortion for the most part or altogether to legalize abortion prior to viability. The most likely effect of the Court's decisions, then, was a very substantial increase in the rate of legal abortions.

Indeed, the number of legal abortions per year increased by about 165 percent between 1972 and 1980. Understandably, people who care about the abortion issue treat the Court as the source of the growth in the abortion rate. But the reality is more complicated, and it is impossible to determine the Court's impact with any precision.[60]

Figure 6-1 underlines that complication. As the figure shows, the rate of increase in abortions was actually greater between 1969 and 1972, before *Roe v. Wade*, than it was afterward. That increase reflected changes in state laws before and during that period, as some states relaxed their general prohibitions of abortion and a few eliminated most restrictions. If the Court had never handed down *Roe*, the number of legal abortions likely would have continued to rise because of further changes in state laws and increasing abortion rates in the states that allowed abortion. But it is impossible to know with any certainty how state laws would have evolved and how abortion rates would have changed if the Court had not intervened.

Figure 6-1 depicts another complication as well. Between 1981 and 2011—the most recent year for which data are available—the numbers of legal abortions declined by about one-third. The rate of abortions per 1,000 women between the ages of 15 and 44 declined by more than 40 percent in those years, and in 2011 it reached the lowest level since 1973.

One source of the decline is the policies of the other branches of government that were discussed earlier in the chapter. For instance, comparisons of states indicate that restrictions on Medicaid funding of abortion and requirements of parental consent or notification before girls under eighteen can obtain abortions reduce the abortion rate.[61] The widespread policy of performing no abortions in government-run

FIGURE 6-1

Estimated Number of Legal Abortions and Related Government Policy Actions, 1966–2011

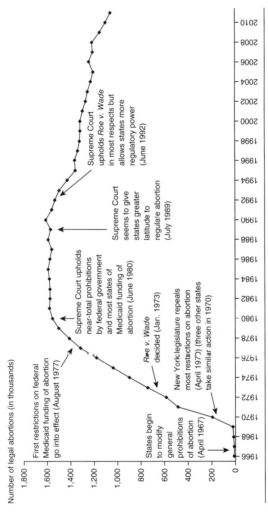

Sources: Estimated numbers of abortions for 1966–1985 are taken from Gerald N. Rosenberg, *The Hollow Hope: Can Courts Bring about Social Change?* 2nd ed. (Chicago: University of Chicago Press, 2008), 180; for 1986–1990, Lawrence B. Finer and Stanley K. Henshaw, "Abortion Incidence and Services in the United States in 2000," *Perspectives on Sexual and Reproductive Health* 35 (January–February 2003): 8; and for 1991–2011, Rachel K. Jones and Jenna Jerman, "Abortion Incidence and Service Availability in the United States, 2011," *Perspectives on Sexual and Reproductive Health* 46 (March 2014): 5. In these sources, numbers for some years are interpolated from numbers for earlier and later years.

medical facilities probably has considerable impact. The growth in state legislation restricting abortion in various ways since 2011 may have brought about further reductions in the numbers of abortions.

Conditions other than government policy also have contributed to this decline.[62] The number of abortions largely depends on the number of unintended pregnancies and on women's choices to seek abortions. Thus, increased use of contraception has made considerable difference. The availability of facilities that perform abortions is also important. Only a small minority of privately owned hospitals perform abortions. Most urban areas have clinics that perform abortions, but many rural areas lack such clinics. And the number of facilities that perform abortions has declined substantially in the past two decades. These patterns reflect the personal beliefs of medical personnel as well as restrictive laws and pressures against providing abortions.

If the Supreme Court helped bring about the increase in legal abortions, it may have contributed to the later decline as well. The Court accepted some policies restricting abortion, including limits on Medicaid funding and some types of parental consent laws. More fundamentally, some commentators—including Justice Ginsburg—think that *Roe* served as a powerful symbol that helped to mobilize the pro-life movement and bring about the restrictive legislation that the movement has supported.[63] Other commentators disagree, pointing out that abortion was becoming a salient and divisive issue even before *Roe*.[64] But *Roe* was one impetus for the development of a mass pro-life movement and perhaps for the broader growth of a social conservative movement. That role is a reminder that the Court's impact can extend beyond the policy issues it addresses to the political process.

Racial Equality. In debates about the Supreme Court's impact, no issue receives as much attention as racial equality. The Warren Court of the 1950s and 1960s did a great deal to combat racial discrimination. It ruled against discrimination in education and voting, it upheld federal laws prohibiting discrimination, and it sought to protect the civil rights movement from legal attacks. To a degree, that line of policy extended back to the Court of the 1940s and forward to the Court of the 1970s. Implicitly, the Court was making a commitment to improve the status of black Americans. To what extent have the Court's policies achieved that goal?

This question has no clear answer, because the picture is complicated. To start with, the extent of change in the status of black Americans since the 1950s is ambiguous. The most dramatic progress has been political. Racial barriers to black voting in the South were overcome.

Partly as a result, the number of black elected officials has grown substantially. The social segregation of American life has broken down unevenly. Official segregation of public schools, the target of *Brown v. Board of Education*, was eliminated. But the level of actual school segregation remains high, and it has increased since the 1990s as active efforts to achieve integration have declined.[65] In the economic arena, reduced employment discrimination and growth in average levels of education have helped to improve the economic status of black Americans. But there remain substantial differences in economic well-being by race. In 2013, the median income of black households was 63 percent of the median for white households, and the poverty rate was nearly three times as high for black individuals as it was for whites.[66]

To the extent that we have come closer to racial equality, there is no reason to think that the Supreme Court was the primary source of that progress. Especially important were the civil rights movement and initiatives by the other branches of government. On the whole, these sources were considerably more powerful than the Court.

The Court's relative weakness is clear in the areas in which it was most active from the 1940s to the 1970s, education and voting. *Brown v. Board of Education* spurred substantial school desegregation in the border states, but in itself it was ineffective in the South. The Court's decisions striking down devices to limit black voting in the South probably had some impact, but the barriers to voting remained strong so long as the Court acted alone. Ultimately, it was enactment of the Civil Rights Act of 1964 and the Voting Rights Act of 1965 and their vigorous enforcement by the Lyndon Johnson administration that broke down official school segregation and made the right to vote effective in the South.

Constitutional protections against racial discrimination apply to the private sector only in part, and even those protections can have little impact without detailed rules and enforcement mechanisms. For that reason, policies to address housing and employment discrimination had to come primarily from the other branches. The most important government action on housing was the Fair Housing Act that Congress enacted in 1968. That statute may have contributed to the substantial decline in segregation between black and white residents since that time.[67] The Court has made several decisions interpreting the Fair Housing Act, and its 2015 ruling that the statute applies to actions that have an unintended effect on racial groups may have substantial impact.[68] But thus far, the Court's role in the housing field has been far more limited than that of the other branches.

By the 1960s many states had enacted laws against racial discrimination in employment. At the federal level Congress took the key action in attacking employment discrimination with the Civil Rights Act of 1964. President Johnson issued an executive order in 1965, which is still in force, that prohibited racial discrimination by employers that do work for the federal government. In the 1970s and early 1980s, the Court generally gave broad interpretations to the laws against employment discrimination. Some evidence indicates that these laws and their state counterparts have improved the economic status of black citizens.[69] The Court's decisions probably enhanced the effects of the federal laws, but in all likelihood its impact was marginal. The same appears to be true of the decisions since the late 1980s that narrowed the reach of employment discrimination laws, in part because Congress overturned some of those decisions.

Perhaps the Court played a major indirect role in furthering racial equality. As some observers see it, its early civil rights decisions—especially *Brown v. Board of Education*—helped to spur passage of federal legislation and served as a catalyst for the civil rights movement. The development of a mass civil rights movement in the South was probably inevitable, and the Supreme Court was hardly the major force contributing to it. But the Court may have speeded the movement's growth. Its decisions in education and other areas created hope for change and established rights to be vindicated by political action. And *Brown* served as a symbol that helped spur litigation campaigns by other social movements.[70]

The series of civil rights laws adopted from 1957 on also may owe something to the Court. In education and voting, the Court took the first significant government action against discrimination in the twentieth century. By doing so, especially in education, the Court helped to create expectations that Congress and the executive branch were pressed to fulfill. Congressional action was the key step in bringing about actual school desegregation in the South. But if the Court had not issued the *Brown* decision, Congress would have had less impetus to act against segregation. In a proclamation commemorating the sixtieth anniversary of *Brown* in 2014, President Obama acknowledged its limitations but concluded that "*Brown's* moral guidance was translated into the enforcement measures of the Civil Rights Act and the Voting Rights Act."[71]

Overall, the Supreme Court has had little direct impact on discrimination in the private sector. Even in the public sector, it has been weak in the enforcement of rights. But the Court helped to initiate and support the processes of change, and its members probably can take some credit for the country's progress toward racial equality. Although the Court's impact has been more limited than many people had hoped, the Court has contributed to significant social change.

Conclusion: The Court,
Public Policy, and Society

It is now possible to reach some tentative conclusions about the role of the Supreme Court as a public policymaker. There are fundamental limits on that role, but the Court is still quite important.

The most obvious limit is that the Court decides relatively few public policy questions. One effect of this limit is that the Court can be only a minor participant in fields such as foreign policy, in which it seldom addresses major issues. Even in its areas of specialization, the Court intervenes only in limited ways. To take two examples, it makes decisions on a small sample of the issues that affect freedom of expression and the rights of criminal defendants.

The Court does address major issues of public policy with some frequency, and some of its decisions mandate significant changes in government policy. The impact of these decisions, however, is mediated by the actions of other institutions and individuals. A ruling that public schools must eliminate organized prayers does not guarantee that those observances will disappear. Congress has reversed several of the Court's interpretations of civil rights laws. And the impact of the Court's decisions on issues such as abortion depends on the actions of people who play a variety of roles in and out of government.

These limitations must be balanced against the Court's strengths. Certainly, a great many Supreme Court decisions have significant effects. The Court influences business practices and the balance of power between labor and management. It affects the state of civil liberties through its rulings on an array of constitutional issues. Decisions on capital punishment are literally a matter of life and death for some people.

The Court's impact is exemplified by its decisions about the political process in the last few decades. Its decision in *Bush v. Gore* resolved a presidential election. Its rulings about how legislative districts are drawn affect the ability of Republicans and Democrats to win seats. The limitations it has imposed on regulation of campaign finance in a series of decisions have helped to transform the funding of political campaigns.

The Court also shapes political and social change. Its partial opposition to government regulation of private business in an earlier era was ultimately overcome, but the Court slowed a fundamental change in the role of government. Although *Roe v. Wade* did not have as much impact as most people think, it has been the focus of a major national debate and struggle for four decades. The Court's decisions have not brought about racial equality, even in conjunction with other forces, but they helped to spur changes in race relations.

As the examples of abortion and civil rights suggest, the Court is perhaps most important in creating conditions for action by others. Its decisions help to put issues on the national agenda so that other policymakers and the general public consider them. The Court is not highly effective in enforcing rights, but it often legitimates efforts to achieve rights. By doing so, it provides an impetus for people to take legal and political action. Its decisions affect the positions of interest groups and social movements, strengthening some and weakening others.

The Supreme Court, then, is neither all-powerful nor inconsequential. Rather, it is one of many institutions that shape American society in significant ways. That is a more limited role than some have claimed for the Court. But the role that the Court does play is an extraordinary one for a single small body that possesses little tangible power. In this sense, the Supreme Court is a remarkable institution.

NOTES

1. *Fisher v. University of Texas* (5th Cir. 2014). The Supreme Court decision was *Fisher v. University of Texas* (2013).
2. Robert Barnes, "Despite Justices' Ruling, Baby Veronica's Case Is Far from Over," *Washington Post*, September 16, 2013, A15. The case was *Adoptive Couple v. Baby Girl* (2013).
3. Paul J. Nyden, "New Trial Ordered in Mining Dispute," *Charleston Gazette*, January 11, 2015, 2A. The case was *Caperton v. A. T. Massey Coal Company* (2009).
4. Matthew E. K. Hall, *The Nature of Supreme Court Power* (New York: Cambridge University Press, 2011).
5. *Latif v. Obama*, 2011 U.S. App. LEXIS 22679, at 98 (D.C. Cir. 2011). See Mark Denbaugh et al., "No Hearing Habeas: DC Circuit Restricts Meaningful Review," Center for Policy & Research, Seton Hall University School of Law (2012), http://law.shu.edu/policyresearch/Guantanamo-Reports.cfm.
6. Kevin T. McGuire, "Public Schools, Religious Establishments, and the U.S. Supreme Court: An Examination of Policy Compliance," *American Politics Research* 37 (January 2009): 50–74; Erik Eckholm, "Battling Anew Over the Place of Religion in Public Schools," *New York Times*, December 28, 2011, A11, A15.
7. *United States v. Olsen*, 737 F.3d 625, 626 (9th Cir. 2013).
8. Douglas Berman, "Split Fourth Circuit Highlights Ugly Mess of SCOTUS 'Crime of Violence' Jurisprudence," Sentencing Law and Policy blog, June 5, 2014, http://sentencing.typepad.com/sentencing_law_and_policy/2014/06/split-fourth-circuit-highlights-ugly-mess-that-is-scotus-crime-of-violence-jurisprudence.html.
9. *Snider v. City of Cape Girardeau* (8th Cir. 2014). The Supreme Court decision was *Texas v. Johnson* (1989).
10. Erik Eckholm, "Juveniles Facing Lifelong Terms Despite Rulings," *New York Times*, January 20, 2014, A1, A3.

11. "As Court Fees Rise, the Poor Are Paying the Price," National Public Radio, May 19, 2014, http://www.npr.org/2014/05/19/312158516/increasing-court-fees-punish-the-poor.
12. Civil Rights Division, United States Department of Justice, *Investigation of the Shelby County Juvenile Court*, April 26, 2012, http://www.justice.gov/opa/pr/department-justice-releases-investigative-findings-juvenile-court-memphis-and-shelby-county.
13. William K. Muir Jr., *Prayer in the Public Schools: Law and Attitude Change* (Chicago: University of Chicago Press, 1967); Richard Johnson, *The Dynamics of Compliance* (Evanston, Ill.: Northwestern University Press, 1967).
14. *Marmet Health Care Center v. Brown* (2012); *KPMG v. Cocchi* (2012); *Nitro-Lift Technologies, L.L.C. v. Howard* (2012).
15. *CLS Bank International v. Alice Corporation Pty. Ltd.*, 685 F.3d 1341, 1356 (Fed. Cir. 2012).
16. The Supreme Court decision was *Alice Corporation Pty. Ltd. v. CLS Bank International* (2014).
17. Seth W. Stoughton, "Policing Facts," *Tulane Law Review* 88 (May 2014): 876–882.
18. Harrell R. Rodgers Jr. and Charles S. Bullock III, *Law and Social Change: Civil Rights Laws and Their Consequences* (New York: McGraw-Hill, 1972), 75.
19. *Green v. School Board* (1968); *Alexander v. Holmes County Board of Education* (1969).
20. *Missouri v. Jenkins* (1990); *Spallone v. United States* (1989).
21. *Board of Education v. Dowell* (1991); *Freeman v. Pitts* (1992).
22. Sara C. Benesh and Wendy L. Martinek, "Context and Compliance: A Comparison of State Supreme Courts and the Circuits," *Marquette Law Review* 93 (Winter 2009): 795–824.
23. This discussion of the impact of *Miranda* is based in part on Richard A. Leo and K. Alexa Koenig, "The Gatehouses and Mansions: Fifty Years Later," *Annual Review of Law and Social Sciences* 6 (2010): 330–335.
24. *People v. Perez* (N.Y. Supreme Ct. 2012); "Subverting the Miranda Rule," *New York Times*, May 3, 2012, A28.
25. See *People v. Neal* (Calif. 2003).
26. Hall, *Nature of Supreme Court Power*, 68–71.
27. Steven B. Duke, "Does Miranda Protect the Innocent or the Guilty?" *Chapman Law Review* 10 (Spring 2007): 562.
28. Marvin Zalman and Brad W. Smith, "The Attitudes of Police Executives toward *Miranda* and Interrogation Policies," *Journal of Criminal Law and Criminology* 97 (2007): 873–942.
29. Matthew R. Christiansen and William N. Eskridge Jr., "Congressional Overrides of Supreme Court Statutory Interpretation Decisions, 1967–2011," *Texas Law Review* 92 (2014): 1317–1541. This discussion of statutory overrides draws from that study and from Richard L. Hasen, "End of the Dialogue: Political Polarization, the Supreme Court, and Congress," *Southern California Law Review* 86 (January 2013): 205–261; and James Buatti and Richard L. Hasen, "Conscious Congressional Overriding of the Supreme Court, Gridlock, and Partisan Politics," *Texas Law Review*, forthcoming.
30. Nancy Staudt, René Lindstädt, and Jason O'Connor, "Judicial Decisions as Legislation: Congressional Oversight of Supreme Court Tax Cases, 1954–2005," *New York University Law Review* 82 (November 2007): 1354.
31. *Paroline v. United States*, 188 L. Ed. 2d 714, 752–753 (2014).

32. The decision was *Graham County Soil and Water Conservation District v. United States ex rel. Wilson* (2010). See Joan Biskupic, "Supreme Court Restricts Whistle-Blower Lawsuits," *USA Today*, March 31, 2010, 7A.

33. Deborah A. Widiss, "Shadow Precedents and the Separation of Powers: Statutory Interpretation of Congressional Overrides," *Notre Dame Law Review* 84 (January 2009): 511–583; Widiss, "Undermining Congressional Overrides: The Hydra Problem in Statutory Interpretation," *Texas Law Review* 90 (March 2012): 859–942.

34. Stolen Valor Act of 2013, 18 U.S.C. § 704(b).

35. Richard M. Re, "The Doctrine of One Last Chance," *Green Bag* 17 (Winter 2014): 173–185.

36. *Shelby County v. Holder*, 186 L. Ed. 2d 651, 673 (2013).

37. The provision on school religion is at 20 U.S.C. § 7904; the provision on the Boy Scouts is at 20 U.S.C. § 7905.

38. Louis Fisher, *The Law of the Executive Branch: Presidential Power* (New York: Oxford University Press, 2014), 205–207; Hall, *Nature of Supreme Court Power*, 105–108.

39. Sean Sullivan, "Elizabeth Warren Gives Liberals the Speech They've Been Waiting For," The Fix Blog, *Washington Post*, September 9, 2013, http://www .washingtonpost.com/blogs/the-fix/wp/2013/09/09/elizabeth-warren-gives-liberals-the-speech-theyve-been-waiting-for-video.

40. Kristen A. Lee, "Indiana Congressman Mike Pence Apologizes for 'Thoughtless' Remark that Compared the Supreme Court's Health Care Decision to 9/11," *New York Daily News*, June 29, 2012, http://www.nydailynews.com/news/national/indiana-congressman-mike-pence-apologizes-thoughtless-remark-compared-supreme-court-health-care-decision-9-11-article-1.1104734.

41. This discussion draws much from the catalog and analyses of congressional action against the Court in Tom S. Clark, *The Limits of Judicial Independence* (New York: Cambridge University Press, 2011), chap. 2.

42. George I. Lovell, *Legislative Deferrals: Statutory Ambiguity, Judicial Power, and American Democracy* (New York: Cambridge University Press, 2003), 162.

43. Clark, *Limits of Judicial Independence*, 49–60. See Stephen M. Engel, *American Politicians Confront the Court: Opposition Politics and Changing Responses to Judicial Power* (New York: Cambridge University Press, 2011), chap. 7.

44. William G. Ross, *A Muted Fury: Populists, Progressives, and Labor Unions Confront the Courts, 1890–1937* (Princeton, N.J.: Princeton University Press, 1994); Jeff Shesol, *Supreme Power: Franklin Roosevelt vs. the Supreme Court* (New York: W. W. Norton, 2010).

45. See Charles Gardner Geyh, *When Courts and Congress Collide: The Struggle for Control of America's Judicial System* (Ann Arbor: University of Michigan Press, 2006).

46. Neil Nagraj, "Justice Alito Mouths 'Not True' When Obama Blasts Supreme Court Ruling in State of the Union Address," *New York Daily News*, January 28, 2010, http://www.nydailynews.com/news/politics/justice-alito-mouths-not-true-obama-blasts-supreme-court-ruling-state-union-address-article-1.194197. See Bethany Blackstone and Greg Goelzhauser, "Presidential Rhetoric Toward the Supreme Court," *Judicature* 97 (January/February 2014): 179–187.

47. Executive Order 13673, "Fair Pay and Safe Workplaces," Sec. 6 (July 31, 2014).

48. U.S. Department of Labor, "Application of the Fair Labor Standards Act to Domestic Service," *Federal Register* 78 (October 1, 2013): 60454–60557. The decision was *Long Island Care at Home, Ltd. v. Coke* (2007).

49. The letter and related materials are available at http://www2.ed.gov/about/offices/list/ocr/letters/colleague-201309.html.

50. Lee Epstein and Joseph F. Kobylka, *The Supreme Court and Legal Change: Abortion and the Death Penalty* (Chapel Hill: University of North Carolina Press, 1992), 87.

51. This discussion draws from the documents and other information at California Department of Corrections and Rehabilitation, "Three-Judge Court Updates," http://www.cdcr.ca.gov/News/3_judge_panel_decision.html.

52. Holly R. Stevens et al., *State, County and Local Expenditures for Indigent Defense Services, Fiscal 2008*, American Bar Association, November 2010, 76; Erinn Herberman and Tracey Kyckelhahn, *State Government Indigent Defense Expenditures, FY 2008–2012—Updated*, Bureau of Justice Statistics, U.S. Department of Justice, NCJ 264684, November 2014.

53. Michael Cooper, "After Ruling, States Rush to Enact Voting Laws," *New York Times*, July 6, 2013, A9.

54. David G. Savage, "Even a Supreme Court Loss Can Propel a Cause," *Los Angeles Times*, January 3, 2007, A10.

55. For two divergent views, see Gerald N. Rosenberg, *The Hollow Hope: Can Courts Bring about Social Change?* 2nd ed. (Chicago: University of Chicago Press, 2008); and Hall, *Nature of Supreme Court Power*.

56. Carlton Fields Jorden Burt (law firm), *The 2014 Carlton Fields Jorden Burt Class Action Survey*, 2014, 30, http://classactionsurvey.com/about.

57. James C. Mohr, *Licensed to Practice: The Supreme Court Defines the American Medical Profession* (Baltimore, Md.: Johns Hopkins University Press, 2013), chap. 11.

58. David Barton, *America: To Pray or Not to Pray?* 5th ed. (Aledo, Tex.: WallBuilder Press, 1994).

59. Ian Vandewalker, *Election Spending 2014: Outside Spending in Senate Races Since Citizens United*, Brennan Center for Justice, New York University, 2015; Douglas M. Spencer and Abby K. Wood, "*Citizens United*, States Divided: An Empirical Analysis of Independent Political Spending," *Indiana Law Journal* 89 (Winter 2014): 315–372.

60. This discussion of abortion is based in part on Rosenberg, *The Hollow Hope*, 175–201; and Matthew E. Wetstein, "The Abortion Rate Paradox: The Impact of National Policy Change on Abortion Rates," *Social Science Quarterly* 76 (September 1995): 607–618.

61. Michael J. New, "Analyzing the Effect of Anti-Abortion U.S. State Legislation in the Post-*Casey* Era," *State Politics & Policy Quarterly* 11 (March 2011): 28–47.

62. See Rachel K. Jones and Jenna Jerman, "Abortion Incidence and Service Availability in the United States, 2011," *Perspectives on Sexual and Reproductive Health* 46 (March 2014): 3–14.

63. Jason Keyser, "Ginsburg Says Roe Gave Abortion Opponents Target," *USA Today*, May 12, 2013, http://www.usatoday.com/story/news/nation/2013/05/11/ginsburg-abortion-roe-wade/2153083.

64. Linda Greenhouse and Reva B. Siegel, "Before (and After) Roe v. Wade: New Questions about Backlash," *Yale Law Journal* 120 (June 2011): 100–159.

65. Gary Orfield and Erica Frankenberg, with Jongyeon Ee and John Kuscera, *Brown at 60: Great Progress, a Long Retreat and an Uncertain Future* (Los Angeles: The Civil Rights Project, University of California at Los Angeles, 2014).

66. Carmen DeNavas-Walt and Bernadette D. Proctor, U.S. Census Bureau, Current Population Reports, P60-249, *Income and Poverty in the United States: 2013* (Washington, D.C.: Government Printing Office, 2014), 6, 12.

67. Jorge De la Roca, Ingrid Gould Ellen, and Katherine M. O'Regan, "Race and Neighborhoods in the 21st Century: What Does Segregation Mean Today?" *Regional Science and Urban Economics* 47 (2014): 138–151.

68. *Texas Department of Housing and Community Affairs v. The Inclusive Communities Project, Inc.* (2015).

69. See William M. Carrington, Kristin McCue, and Brooks Pierce, "Using Establishment Size to Measure the Impact of Title VII and Affirmative Action," *Journal of Human Resources* 35 (Summer 2000): 503–523; and David Neumark and Wendy A. Stock, "The Labor Market Effects of Sex and Race Discrimination Laws," *Economic Inquiry* 44 (July 2006): 385–419.

70. David S. Meyer and Steven A. Boutcher, "Signals and Spillover: *Brown v. Board of Education* and Other Social Movements," *Perspectives on Politics* 5 (March 2007): 81–93; Martha Minow, *In Brown's Wake: Legacies of America's Educational Landmark* (New York: Oxford University Press, 2010).

71. Office of the Press Secretary, The White House, "Presidential Proclamation—60th Anniversary of Brown v. Board of Education," May 15, 2014, http://www.whitehouse.gov/the-press-office/2014/05/15/presidential-proclamation-60th-anniversary-brown-v-board-education.

Glossary of Legal Terms

Affirm: In an appellate court, to reach a decision that agrees with the outcome for the parties in the lower court whose decision is being reviewed.

Amicus curiae: "Friend of the court." A person, private group or institution, or government agency that is not a party to a case but that participates in the case at the invitation of the court or, more often, on its own initiative. That participation is usually in the form of a brief, but amici in the Supreme Court (most often, the federal government) sometimes participate in oral argument.

Appeal: In general, a case brought to a higher court for review. In the Supreme Court, a small number of cases are designated as appeals under federal law; these cases fall under the Court's mandatory jurisdiction, so the Court must reach some kind of decision on the merits.

Appellant: The party that appeals a lower-court decision to a higher court. In the Supreme Court, the parties to cases are designated as appellants and appellees in appeals, cases that the Court is required to hear.

Appellee: A party to an appeal that wishes to have the lower-court decision upheld and that responds when the case is appealed. (See *Appellant.*)

Brief: A document submitted to a court, usually by attorneys, that argues in support of one of the parties to a case. The Supreme Court receives briefs at the stage in which it decides whether to hear a case and at the stage in which it actually decides cases.

Certiorari, Writ of: A writ issued by the Supreme Court, at its discretion, to order a lower court to send a case to the Supreme Court for review. The overwhelming majority of cases come to the Court as petitions for writs of certiorari.

Civil cases: All legal cases other than criminal cases.

Class action: A lawsuit brought by one person or group on behalf of all people who are in similar situations.

Concurring opinion: An opinion by a member of a court that agrees with the outcome for the parties in a court's decision but that offers its own rationale for the decision. A "regular" concurring opinion agrees with the court's opinion as well as the outcome; a "special" concurring opinion disagrees with the court's opinion.

Decision on the merits: A court's decision on which party should win a case. In the Supreme Court, after the Court agrees to hear a case it then reaches a decision on the merits.

Dicta: See *Obiter dictum.*

Discretionary jurisdiction: Jurisdiction that a court may accept or reject in particular cases. The Supreme Court has discretionary jurisdiction over the great majority of cases that come to it, cases in which it decides whether or not to issue a writ of certiorari and hear the case.

Dissenting opinion: An opinion by a member of a court that disagrees with the outcome for the parties in the court's decision.

Habeas corpus: "You have the body." A writ issued by a court to inquire whether a person is lawfully imprisoned or detained. The writ demands that the persons holding the prisoner justify the detention or release the prisoner.

Holding: In a majority opinion, the rule of law necessary to decide the case. That rule is binding as precedent in future cases, though a court sometimes decides to overrule a precedent it had established in an earlier case.

In forma pauperis: "In the manner of a pauper." In the Supreme Court, cases brought in forma pauperis by indigent persons are exempt from the Court's usual fees and from some formal requirements. These requests for hearings are called paupers' petitions or unpaid petitions.

Judicial review: Review of legislation or other government action to determine its consistency with the federal or state constitution; includes the power to strike down policies that are inconsistent with a constitutional provision. The Supreme Court reviews government action only under the federal Constitution, not state constitutions.

Jurisdiction: The power of a court to hear a case in question.

Litigants: The parties to a court case.

Majority opinion: An opinion in a case that is subscribed to by a majority of the judges who participated in the decision. Also known as the opinion of the court.

Mandamus: "We command." An order issued by a court that directs a lower court or other authority to perform a particular act.

Mandatory jurisdiction: Jurisdiction that a court must accept. Cases falling under a court's mandatory jurisdiction must be decided officially on their merits, although a court may avoid giving them full consideration.

Merits decision: See *Decision on the merits.*

Modify: In an appellate court, to reach a decision that disagrees in part with the outcome for the parties in the lower court whose decision is being reviewed.

Moot: A moot case is one that has become hypothetical so that a court cannot decide it.

Obiter dictum: (Also called *dictum* [sing.] or *dicta* [pl.].) A statement in a court opinion that is not necessary to resolve the case before the court. Dicta are not binding in future cases.

Original jurisdiction: Jurisdiction as a trial court. The Supreme Court has original jurisdiction over a few types of cases.

Paupers' petitions: See *In forma pauperis.*

Per curiam: "By the court." An opinion of the court that is not signed by a specific judge. Per curiam opinions are sometimes quite brief.

Petitioner: One who files a petition with a court seeking action or relief, such as a writ of certiorari. Parties whose cases have been accepted by the Court through a grant of certiorari continue to be referred to as petitioners when their case is decided on the merits.

Remand: To send back. When a case is remanded, it is sent back by a higher court to the court from which it came, for further action.

Respondent: The party in opposition to a petitioner. See *Petitioner*.

Reverse: In an appellate court, to reach a decision that disagrees with the outcome for the parties in the lower court whose decision is being reviewed.

Standing: A requirement that the party who files a lawsuit have a legal stake in the outcome.

Stare decisis: "Let the decision stand." The doctrine that principles of law established in earlier judicial decisions should be accepted as authoritative in subsequent similar cases.

Statute: A law enacted by a legislature.

Stay: To halt or suspend further judicial proceedings. The Supreme Court sometimes issues a stay to suspend action in a lower court while the Court considers the case.

Vacate: To make void or annul. The Supreme Court sometimes vacates a lower-court decision, requiring the lower court to reconsider the case.

Selected Bibliography

General

Cushman, Clare. *Courtwatchers: Eyewitness Accounts in Supreme Court History.* Lanham, Md.: Rowman & Littlefield, 2011.

Epstein, Lee, Jeffrey A. Segal, Harold J. Spaeth, and Thomas G. Walker. *The Supreme Court Compendium: Data, Decisions, and Developments.* 6th ed. Washington, D.C.: CQ Press, 2016.

Lamb, Brian, Susan Swain, and Mark Farkas, eds. *The Supreme Court: A C-Span Book Featuring the Justices in Their Own Words.* New York: PublicAffairs, 2010.

Savage, David G. *Guide to the U.S. Supreme Court.* 5th ed. Washington, D.C.: CQ Press, 2010.

Chapter 1

Davis, Richard, ed. *Covering the United States Supreme Court in the Digital Age.* New York: Cambridge University Press, 2014.

Davis, Richard. *Justices and Journalists: The U.S. Supreme Court and the Media.* New York: Cambridge University Press, 2011.

Gibson, James L., and Gregory A. Caldeira. *Citizens, Courts, and Confirmations: Positivity Bias and the Judgments of the American People.* Princeton, N.J.: Princeton University Press, 2009.

Peppers, Todd C., and Artemus Ward, eds. *In Chambers: Stories of Supreme Court Law Clerks and Their Justices.* Charlottesville: University of Virginia Press, 2012.

Slotnick, Elliot E., and Jennifer A. Segal. *Television News and the Supreme Court: All the News That's Fit to Air?* New York: Cambridge University Press, 1998.

Solberg, Rorie Spill, and Eric N. Waltenburg. *The Media, the Court, and the Misrepresentation: The New Myth of the Court.* New York: Routledge, 2014.

Chapter 2

Abraham, Henry J. *Justices, Presidents, and Senators: A History of the U.S. Supreme Court Appointments from Washington to Bush II.* 5th ed. Lanham, Md.: Rowman & Littlefield, 2008.

Collins, Paul M., Jr., and Lori A. Ringhand. *Supreme Court Confirmation Hearings and Constitutional Change.* New York: Cambridge University Press, 2013.

Farganis, Dion, and Justin Wedeking. *Supreme Court Confirmation Hearings: Reconsidering the Charade.* Ann Arbor: University of Michigan Press, 2014.

McMahon, Kevin J. *Nixon's Court: His Challenge to Judicial Liberalism and Its Political Consequences.* Chicago: University of Chicago Press, 2011.

Nemacheck, Christine L. *Strategic Selection: Presidential Nomination of Supreme Court Justices from Herbert Hoover through George W. Bush.* Charlottesville: University of Virginia Press, 2007.

Ward, Artemus. *Deciding to Leave: The Politics of Retirement from the United States Supreme Court.* Albany: State University of New York Press, 2003.

Yalof, David Alistair. *Pursuit of Justices: Presidential Politics and the Selection of Supreme Court Nominees.* Chicago: University of Chicago Press, 1999.

Chapter 3

Baird, Vanessa A. *Answering the Call of the Court: How Justices and Litigants Set the Supreme Court Agenda.* Charlottesville: University of Virginia Press, 2007.

Black, Ryan C., and Ryan J. Owens. *The Solicitor General and the United States Supreme Court: Executive Branch Influence and Judicial Decisions.* New York: Cambridge University Press, 2012.

Collins, Paul M., Jr. *Friends of the Supreme Court: Interest Groups and Judicial Decision Making.* New York: Oxford University Press, 2008.

Lawrence, Susan E. *The Poor in Court: The Legal Services Program and Supreme Court Decision Making.* Princeton, N.J.: Princeton University Press, 1990.

McGuire, Kevin T. *The Supreme Court Bar: Legal Elites in the Washington Community.* Charlottesville: University Press of Virginia, 1993.

Pacelle, Richard L., Jr. *Between Law and Politics: The Solicitor General and the Structuring of Civil Rights, Gender, and Reproductive Rights Litigation.* College Station: Texas A&M Press, 2003.

Walker, Samuel. *In Defense of American Liberties: A History of the ACLU.* 2nd ed. Carbondale: Southern Illinois University Press, 1999.

Chapter 4

Bailey, Michael A., and Forrest Maltzman. *The Constrained Court: Law, Politics, and the Decisions Justices Make.* Princeton, N.J.: Princeton University Press, 2011.

Black, Ryan C., Timothy R. Johnson, and Justin Wedeking. *Oral Arguments and Coalition Formation on the U.S. Supreme Court: A Deliberate Dialogue.* Ann Arbor. University of Michigan Press, 2012.

Brenner, Saul, and Joseph M. Whitmeyer. *Strategy on the United States Supreme Court.* New York: Cambridge University Press, 2009.

Clark, Tom S. *The Limits of Judicial Independence.* New York: Cambridge University Press, 2011.

Danelski, David J., and Artemus Ward, eds. *The Chief Justice: Appointment and Influence.* Ann Arbor: University of Michigan Press, 2015.

Epstein, Lee, and Jack Knight. *The Choices Justices Make.* Washington, D.C.: CQ Press, 1998.

Friedman, Barry. *The Will of the People: How Public Opinion Has Influenced the Supreme Court and Shaped the Meaning of the Constitution.* New York: Farrar, Strauss, & Giroux, 2009.

Hansford, Thomas G., and James F. Spriggs II. *The Politics of Precedent on the U.S. Supreme Court.* Princeton, N.J.: Princeton University Press, 2006.

Harvey, Anna. *A Mere Machine: The Supreme Court, Congress, and American Democracy.* New Haven, Conn.: Yale University Press, 2013.

Maltzman, Forrest, James F. Spriggs II, and Paul J. Wahlbeck. *Crafting Law on the Supreme Court: The Collegial Game.* New York: Cambridge University Press, 2000.

Pacelle, Richard L., Jr., Brett W. Curry, and Bryan W. Marshall. *Decision Making by the Modern Supreme Court.* New York: Cambridge University Press, 2011.
Segal, Jeffrey A., and Harold J. Spaeth. *The Supreme Court and the Attitudinal Model Revisited.* New York: Cambridge University Press, 2002.

Chapter 5

Epp, Charles R. *The Rights Revolution: Lawyers, Activists, and Supreme Courts in Comparative Perspective.* Chicago: University of Chicago Press, 1998.
Kahn, Ronald, and Ken I. Kersch, eds. *The Supreme Court and American Political Development.* Lawrence: University Press of Kansas, 2006.
Keith, Linda Camp. *The U.S. Supreme Court and the Judicial Review of Congress.* New York: Peter Lang, 2008.
McCloskey, Robert G. *The American Supreme Court.* 5th ed. Revised by Sanford Levinson. Chicago: University of Chicago Press, 2010.
Pacelle, Richard L., Jr. *The Supreme Court in a System of Separation of Powers: The Nation's Balance Wheel.* New York: Routledge, 2015.
Pacelle, Richard L., Jr. *The Transformation of the Supreme Court's Agenda: From the New Deal to the Reagan Administration.* Boulder, Colo.: Westview Press, 1991.
Whittington, Keith E. *Political Foundations of Judicial Supremacy: The Supreme Court and Constitutional Leadership in U.S. History.* Princeton, N.J.: Princeton University Press, 2007.

Chapter 6

Canon, Bradley C., and Charles A. Johnson. *Judicial Policies: Implementation and Impact.* 2nd ed. Washington, D.C.: CQ Press, 1999.
Geyh, Charles Gardner. *When Courts and Congress Collide: The Struggle for Control of America's Judicial System.* Ann Arbor: University of Michigan Press, 2006.
Hall, Matthew E. K. *The Nature of Supreme Court Power.* New York: Cambridge University Press, 2011.
Leo, Richard A. *Police Interrogation and American Justice.* Cambridge, Mass.: Harvard University Press, 2008.
Miller, Mark C. *The View of the Courts from the Hill: Interactions between Congress and the Federal Judiciary.* Charlottesville: University of Virginia Press, 2009.
Pickerill, J. Mitchell. *Constitutional Deliberation in Congress: The Impact of Judicial Review in a Separated System.* Durham, N.C.: Duke University Press, 2004.
Rosenberg, Gerald N. *The Hollow Hope: Can Courts Bring about Social Change?* 2nd ed. Chicago: University of Chicago Press, 2008.
Sweet, Martin J. *Merely Judgment: Ignoring, Evading, and Trumping the Supreme Court.* Charlottesville: University of Virginia Press, 2010.

Sources on the Web

There are many sources on the Supreme Court on the World Wide Web. Some of the most useful websites are listed here. Access to each of these websites is available without charge.

Many colleges and universities subscribe to the LexisNexis Academic database, which provides access to all published court decisions as well as articles in newspapers, law reviews, and other sources. The database includes the text of briefs submitted to the Supreme Court in cases with oral arguments.

As is true of websites in general, the content of these sites can change over time, and websites sometimes disappear altogether. However, most of the following sites have been maintained for many years.

Supreme Court of the United States (www.supremecourtus.gov). This is the Court's official website. The site includes the Court's rules and the calendar for oral arguments in the current term. The website also includes the docket sheets for each case that comes to the Court—sheets that list all the briefs filed and the actions taken by the Court. The site provides transcripts and audio of oral arguments, the Court's opinions, and other information about the Court and its cases. In the near future the Court will begin putting all materials filed with it on the website.

SCOTUSblog (www.scotusblog.com). This site is the most extensive source of material about the Court. Postings provide a great deal of information and analysis on cases that the Court has accepted and decided since the 2007 term and some information on other cases filed in the Court. The site includes briefs, oral arguments, decisions, statistics on the Court's work, and news and commentary on the Court. Material on each case accepted by the Court is pulled together under "merits cases," organized by term.

FindLaw (www.findlaw.com/casecode/supreme.html). This website includes a database of opinions in Supreme Court decisions since 1893.

Legal Information Institute (https://www.law.cornell.edu/supremecourt/text/home). The law school at Cornell University provides this website, which includes collections of Supreme Court decisions and other kinds of information about the Court such as previews of cases that the Court will hear.

Oyez (www.oyez.org). This site, housed at IIT Chicago–Kent College of Law, provides several types of information about cases and decisions in the Supreme Court. The most distinctive feature is a collection of audios of oral arguments and announcements of decisions in the Court. The site also shows the membership of the Court over time and provides biographical information about the justices.

The Constitution of the United States of America: Analysis and Interpretation (https://www.congress.gov/constitution-annotated). This publication, also known as the *Constitution Annotated*, is compiled by the Congressional Research Service of the Library of Congress. It provides a highly detailed summary of the Supreme Court's interpretations of each provision of the Constitution, along with citations of the relevant cases. Also included are lists of all federal, state, and local statutes that the Court has declared unconstitutional and all Supreme Court decisions that have been overruled by subsequent decisions.

Case Index

Case titles are followed by case citations. These begin with the volume of the reporter in which the case appears. This is followed by the abbreviated name of the reporter; "U.S." is the *United States Supreme Court Reports*, the official reporter of Supreme Court decisions. The last part of the citation is the page on which the case begins. Decisions are published and given full citations in the *United States Supreme Court Reports* several years after the Court issues them; for that reason, recent Supreme Court decisions are cited to unofficial reporters. In this text, the *United States Supreme Court Reports, Lawyers' Edition* (L. Ed. 2d) is the unofficial reporter used for that purpose. Lower court decisions have their own reporters, including the *Federal Reporter* (F.3d) for the federal courts of appeals and various regional reporters for decisions of state supreme courts. For lower courts, the year of the decision is preceded by a designation of the specific court—the circuit for the federal courts of appeals, the district for the federal district courts, and the state for state supreme courts.

Index